business
genius

business
genius

A more inspired approach to
business growth

peter fisk

CAPSTONE

Copyright © 2008 by Peter Fisk

First published in 2008 by Capstone Publishing Ltd. (a Wiley Company)
The Atrium, Southern Gate, Chichester, PO19 8SQ, UK.
www.wileyeurope.com
Email (for orders and customer service enquires): cs-books@wiley.co.uk

The right of Peter Fisk to be identified as the author of this book has been asserted in accordance with the Copyright, Designs and Patents Act 1988

Other Wiley Editorial Offices

John Wiley & Sons Inc., 111 River Street, Hoboken, NJ 07030, USA
Jossey-Bass, 989 Market Street, San Francisco, CA 94103-1741, USA
Wiley-VCH Verlag GmbH, Boschstr. 12, D-69469 Weinheim, Germany
John Wiley & Sons Australia Ltd, 42 McDougall Street, Milton, Queensland 4064, Australia
John Wiley & Sons (Asia) Pte Ltd, 2 Clementi Loop #02-01, Jin Xing Distripark, Singapore 129809
John Wiley & Sons Canada Ltd, 22 Worcester Road, Etobicoke, Ontario, Canada M9W 1L1

Wiley also publishes its books in a variety of electronic formats. Some content that appears in print may not be available in electronic books.

Library of Congress Cataloging-in-Publication Data
Fisk, Peter (Peter Robert)
Business genius : a more inspired approach to business growth / Peter Fisk.
p. cm.
Includes index.
ISBN 978-1-84112-790-3 (pbk. : alk. paper)
1. Industrial management. I. Title.
HD31.F5364 2008
658.4'063--dc22

2008001338

A catalogue record for this book is available from the British Library.

ISBN 13: 978-1-84112-790-3

Typeset in Agfa Rotis Sans Serif by Sparks – www.sparkspublishing.com
Printed and bound in Great Britain by TJ International Ltd, Padstow, Cornwall

Substantial discounts on bulk quantities of Capstone Books are available to corporations, professional associations and other organizations. For details telephone John Wiley & Sons on (+44) 1243-770441, fax (+44) 1243 770571 or email corporatedevelopment@wiley.co.uk

Contents

Credits

To Alison, Anna and Clara.

And to all the people around the world in organizations large and small, who believe in creating a better approach to business, and have ideas they would love to make happen.

I hope, in some small way, that this book inspires you.

About the author

Peter Fisk is a highly experienced business strategist, consultant to business leaders worldwide, an inspirational business speaker and a business entrepreneur. He has spent many years working with the likes of British Airways and Coca-Cola, Marks & Spencer and Microsoft, Virgin and Vodafone.

He is author of the best-selling book *Marketing Genius*, which has been translated into 24 languages, and *The Complete CEO*. He is described by *Business Strategy Review* as 'one of the best new business thinkers'.

Peter started his career as a nuclear physicist, before getting into the supersonic world of marketing at British Airways with roles in brands and marketing, strategy and leadership development.

He was CEO of the world's largest professional marketing organization, the Chartered Institute of Marketing. He also led the global strategic marketing consulting team of PA Consulting Group, was managing director of Brand Finance, and a partner of strategic innovators The Foundation.

He is founder and CEO of The Genius Works, helping business leaders around the world to think differently – to develop and implement more inspired strategies, innovation and marketing. He recently launched *The Marketing Fast Track* and hosts CNBC's *The Marketing Show*.

He is an accomplished international speaker on all aspects of business strategy and leadership, innovation and marketing, customers and brands. He is thoughtful and considered, provocative and entertaining – capturing what's hot, what works, and what's next.

He defines the emerging agenda for business, working across the world with companies and their leaders, to make the best ideas happen practically and successfully.

For more information visit www.thegeniusworks.com or email peterfisk@peterfisk.com.

Inspiration

Osaka, Japan.

I am watching the race to be the fastest man on the planet.

It is a hot and humid evening in the magnificent Nagai Stadium. The night sky is clear and there is a warm breeze, although not enough to help the athletes. The large, knowledgeable crowd fall silent as the eight contenders approach their starting blocks. They look focused and confident, but also nervous or scared. Who will become the world 100m champion?

In the commentary box, Michael Johnson, a sprint legend – nine times world champion himself, and still a double world record holder – watches the athletes closely. He knows that they are all in superb physical shape, they each have excellent records in previous competitions, and he can reel off the times they have previously run to one hundredth of a second.

But those statistics will not determine the winner tonight.

He is watching their body language. How they walk, hold their heads, the look in their eyes. Who has the strength and fitness, the passion and desire, but also the focus and control to win? The Jamaican looks too relaxed, he thinks, the Briton seems to be a bundle of nerves, the Slovenian appears completely overawed, whilst the American looks quietly ahead at the finish line in the distance.

Johnson always ran with his head held high. The sign, he says, of an athlete who knows he will win. It is not just about running fast, it is about being able to execute the right plan at the right time. It is not just about capability and confidence, but the ability to think smarter and act faster than others.

I think about how 'genius' can be applied to business.

Who are the most successful businesses today? What do their people do differently? How can big companies learn from small ones, and vice versa? What can creative entrepreneurs and experienced business leaders learn from each other? What makes a great business strategy? And how do they drive more profitable, more sustainable growth?

Faster.

Of course there are many answers, and many different, great role models, from Dietrich Mateschitz and his secret of Red Bull to Jeff Immelt and the creative transformation of General Electric, Ray Davis and the extraordinary story of Umpqua Bank, or Zara's Spanish king of fast fashion, Amancio Ortega.

There are future-back strategies that find the emerging markets first, and outside-in propositions that touch people more deeply. There are right-brain leaders who play a more collaborative role in their businesses, and energized people who deliver radical action and extraordinary results.

So where should we start?

More specifically, what's an inspirational way to start a business? Indeed, what's an inspirational way to start every day?

If you're a rock star you might throw on your shades and head off to the recording studio. If you're a dedicated athlete, you might kick on your running shoes for the morning training session. If you are the cool entrepreneur Renzo Rosso, you might sip your espresso as you plan your next Diesel brand extension. Or if you are the king of all things digital, Steve Jobs, you might already be in deep thought about which market to transform next.

Or you could be you, heading for your office, switching on your laptop.

Each morning you start with a clean sheet of paper, the hours ahead of you are opportunities to grow – to do something better, to develop your ideas further, to improve your own capabilities, or to grow your business faster. Every activity, every meeting, every decision is an exciting opportunity.

Somehow it doesn't often feel like that. Most people in most businesses head straight for the coffee machine, then to their email-laden inboxes, or start a sequence of hour-long review meetings, or click open their hundred-page documents.

Why do we do this?

We spend most of our business lives with our heads down. Doing what we do, reviewing what we have done, doing more of what we have always done. The endless pursuit of more information, more detailed analysis, faster reporting, and efficient optimization, catches us in a spreadsheet trap.

We have little time to think.

We rarely step back and consider the possibilities, use our intuition rather than analysis, our own insights as opposed to the latest research, our imaginations rather than our artificially-enhanced intelligence. The endless treadmill of meetings and deadlines, the demand for speed and precision, leaves little time to talk, to learn, to listen, to imagine.

Is this really the route to competitive advantage? Is it the environment for innovation and growth, or for efficiency and commoditization?

When was the last time you listened to a truly inspiring person? Spent time talking to individual customers about their ambitions; not just their needs? Learnt from a completely different business or environment? Sat down with a team and talked about the future not the past? Had a truly original idea that you actually made happen? Left work so energized that you were desperate to get back next morning?

Business needs more inspiration.

We need to spend more time with our heads up. We need to break the routine of our daily schedules, use the spreadsheets as a platform from which to think more creatively, to trust our intuition as well as the data. We need to get out of self-limiting sectors, with our self-defined conventions and our self-depressing schedules, to be human, thoughtful and imaginative.

How else can we make our brightest ideas happen, stand out from the competition, go beyond the conventions of today, make a bigger difference to the lives of real people, influence the way the world works, and generate significant wealth for our society, shareholders and selves?

The human body is an amazing machine. The human brain is an incredible device. With both our intelligence and imagination we should be able to create outputs that are much more than ordinary: we should be able to create extraordinary results.

Think differently

I wrote this book because I want to inspire people to think differently, to get more out of themselves, and to make a bigger and better contribution to their businesses and markets.

My own inspiration comes from a career that started in the beautiful countryside of Northumberland, with its rolling hills and sheep farms, its unspoilt sandy beaches and ancient castles. Slightly further south, the old industries of Tyneside, coal mining and shipbuilding, were in decline and the search was on for new sources of wealth creation.

As I grew up, my inspiration came from my parents, both teachers, who constantly sought to make a difference to each child who progressed through their schools, not just intellectually, but as rounded young people too.

I enjoyed and did well at school, but my inspiration came from sport. Like my dad, I was a runner, inspired by the world record years of Sebastian Coe and Steve Ovett. I trained morning and night in the pursuit of the extra seconds that would give me an edge in the road, cross country or track races each weekend. At my local track, I would watch Steve Cram train. Just a little older than me, he would soon be breaking the records of Coe and Ovett, and becoming World Champion too.

Whilst I didn't have the world record-breaking DNA of my heroes, I worked and dreamed hard. In the years ahead in business, it was my passion, motivation and competitiveness, developed through sport, that drove me to progress, more than any qualifications or training programmes.

After an initial foray into the intriguing but painstakingly slow world of nuclear physics, I got into the more exciting and kerosene-fuelled world of business with British Airways. At the time, 'the world's favourite airline' offered an exhilarating world of global travel, jet set executives and supersonic aircraft.

Nothing beat flying Concorde from London to JFK for a meeting, then returning the same day.

As I progressed through roles at the airline, from market analyst to corporate sales, brand development and market strategy, I was always excited but usually deflated by the narrow ways in which people saw these roles – 'you're an analyst, leave the creativity to us'; 'we don't trust the commercial skills of marketing people'; 'strategists don't understand the practicality of operations'.

I resented the prejudices, putting people into boxes, the blinkered thinking, and was amazed how few people wanted or were able to see the bigger picture, how things could integrate and complement, how analysis and creativity worked together, how strategy had to fuse with action.

And then I read about Coe, and how his coach pursued not just the development of him as an athlete who could run fast but as a 'Renaissance man' who could think too. From Aristotle to

Michelangelo, the greats of the past had been rounded characters, athletic and intellectual, intelligent and imaginative.

As I worked with some of the business giants – American Express and Coca-Cola, Microsoft and Marks & Spencer, Philips and Shell, Virgin and Vodafone – the leaders and managers, brands and businesses that have impressed me most are the ones who see a bigger picture.

They see things differently and do different things. They connect the unconnected, challenge the conventions, look for new opportunities, are not afraid to try new ideas and they have inspiring leaders. They are inspired businesses, with a sense of 'genius' about them.

Intelligence and imagination

What is common about the thinking styles that produced Venice's Sixteenth Chapel and the Theory of Relativity, that gave us penicillin and the World Wide Web?

Academics and philosophers have long tried to bottle 'genius'. Russian scientists, through the analysis of child protégés, claim to have identified the 'genius gene'; whilst others argue that genius is, as Thomas Edison believed, down to hard work: 'One per cent inspiration; ninety nine per cent perspiration'.

However there are some clues as to what drives genius, and its extraordinary results. Whilst genius is often thought to equate purely to intelligence, it is certainly not necessary to have an extraordinarily high IQ, to speak 15 languages by the age of 8 or to master the intricacies of quantum mechanics.

Genius typically involves both intelligent and creative thought, and the combination of the two, to whatever degree, can create so-called 'genius'. From Archimedes to Warhol, Mozart to McCartney, there are some regular characteristics of genius:

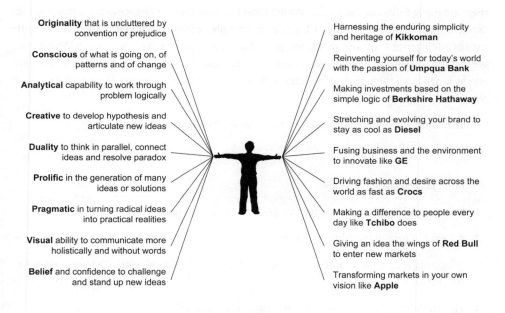

Originality that is uncluttered by convention or prejudice

Conscious of what is going on, of patterns and of change

Analytical capability to work through problem logically

Creative to develop hypothesis and articulate new ideas

Duality to think in parallel, connect ideas and resolve paradox

Prolific in the generation of many ideas or solutions

Pragmatic in turning radical ideas into practical realities

Visual ability to communicate more holistically and without words

Belief and confidence to challenge and stand up new ideas

Harnessing the enduring simplicity and heritage of **Kikkoman**

Reinventing yourself for today's world with the passion of **Umpqua Bank**

Making investments based on the simple logic of **Berkshire Hathaway**

Stretching and evolving your brand to stay as cool as **Diesel**

Fusing business and the environment to innovate like **GE**

Driving fashion and desire across the world as fast as **Crocs**

Making a difference to people every day like **Tchibo** does

Giving an idea the wings of **Red Bull** to enter new markets

Transforming markets in your own vision like **Apple**

Like Galileo and da Vinci, Einstein and Picasso, genius requires an inner strength of conviction in order to stand by the radical ideas and actions that are at odds with received wisdom, that challenge the status quo, that could easily be compromised on by a lesser willed person. In any walk of life, it is rare for people to immediately like significant change in their surroundings, practices or beliefs. We prefer the safety and convenience of what we know to what we don't. But we gradually see the possibility, the logic and the benefit in different thinking, and we accept it and, eventually, engage in it. A genius reaches out beyond today, and slowly people follow and embrace what is new, different and better.

'Genius' is about applying intelligence in more imaginative ways.

There are many definitions of genius. Whilst some focus on the intelligence aspects of genius, for example the attainment of a high IQ, genius is typically defined as being less about an absolute level of intelligence and more about the application of intelligence in creative ways. Whilst some suggest that one is born with genius, or with the aptitude to achieve it, most argue that genius is primarily achieved through carefully chosen hard work that blends deeper thinking with radical creativity.

Genius uniquely combines these extremes to deliver extraordinary results.

gen·ius

noun pl. geniuses

1 Exceptional intellectual or creative power or other natural ability.

2 An exceptionally intelligent or able person.

3 (pl genii/jeeni-i/) (in some mythologies) A spirit associated with a person, place or institution.

4 The prevalent character or spirit of a nation, period, etc.

Source: *Oxford English Dictionary*

The combination of intelligence and imagination, the connection of opposites, in positive and reinforcing ways, is the source of new insights, of unusual ideas, and of extraordinary results.

Extraordinary results

It is little more than 10 years ago since we wrote letters rather than emails, browsed CDs in the music store rather downloaded our favourite tracks, and relied upon a small number of media channels, retail outlets and brand owners to run our lives.

We now live and work in flux – markets come and go, converge and fragment at unbelievable speed, and in unpredictable ways. Kodak used to be a market leader and is now unsure what market it is in, Google went from zero to corporate hero in a few years, Apple rose from uncertainty and reinvented the world of music, and YouTube became our favourite place to watch movies within months.

Satisfaction and improvement, derivatives and incentives are not enough. Incremental business improvement, maintaining existing revenues, even if it is delivered more efficiently, doing what you've always done, maybe a little better, can be the quickest way to a painful death.

Just meeting existing consumer needs or being a little better than existing competitors is not a recipe for success. Stretching, refreshing and exploiting the brand as no more than a name and logo, putting an advertising gloss on commoditized products, exhorting your sales teams to work harder, or resorting to price competition is a not even a recipe for survival. We need to do more.

It's time to rethink business, to reenergize our own minds too.

Applying the ideas of 'genius' to business requires us to start from a new perspective – from the future rather than today, and from the outside rather than the inside. It also requires us to interpret and apply these new perspectives more powerfully, seeing the bigger picture, making new connections and ensuring that the radical part of ideas are not lost in practical focus of action.

Genius is therefore about fusion – connecting opposites that together are more than the component parts.

These connections typically bring together a more intelligent and more imaginative approach to business. And given that in recent years, business has typically embraced intelligence more than imagination, it also requires some adjustment, favouring the more imaginative side of the equation.

Genius = intelligence + imagination = extraordinary results.

'Yin' and 'yang' are not alternatives; they cannot exist without each other. They are complementary, they are mutually reinforcing, they are about balance. They are about creating more together than apart. Yin and yang bring together attributes that are rational and emotional, conscious and unconscious. Masculine and feminine.

Business Genius explores the four yin-yang fusions that together deliver a more inspired business, and their implications for individuals and collectively. It then explores how to apply these fusions to the essential disciplines of strategy and innovation, customers and propositions, people and change, which are required to deliver sustained, profitable growth and extraordinary results.

At a personal level, 'genius' delivers a more inspired way of thinking and behaving:

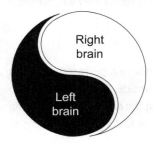

Right brain and left brain. Taking a more thoughtful, creative and holistic approach to your challenges. Embracing new ideas rather than being a slave to numbers. Freeing your creative side, to focus your imagination on what matters most.

Right brain > left brain

Right brain + left brain = holistic thinking

Radical ideas and practical action. Taking a more thoughtful, bolder approach to business challenges. Making the best ideas happen without compromise. Making every action count, ensuring that radical ideas deliver more significant impact.

Radical ideas > practical action

Radical ideas + practical action = dramatic impact

At a business level, 'genius' delivers a more inspired way of planning and operating:

Future back and now forward. Starting from possibilities, unlimited by the rules and conventions, or existing capabilities. Seizing and shaping the best market opportunities before others. Creating tomorrow whilst also delivering today.

Future back > now forward

Future back + now forward = enlightened innovation

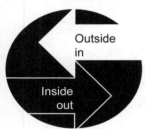

Outside in and inside out. Defining strategy based on the best markets, customer needs and competitive difference, rather than what you have always done, or think you should do. Doing business on customers terms rather than your own.

Outside in > inside out

Outside in + inside out = engaged customers

Anyone could be a business genius.

There are no child protégés in the boardrooms, just people who work hard and smart. However, the business world now works by new rules; no longer is it enough or even appropriate to follow the old conventions and etiquettes. Indeed the winners of tomorrow might seem a little crazy compared to the leaders of the past.

The twenty-first century workplace should be an inspirational place to start each day, with markets and innovations unbounded by physicality, full of possibilities limited only by your imagination.

The four yin-yang dimensions will shape the four sections to this book. You can explore how effectively you are currently tapping into them in the *Business Brainscan* at the back of the book, and you can explore them more personally and practically by attending one of the *Genius Live* workshops around the world, or by visiting *The Genius Lab* online.

Go for walks in the mountains like Albert Einstein and break all the rules like Pablo Picasso. Not just occasionally, but as a way of life. See things differently, make new connections, and have the confidence to make your best ideas happen.

'Think different' is what Apple told us in a salute to the people – like Einstein and Picasso, Ghandi and Mandela, Chaplin and Lennon, Ford and Branson – who change things:

'Here's to the crazy ones.

'The misfits. The rebels. The troublemakers. The round pegs in the square holes.

'The ones who see things differently.

'They're not fond of rules. And they have no respect for the status quo.

'You can praise them, disagree with them, quote them, disbelieve them, glorify or vilify them.

'About the only thing you can't do is ignore them.

'Because they change things.

'They invent. They imagine. They heal. They explore. They create. They inspire. They push the human race forward.

'Maybe they have to be crazy.

'How else can you stare at an empty canvas and see a work of art?

'Or sit in silence and hear a song that's never been written?

'Or gaze at a red planet and see a laboratory on wheels?

'While some see them as the crazy ones, we see genius.

'Because the people who are crazy enough to think they can change the world, are the ones who do.'

I hope you enjoy this book. I hope it helps and inspires you to see things a little differently, think a little more radically, and in your own way, do something extraordinary.

Be bold. Be brave. Be brilliant.

Peter Fisk

Email: peterfisk@peterfisk.com

Website: www.thegeniusworks.com

Right brain, left brain

PART 1

▶ Right brain, left brain

'The test of a first-rate intelligence is the ability to hold two opposed ideas in mind at the same time'

F. Scott Fitzgerald

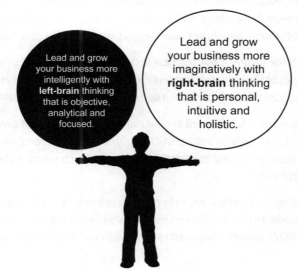

Lead and grow your business more intelligently with **left-brain** thinking that is objective, analytical and focused.

Lead and grow your business more imaginatively with **right-brain** thinking that is personal, intuitive and holistic.

- ▶ The human brain is an extraordinary result of natural evolution, and of course its structure is far more complicated than a simple left-right division. Indeed neuroscience has developed rapidly in the last few decades, and we are continually learning how to interpret our thoughts and actions, and improve them.

- ▶ Left and right brain thinking is still a useful metaphor in considering how we think. 'Right brain' is the more 'imaginative' side – subjective, intuitive, holistic and divergent – whilst 'left brain' is the more 'intelligent' side – objective, interactive, analytical and convergent.

- ▶ We approach the future of our business and markets with our eyes wide shut. We need to open our minds to the bigger picture – the world around us, what other companies do, what will drive and sustain our growth, and our role in it. This is a right brain opportunity.

- ▶ Business has become too focused and mechanical (left brain), not giving enough time and space to think more broadly and holistically (right brain). Of course we need both – left and right brain, intelligence and imagination – but it is the connections between the two that make the difference.

- ▶ If we want to succeed in business today – to make sense of our changing and confused, fast and fragile world; to be effective entrepreneurs and business leaders in it; and to create and sustain profitable growth – we need to think with our whole brain, not just part of it.

Driving and accelerating business growth

'You either step forward into growth or you will step back into safety'

Abraham Maslow

A more **intelligent** approach to **growth** that embraces stronger *left brain* thinking	A more **imaginative** approach to **growth** that embraces stronger *right brain* thinking
• Maximize the economic value creation for stakeholders	• Shape the future in your vision, rather than live by somebody else's
• Focus on best market, customer and product opportunities	• Identify and capture new market opportunities first
• Add more distinctive value to your products and services	• Disrupt the accepted rules, conventions and business models
• Strengthen the purpose and competitive position of your brand	• Exploit your intangible business assets in more powerful ways
• Extend into adjacent categories and markets	• Collaborate with different and interesting partners
• Manage growth as a process and as a diverse portfolio	• Accelerate growth through platforms and accelerators
• Ensure that your growth is profitable, sustainable and creates value.	• Grow your business through 'The Seven Lives of Business'

Growth is easy, isn't it?

Discount your prices and your revenue goes up. Recognizing that you also need to make a profit, you cut your costs and the margins quickly improve. Wanting to drive even more dramatic growth, you acquire another company and you can double your size in no time. But it doesn't last.

Sustaining growth is not easy. Sustaining profitable growth is hard. Creating significant and sustainable growth is the imperative for every small business, and indeed the challenge for every large business today.

Achieving great results creates the expectation that you can do it again and again. You need to sustain it. Investors want to see evidence of the future profit streams that will give them a decent long-term return on their investments. Customers recognize that growing companies are doing something right and want to be part of it. Employees know that growth creates a bigger pie in which they can take a thicker slice.

Yet few companies manage to sustain profitable growth. They appear to reach a stumbling block when they reach the perceived limits of their current world, their existing markets and models, capabilities and ambitions, energy or inspiration.

With their heads down and spreadsheets buzzing, they seek to squeeze more out of their existing markets – an extra point of market share, another derivative product development or a more efficient process, that might secure a slightly greater margin. These things matter, but they don't create growth that is significant and sustainable.

The obsession with doing more of the same, through optimization or small improvements, is a significant obstacle growth. Fractions of market share or profit margins will help, but won't make the real difference. The danger is that we plough the same furrow, exploiting what we know best, delivering the same products, doing what we have always done slightly better.

We lose sight of the changing world outside.

We end up playing the old game, whilst oblivious to a new game – a new market, a new customer desire, a new business model. And because we prefer to make the most of what we have, we become hindered by our existing business, locked in our past and current success. The real danger is that incrementalism leads to irrelevance.

So how does a business, large or small, create and sustain profitable growth?

The answer is already in our heads. As human beings we have an enormous capacity to think, to sense and respond, to innovate and change. We each have 100 trillion brain cells, and probably use about 1% of them at any time. At an incredibly simple level we can categorize our brains into left and right sides – reflecting our ability to think intelligently and imaginatively, analytically and intuitively, sequentially and holistically.

Yet it is the connections between these that really matters. In Einstein's case, his brain remained the object of fascination and research for many years, scientists concluding that it was in some ways different – not simply bigger, but better connected. The grey matter in our heads is connected by white matter. So it is perhaps this white stuff, the connective tissue, that holds more clues to our own genius, and the best opportunities for personal and business growth.

The successful growth business is firstly an imaginative business. It then intelligently focuses on the best opportunities. Whilst most of today's businesses are dominated by left-brain thinking, it is the right-brain thoughts that unlocks newness and enables them to start new things, and make the leaps forward.

Growth businesses succeed by thinking more broadly – seeing a bigger picture, a more holistic view of the market challenges and opportunities. They see a broader context, and by doing so they see more opportunities to exploit, more ways to be different, more sources of future profit.

And the more you have to choose from, the richer your options, the more likely you are to find the best, and the more sustainable you can be in exploiting them.

This might seem overly ambitious, particularly for a small business struggling to survive. Yet, even a few people with dedicated time can apply enormous brainpower to thinking more broadly, deeply and clearly – new thinking that could deliver extraordinary results.

Large businesses need a mix of people with left- and right-brain preferences, or ideally both. Small businesses must choose their colleagues with even more care. The visionary, creative, intuitive entrepreneur – from Richard Branson to Bill Gates – has always sought a more focused, analytical manager to be their side-kick.

More intuitive, more divergent, more holistic thinking enables us to see things differently, and thereby to think and do different things – to challenge conventions, to explore new possibilities, to hypothesize alternatives. More logical, more convergent, more focused thinking then enables you to choose the best markets, products, customers and approaches to focus your resources to be successful in this wider world.

Today's high growth business is an inspired business, fusing imaginative stretch and intelligent focus in order to deliver extraordinary results.

Imaginative with your right brain. Intelligent with your left brain. Inspired whole brain thinking.

1.1   THE SEVEN LIVES OF BUSINESS
The challenge of growth, the challenge of change

The origins of business thinking go far back. Three thousand years ago, the Chinese developed their word for 'business', based on two ancient symbols – the first refers to 'birth' and 'life' and the second to 'meaning'. It seems that the Chinese recognised that growth, sustained with an enduring purpose, is fundamental to business success back then, just like we do today.

Growing businesses have different characteristics, challenges and opportunities, as they evolve from start-ups into much larger organizations. Most companies don't recognize the growth phases that they move through; they suffer from the growing pains without recognizing what to do, and they miss the best opportunities which each phase uniquely offers.

- What is required to sustain a growing business?

- What are the biggest challenges and opportunities at each phase?

- What are the most appropriate styles of leadership and management as it grows?

There are typically seven stages in the life of a business. Of course, every organization and market is different, and some companies will choose to stay small, whilst others will grow huge, and may well be split up to become small businesses that can grow again. Just like the mountaineer setting out from base camp, the gentle foothills will require very different skills, different clothing and a different pace from climbing the icy peaks.

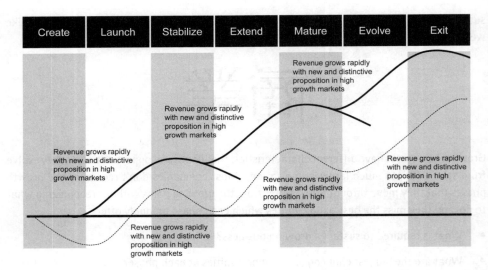

| Create | Launch | Stabilize | Extend | Mature | Evolve | Exit |

Revenue grows rapidly with new and distinctive proposition in high growth markets

Revenue grows rapidly with new and distinctive proposition in high growth markets

Revenue grows rapidly with new and distinctive proposition in high growth markets

Revenue grows rapidly with new and distinctive proposition in high growth markets

Revenue grows rapidly with new and distinctive proposition in high growth markets

Revenue grows rapidly with new and distinctive proposition in high growth markets

THE SEVEN LIVES OF BUSINESSES

While each life-stage is partly a result of the business's age, size and performance, it is also distinguished by its structure and sophistication. Some companies will evolve rapidly and others slowly, some will leap through life. Some evolved companies will still be small, maybe virtual, whilst some large companies might still be quite primitive. You can probably think of a few.

Their challenges are different. Small businesses want to get noticed, capture a new market, gain customers, and ensure that they drive enough cash flow to survive, and hopefully thrive. Large companies have an equally tough challenge in seeking to remain innovative, find new markets and to take their organizations with them.

The objectives of each life-stage are different and, therefore, the approach is too. Unlike the natural world, this is rarely a natural evolution. It requires deliberate thought and desire, hard choices and decisive management. Moving from one phase to the next will require change – in strategy, people, activities, leadership and even ownership.

Some of the changes as companies seek to evolve will be painful.

Entrepreneurs love their small, chaotic, personal worlds. Small teams don't like being torn apart or having more structures and processes imposed on them. Large companies don't like having to make choices, to delete certain product lines, pull out of certain markets, make people redundant.

Yet we choose to evolve because each life-stage brings new opportunities for growth.

Additional investment allows the company to extend its offerings, recruit more people, launch new ventures. Clearer structures and processes improve focus and efficiency, giving people their own teams to run and markets to manage. New leaders bring valuable experience and fresh ideas, and often allow the founding entrepreneurs to focus their creativity, without the admin.

Growth brings its rewards too, and part of the skill is linking the right rewards to the growth model so that it encourages the positive, evolutionary behaviours that the organization needs. Ensuring that all employees, and even wider business partners, have a stake in the business is one effective way of ensuring that everybody focuses on the same goal, supports growth, and shares in the rewards.

	Create	Enter	Stabilize	Expand	Optimize	Extend	Evolve
Priorities	• Evaluate best market opportunities • Articulate business purpose and strategy • Develop initial concept for launch	• Building awareness and initial sales • Delivering on the promise • Maximizing impact of brand launch	• Consolidate and grow best customers • New strategy for secondary growth • Improve process efficiency	• Enter new markets and categories • Drive innovation and service delivery • Find more partners to extend reach	• Focus on best markets, customers • Manage/rationalize product portfolio • Fully exploit key business assets	• Extend growth into new markets • Drive strategic innovation • Venturing and new partnerships	• Evaluate options for exit and renewal • IPO, trade sale or break up • Or continue to next phase of growth
Challenges	• Getting the business set up • Developing an initial business plan • Securing start-up funding if needed	• Marketing on a limited budget • Limited resources, everyone hands on • Managing cashflow closely	• Getting beyond steady revenues • Tension between founders and staff • Retain customers and best people	• Managing complex, diverse activities • Maintain focus on best opportunities • Consider mergers and acquisitions	• Dispose of non-value creating areas • Simplifying internal structure, strategies • Transparent KPIs and management	• Rethink what is the core business • Drive fundamental change • Reenergize people and leaders	• Evaluate all options independently • Maximize value of business assets • Consider best form and timing of exit
Proposition	• Identifying first audience to target • Articulating brand and proposition • Developing initial product(s)/service(s)	• Build awareness of new brand • Use affinity and channel partners • Deliver initial product(s)/service(s)	• Identify new market and product options • New propositions for new segments • Partner with established brands	• International, multi-segmented CVPs • Portfolio of quality products/services • Licensing through third parties	• Rationalise portfolio of customers • Rationalise portfolio of products • Refresh brand and propositions	• Emerging markets and whitespaces • Innovation of business model • Customized solutions, channels	• Innovative brands and propositions • Strong customer relationships • Well protected rights and patents
Investment	• Expense of start-up and personal time • Cost of R&D and prototyping • Design of brand, website, materials	• Cost of marketing and sales • Cost of outsourcing back office	• Cost of new product development • Cost of outsourcing back office	• Cost of entering new markets • Recruit more people to support • Cost of loans to support growth	• Cost of brand and web refresh • Cost of databases and analytics	• Cost of significant business change • Cost of ventures and partnerships	• Cost of professional advice

CHALLENGES AT EACH BUSINESS LIFE-STAGE

The potential characteristics of each life-stage are illustrated in the table, although there will obviously be variations on the theme. Where is your business? Maybe different parts of it are at different stages, with your structure lagging behind your market ambitions, or your investments out of kilter with your strategic opportunities.

The life-stages flex between periods of rapid growth, where innovation and extension are important, followed by periods of consolidation where the organization has to regroup in order to build a new platform for another stage of growth. The focus and culture of the business will therefore differ by stage, and the challenges in moving to the next stage will be different each time.

Stage 1: 'Create' reflects the birth of a new business, driven with entrepreneurial ambition. The founders shape their ideas and establish the business. The focus will be on creativity, whilst big obstacles to growing to the next stage will include funding.

Stage 2: 'Enter' is about getting the business going, launching itself into markets, building awareness, delivering its services, and generating some income. The focus will be on building, whilst obstacles to evolving the business will often include the founders' own relentless passion.

Stage 3: 'Stabilize' seeks to bring some order to a small, probably fairly chaotic business. The founders might not notice, but others are struggling. The focus will be on consolidation, whilst the obstacles to growing will include learning to empower people.

Stage 4: 'Expand' marks a second phase of rapid growth, extending the business in new ways, reaching out to new products and extending the range. The focus is on innovation, whilst the obstacles to moving on will now include the resistance to more formal control.

Stage 5: 'Optimize' takes stock of all of this expansion to focus resources on the markets, products and customers that matter most. It may also involve stopping doing other things. The focus is on prioritization, whilst obstacles now include the bureaucracy that inevitably creeps in.

Stage 6: 'Extend' is back on the innovation track, looking for more strategic ways to innovate the business, shaping markets and business models. The focus is on strategic innovation, and the obstacle now is size, lacking the agility and single-mindedness of small business.

Stage 7: 'Evolve' is the alternative to death. There is no limit to how far a business can evolve, how high it can fly, the focus is on deciding where to go next – to sell, merge, break up, or keep extending into new domains, limited only by the imagination of its people.

business
genius

Most companies die young. They should be able to live for 200 to 300 years according to Arie de Geus in *The Living Company*, yet few organizations survive this long, falling victim to blinkered strategies in changing worlds, or the inability to evolve as they grow.

Imagine the changes that a company like Kikkoman, the Japanese soy sauce company, has lived through, from the days as a family business on the banks of the Edo River to the global corporation of today. Consider the journeys of some of the world's oldest companies, together with the relative youth of some of the best known companies today:

THE LIVES OF BUSINESS LEADERS

Founded	Company	Sector	Country
578	Kongo Gumi	Construction	Japan
1288	Stora Enso	Paper	Finland
1385	Antinori	Wines	Italy
1526	Pietro Beretta	Guns	Italy
1623	Zildjian	Cymbals	Turkey
1630	Kikkoman	Soy sauce	Japan
1734	Taittinger	Champagne	France
1748	Villeroy & Boch	Tableware	Germany
1802	DuPont	Chemicals	USA
1853	Levi Strauss	Clothing	USA
1886	Coca-Cola	Soft drinks	USA
1892	GE	Electrical	USA
1975	Microsoft	Technology	USA
1977	Apple	Technology	USA
1998	Google	Technology	USA

Source: Centuries of Success, William O'Hara

Insight 1: CROCS
Fast growth by three men in a boat

The growth of Crocs is phenomenal by any measure. Not the rough skinned, wide jawed reptiles, but the slightly ugly, multicoloured variety that have taken the footwear world by storm.

Islas Mujeres, Mexico. 2002.

Three guys from Boulder, Colorado decide to go sailing. Lyndon Hanson, Scott Seamans and George Boedecker take off from their stressful jobs and head for the Caribbean. On arriving at their boat, they unpack their bags, including a pair of foam clogs that one of them found whilst in Canada.

As the days, waves and beers pass by, they are inspired to build a business around the funky, foam-made shoes with the Swiss-cheese perforations. They are incredibly comfortable, non-slip, lightweight, washable and never smell. The perfect boat shoe.

They need a name. 'Crocs' is chosen because crocodiles are tough and strong with no natural predators. Equally good in the land and water, they live for a very long time.

Fort Lauderdale, Florida. 2003.

The three friends are staggered by their astonishing success: $1.2 million sales in their first year, and they are still treating the business like a part-time job. They launch their shoes at the Fort Lauderdale boat show – but soon everyone from doctors to gardeners to waiters wants them.

They lease a warehouse in Florida, so that they can combine business and pleasure, but are struggling to cope with demand. Celebrities like Brad Pitt and Britney Spears adopt them. Kids adore them.

Crocs are not just functional but suddenly the height of fashion too.

27

Sydney, Australia. 2004.
Crocs are growing incredibly quickly with $13.5 million turnover by end of the second year, although with a small loss. Word of mouth continues to spread the desire for Crocs like wildfire.

Ron Snyder, a former college friend, has joined as CEO. He previously ran the global business of Flextronics and oversaw its growth from $3 billion to $16 billion in four years. He sees similar potential with Crocs.

Snyder decides to buy the Canadian company, Foam Creations, who make Crocs from a special 'closed-cell resin' called Croslite. In the past Crocs had basically distributed their products; now it has its own unique process, material, design and distribution.

Crocs are now ready for even faster and more profitable growth.

Beijing, China. 2005.
Revenue leaps to $108.6 million and profits to $17 million. The rubbery clogs and flip-flops can now be found in over 40 countries. The range and colours diversify too – and with prices ranging from $30 to $60 a pair, they are cheap enough for people to buy two, three or four pairs.

Strong branding and high profile sponsorships that link closely with target audiences help to raise curiosity, visibility and desire further – from baseball, football and motor racing, to the latest kids movies from Disney.

'Think bigger than you are' is a lesson Snyder brought with him. He registers Crocs as a trademark in countries around the world, and establishes manufacturing capability from Mexico to China to support still faster growth. However they are still struggling to keep up with demand.

Wall Street, New York. 2006.
Now a global phenomenon, everybody wants Crocs. Shops sell out before new supplies arrive.

Sales are phenomenal too, selling 20 million pairs, and tripling revenue to $354.7 million and profit margins growing to 18%.

People love their Crocs. Jibbitz, for example, started as a tiny, home-made collection of clay and rhinestone that clipped onto the shoes and enabled people to customize them. It grew even faster than the shoe company, so much so that Crocs snapped up the kitchen company for $20 million.

Crocs goes public, with an IPO initially valuing the company at an eye-catching $1 billion, and grows rapidly on trading. Some say it is an outrageous valuation, the company is riding on a fashion trend that cannot last, and investors have been seduced by a funky brand. Only time will tell.

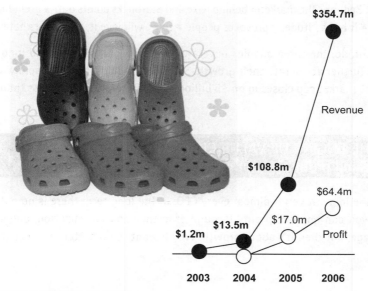

$354.7m

Revenue

$108.8m

$64.4m

$13.5m $17.0m

$1.2m   Profit

2003   2004   2005   2006

FAST, PROFITABLE GROWTH OF CROCS

Niwot, Colorado. 2007.

On the Lovemarks.com website, Crocs has rapidly become a popular choice with consumers in selecting their most loved brand. Rachel is a typical advocate:

> 'Absolutely the most comfortable shoes I've ever experienced. They soon adopted the shape of my feet, support my back, are so easy to take care of, and are created in the most detailed and beautiful rainbow of colours. One for every outfit.'

However, no brand can be loved by everyone:

> 'Oh nooooooo, I can't stand Crocs! Despite arguments that they might be comfortable – I think they look totally hideous. I wouldn't be seen dead wearing them.'

But as Scott Bedbury, the marketer behind Nike and Starbucks points out, 'a great brand polarizes people – it has attitude, it provokes people – some will love it, and others hate it.'

Back in Colorado, the three buddies have a whole boat load of ideas and innovations to develop, to further accelerate their growth. Sales continue to increase rapidly and profitably, and the market cap closes in on $5 billion. Not bad for a company less than five years old.

1.2 THE ENGINE OF VALUE CREATION
Revenue and profits are not enough, value is what matters

Growth is the imperative for almost every CEO. In the long term there is no option but to grow. Yes, you can improve profits through efficiency and optimization, and shrink to a smarter shape, but then it's about growth. We all want to do better this year than we did last year.

We typically measure growth in revenue – our sales turnover, product volumes. Of course, it feels good to sell more and more – but not if it's ultimately unprofitable. Sometimes, you will decide to sustain unprofitable sales in order to establish yourself in a market, but at some point it has to turn positive.

Continuing to sell unprofitably is a recipe for disaster. Yet lots of people do it, at least in parts of their business if not all. Finding the products, categories, segments and markets for profitable growth is therefore a priority – as is eliminating the unprofitable ones.

Similarly, stock markets work in a way that rewards companies that deliver beyond expectations. If you are a shareholder, then you expect a return significantly better than you would get it if you kept it securely in a long-term savings account. This is your basic requirement. You want a return more than this. Therefore, growth needs to be even more profitable and significant.

And it needs to be sustainable too. There are plenty of one-trick ponies. Any fool can discount the prices and sell lots. Any fool can take a huge loan, buy a competitor's business, and double revenue in the short term. But is that sustainable? Not often. This is why organic growth, growth driven by improving and extending your core business is what succeeds.

	% of companies	Market/book ratio
Outperformers on revenue growth or profitability	12.8	
Outperformers on revenue growth	2.8	1.9
Outperformers on profitability	9.2	3.0
Outperformers on both	0.8	4.1

Source: McKinsey Quarterly, 2007 (based on the 10 year performance across industry sectors)

Sustainable, profitable growth is incredibly elusive, yet research shows that companies that can outpace their rivals in terms of both growth and profitability achieve the best stock market performances. Revenue growth alone is not enough, it needs to profitable too.

This is demonstrated by a recent McKinsey survey which found that only 0.8% of the companies researched were able to outperform their competitors in terms of both revenue and profit growth over a decade. Whilst 9.2% of companies delivered better profit performance compared to peers, only 0.8% of companies were able to deliver revenue growth too.

Most significantly, exploring the stock market performance of these companies over the same period (by compared their market value to their book value) showed that companies that can deliver growth in revenue and profitability deliver the best returns to shareholders.

Sustaining growth becomes a dynamic system.

An obsessive, single-minded approach to make as much as much money as quickly as possible for the business owners, be they founders or shareholders, is not a healthy approach. Employees will quickly become disenchanted with working hard for relatively low wages whilst the owners roll in their riches. Customers too want to see a constant stream of better, innovative solutions, delivered with high-quality service and support.

Business is a 'value exchange', creating value for many 'stakeholders' – each with a stake in the system through which they give something and get returns.

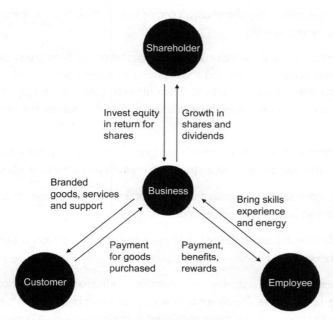

BUSINESS AS A VALUE EXCHANGE BETWEEN STAKEHOLDERS

Customers will pay more for great products and service, a brand they trust and a solution that best meets their needs. Employees give their time and effort, ideas and skills, in return for pay and other benefits. Shareholders invest in the business, in the belief that they will get a better return on their money from it than by investing elsewhere.

The value exchange requires balance. If any stakeholder feels that they are not getting a fair return for what they put in, then the whole system begins to falter. Customers don't feel that they are getting a good deal so go elsewhere, there are insufficient funds to pay employees so their productivity declines, and shareholders decide to take their funds elsewhere. Without a fair balance, the system will fail.

The value exchange is also dynamic because the expectations of each group continue to rise – customers want better solutions and lower prices, employees want salary rises and more benefits, and investors want better returns. Many other stakeholders also play an increasingly important role too – suppliers, business partners, governments, local communities and society in general.

Distributing a fair return to stakeholders can be done in two ways – by imaging a 'value cake' and how it should be shared between all those who contribute to the business success:

- The greedy shareholder will demand an ever-thicker slice of the same cake, to the disgust of everyone else who gets a smaller one.

- The wise shareholder recognizes that a smarter way to get a big piece is to 'grow' a bigger cake, where everyone else can have a big slice too.

Simple analogies aside, the ways in which companies are managed determine their sustainability and long-term success. The choice of how much dividend to return to shareholders, how much to give as bonuses, and how much to reinvest in the business, is an important one. What is indisputable is that companies must sustain profitable grow to create lasting value.

'Value' is an important word at this point.

'Economic value' reflects the sum of future profits that the company is likely to generate. More accurately, it is the net present value of this future performance, taking into account the certainty (i.e. risk) that it will actually be delivered.

Economic value reflects the future potential of the organization and is driven by the strategic choices, the healthy performance, and the investments made for future results. Virtually every action of the business will have a short- and longer-term impact, which should both be considered. Growing businesses in particular may need to favour the long term, even at the expense of short-term gains.

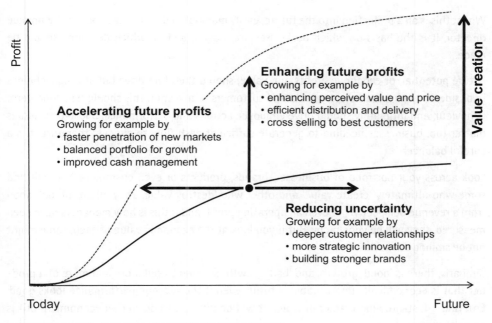

ECONOMIC VALUE, THE SUM OF LIKELY FUTURE PROFITS

Investors are therefore most interested in the future performance of the business – the markets you will enter, the products you are developing, and the strength of brands and relationships to ensure that these future activities will deliver profitable sales.

Investors also expect a return on their investment greater than they would receive from a safe investment (like a savings account or investing in low-risk bonds). We call this the cost of capital, and therefore need to include it in our thinking. They expect 'economic profit', i.e. operating profits minus the cost of capital (typically around 8–12% depending on the future certainty of your markets).

Whilst this is all a projection into the future, easily manipulated in the black box of the finance director, it is the basis on which businesses are judged, and on which decisions should be made.

Future potential, or economic profits and value, should therefore drive our strategic choices in business – which markets, products and customers to invest in. This should be a long-term behaviour, and ultimately should drive employee actions and performance. Short-term issues matter too, businesses needing to generate sufficient cash flow to survive; therefore it is a careful balance.

Look across your portfolio of businesses, brands, products or even customers. You will find some who ultimately 'create value' and other who 'destroy value.' They might all look good from a revenue perspective, or even an operating profit, and if this is how managers have been measured, they will be very happy. But if you look at the economic value of each, some might not be smiling so much.

Similarly, there is 'good' growth, and 'bad' growth. Seeking to sell more and more of a product that is economically unprofitable is futile, even if the revenue performance looks good. Entering a fast-growing market in which it will be difficult to deliver an economic profit is pointless too.

Growth is not easy, nor is growth obvious. Growth isn't something that just happens. It's not simply the output of doing business. It is more than a result. It needs to be managed – it needs a process and strategy too. There is ultimately only one way to deliver over the long term to shareholders. Sustained, profitable growth becomes the business lifeblood.

Insight 2: RED BULL
Entrepreneurial growth of 'liquid cocaine'

'Red Bull gives you wings'

It had been a long flight from Vienna to Bangkok, so Dietrich Mateschitz sat down in the hotel bar, definitely lacking any wings. He asked the Thai waitress what she would recommend to revive him. She laughed and suggested a glass of 'Krating Daeng' (the Thai for red bull) which was popular with Thai farmers, builders and truck drivers who wanted to combat mental and physical fatigue.

The drink, developed in 1962 by Chaleo Yoovidhya, now the CEO of TC Pharmaceutical, was based on Lipovitan, which had originally arrived from Japan. Tasting of citrus and herbs and containing twice the caffeine of a regular can of Coke, it was already a fast-growing drink throughout Asia.

Meteschitz found it a great cure for jet lag, although a little too sweet. As international marketing director of Blendax, a German toothpaste company, he was in town to agree a new licensing agreement with Chaleo. Instead, the two men talked about the potential of the energy drink.

In 1984 the two men started taking the Asian drink to a European audience, each investing $500,000 of their savings in Red Bull GmbH. Initial market testing was not good. The thin brown colour was seen as totally unappetizing, the 'sticking mouth' feeling and aftertaste were disgusting, and the concept of 'stimulates body and mind' was seen as irrelevant.

No product had ever tested quite so badly.

However Mateschitz, who had taken on the running of the business, was determined. For three years he lived with consumer abuse and endless quarrels with government health officials over the contents. 'The worst years of my life,' he would say later.

37

Eventually he threw away his textbooks and ignored convention. This was a drink that would invent a new category – a legal, yet cool stimulant. It looked and tasted like nothing before. Rather than compete against soft drinks, he priced it closer to designer alcohol drinks, 8–10 times more than Coke.

He launched the Austrian version of Red Bull in 1987. The drink was carbonated and less sweet than the original version and packaged in its distinctive 250ml can. Some markets, such as Germany, took as many as five years to overcome health concerns – although Mateschitz didn't always help by joking, 'I had to fly to Pamplona to source bulls' testicles', but he argued that the rumours never hurt.

One young Mexican drinker enthused:

> 'Red Bull is an outrageous drink. I love how it makes me feel always, and really gives me more energy. I drink it after exercise, when I'm out partying with friends, or when I'm working late. When I wake up in the morning and I find out I'm running late for class and I'm still kind of sleepy, I always drink a Red Bull and it keeps me going. I love Red Bull!'

His marketing campaigns were radical and provocative too, ranging from appearances in Play-Station games to Formula 1 motor racing sponsorship, 'The Art of the Can' competition to make sculptures out of empty cans and Red Bull Festival Air Days. The brand seeks to play a role in people's lives rather than just creating aspirational images, conveying the adrenalin-inducing personality.

The myth-building and controversy were all part of the plan, as Jeff Edwards suggested in his book about the growth of the business, *Liquid Cocaine*:

> 'Here is a product that's managed to acquire a reputation as an over-the-counter amphetamine, a surefire wild-times elixir, all the while squirming its way into bars as if it were the latest offering from Anheuser-Busch ... a party drink, a stimulant, an aphro-

disiac, a raver's 'smart drink' gone mainstream ... Red Bull has carefully and intentionally cultivated the mystery surrounding its products, the public has filled in the blanks with speculation and innuendo.'

Meanwhile Red Bull sells and sells.

Mateschitz, sitting in his team space overlooking Austria's Fuschl am See, can look back at his good fortune in taking the jet lag advice of the Thai waitress. He leads a 4000 person company that has not lost its entrepreneurial spirit, with little hierarchy and much 'organized chaos'. It is a caffeine-fuelled business on a mission, but with a simple will to win, rather than a mission statement.

Another Red Bull enthusiast, this time a Polish female, went even further:

'Red Bull is like a potion to me. I don't really care about the extra energy it is supposed to provide my body with. When I drink it I feel like Alice in Wonderland. I use it as a mood enhancer. It makes me feel better and different. For a few moments I can completely forget myself. And I love its taste and smell. It's not delicious, it's specific – and that's exactly the way the real "miracle liquid" should taste.'

By 2006, over three billion cans had been sold in 130 countries. Mateschitz has redefined the market for energy drinks and also made himself a $5 billion fortune. Chaleo, his Thai partner, has made even more, as the original Krating Daeng drink continues to grow across Asia.

1.3 PLATFORMS FOR ACCELERATING GROWTH
Incremental and innovative ways to grow your business

Whilst the options for growth are commonly grouped into organic and inorganic – internally and externally sourced growth – this distinction is much more blurred today.

Organic growth in the sense of 'building on what you've got' is usually the easiest and quickest, but it also delivers small increments of improvement. Of course this does not have to be the case – moving from a product-pushing to solution-selling model can quickly establish superior revenue, significantly greater profits, add differentiation to your offer and engage customers more deeply too. Boeing has found this, for example, when it started offering aircraft leasing and service-based contracts, as did IBM when it started offering business consulting solutions rather than just the technology.

Inorganic growth in the sense of 'acquiring something different' is most often seen in the form of business acquisitions, although they are often presented as friendlier mergers (accounting regulations dictate that one company should be the acquirer). Such transactions are fraught with dangers: whether or not they will work together and whether or not the organizations can extract the 'synergies', not just in terms of cost savings, but in terms of fusing capabilities and portfolios to do something more together than they could apart. The M&A troubles of the likes of Daimler and Chrysler, AOL and Time Warner, or HP and Compaq are well documented. Enormous sums of money and reputations are at risk.

Sometimes, of course, they do succeed – as in the coming together of P&G and Gillette – where there is clearly positive reasons to marry: complementary capabilities (P&G were scientists, Gillette were engineers), product portfolios (P&G were more about women's personal care, Gillette more about men), and market penetration (P&G were dominant in the large superstores of mature markets, whilst Gillette had greater distribution in the small shops and emerging markets). The results followed too. They learnt from each other, they fused their best bits and eliminated others, and real growth (in addition to their combined volumes) followed, as did improved profits and, most significantly, share price.

There are three broad platforms for growth. These should not be viewed as alternatives but as a range of opportunities from which the organization should select a number at each level. The platforms are distinguished by the time and effort required to deliver growth, and the risk and reward involved.

Operational Growth	Innovative Growth	Strategic Growth
Growing through stronger differentiation and deeper customer engagement:	Growing by redefining context and developing new concepts:	Growing by transforming markets with disruption and breakthrough ideas:
• New customers • New channels • New propositions • New products • New communication • New pricing	• New concepts • New applications • New markets • New partners • New processes • New structures	• New ventures • New categories • New businesses • New acquisitions • New capabilities • New business models

PLATFORMS FOR PROFITABLE, SUSTAINABLE GROWTH

The three 'growth platforms' are:

1 **Operational growth.** Doing more of what you do.

- Adding. Getting customers to buy more – Starbucks' broader range of food and accessories encourages larger and more regular purchases.

- Retaining. Retaining your best customers – Lexus focuses on personal service to retain customers for servicing and future renewals.

- Broadening. Engaging new customer segments – Coca-Cola reaches out to new customer segments with new reasons to drink and things to drink.

41

- Extending. Reaching further with new channels – Top Shop extends its reach to young people around the world through franchising and in-store partners.

- Globalizing. Entering new geographic markets – Zara is rapidly extending its store portfolio to every corner of the earth.

- Differentiating. Communicating a new proposition – Skoda revitalized its brand from 'old Communist rust-bucket' to 'solid cars with attitude'.

- Streamlining. Improving business efficiency – Delta fundamentally restructured its airline to reduce costs and improve efficiencies.

2   **Innovative growth.** Do what you do differently.

- Inventing. Developing new products and services – HSBC constantly seeks to develop new financial services for its many audiences.

- Reapplying. Creating new applications for products – Philips explores how its existing products and technologies can be used in new ways.

- Collaborating. Developing solutions with new partners – Disney constantly works with licensees to take its properties into new markets.

- Diversifying. Launching additional diffusion brands – Versace recognized that it needed secondary brands to reach different audiences.

- Concepting. Designing a new business model – Boeing redesigned its business model to focus on collaborative services.

- Sharing. Forming alliances to share resources – Cisco formed alliances with communication partners around the world.

- Partnering. Riding on an affinity partner's back – Samsung reaches out to new markets using partners with strong customer bases.

3   **Strategic growth.** Doing different things.

- Shaping. Shaping new markets in your vision – Apple fundamentally rethinks markets and how to shape them in its own vision.

- Focusing. Becoming a specialist in one area – ICI stripped down their business to focus on a core area.

- Extending. Diversifying into adjacent categories – Nike takes its brand to more and more different sports.

- Acquiring. Buying up your direct competitors – HP acquired Compaq in the hope that they could dominate PCs and printers.

- Connecting. Finding a complementary business – P&G tied up with Gillette to offer men and women the best they can get.

- Venturing. Creating new venture businesses – Google constantly experiments with new businesses by setting up ring-fenced teams.

- Moving. Shifting the business to new markets – IBM recognised that its heritage was not its future, and got out of the PC business.

Collectively these initiatives deliver a 'growth portfolio' – a collection of different initiatives that will deliver growth short- and long-term, with varying levels of effort and risk. How they are achieved depends on the organization, but most can turn to internal and external means, depending on what is right for the market and organization.

Ultimately, growth is very simple – how can you use the assets you have, including brands and relationships, and match them with the best market opportunities for profitable growth?

Matching assets and opportunities is a creative process, most simply about matching the strongest assets with the best opportunities, and then innovatively exploring how the different combinations might deliver growth.

The best initiatives, shaped and evaluated together, form a portfolio of initiatives: 'Operational' growth will typically deliver results fastest but with least impact. You want some of this to show you are delivering. 'Innovative' growth will take a little longer, but has the potential to make more difference. You want some of that too. 'Strategic' growth will be an even slower process, but the results will make people stand up and say 'Wow!' You definitely want some of that too.

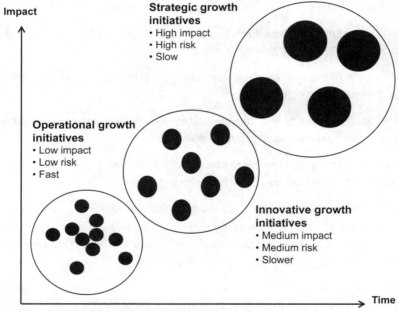

A GROWTH PORTFOLIO BALANCES IMPACT, RISK AND TIME

Like any managed portfolio, the challenge is to create a balance between fairly simple 'no brainers' and more strategic 'big bets'. Growth is required to become a dedicated part of strategic planning, putting all the initiatives on the table, and evaluating their relative strengths and weakness.

Only that way does the portfolio emerge, and only that way can growth be managed.

Who should manage growth in the business?

Because growth is so often seen only as an output, a measure, rather than a process and manageable activity, it is usually left unmanaged, or comes under the responsibility of the CEO or finance director.

Growth needs dedicated management by people with the best growth mindset are those closest to the market opportunities, to the ability to drive innovation and sales. The most sensible 'chief growth officer' is often the 'commercial director'. Whilst this is still an emerging role in organisations, it is a role that can combine a focus on sales and marketing, pricing and profitability, today and tomorrow – and to champion growth across the whole business.

Acceleration

In the continuous search for more value creation, there are three ways to increase the economic value of the business, the likely future cash-flows – one is to improve the margins, another is to reduce the risk, whilst the best is to accelerate growth.

Accelerating growth might seem obvious – just work harder and it will happen sooner – however, businesses can only work at the pace of markets, even if they can influence them.

An effectively managed growth portfolio can be accelerated in different ways. Indeed the three growth platforms can be viewed like the propellers on a turbine. Rather than doing the easy things first, and then moving onto the more difficult challenges, acceleration can be achieved by doing them together.

The blades of the 'propeller' build a momentum and, like an aircraft which the propeller drives, the growth curve starts to rise exponentially.

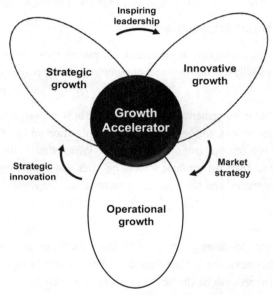

ACCELERATING GROWTH THROUGH STRATEGY, INNOVATION AND LEADERSHIP

Examples of growth 'accelerators' include:

- Faster decisions – large organizations are notoriously slow to seize opportunities, particularly when growth only gets addressed within the planning cycles.

- Rapid development – reducing the time to market or new products, processes and systems by overlapping stages, outsourcing activities, in-market testing and evolving.

- Market sensing – having a quicker, faster sense of market changes, being able to sense and respond to changing customer needs, competitor actions and emerging markets.

- Dual segmenting – evaluating potential audiences not only in terms of their characteristics, motivations and value, but consideration of how this will evolve too.

- Slipstreaming – driving innovations so that product and service enhancements can be launched in parallel with, for instance, a strategic venture which may take longer to catch on.

- Internal creativity – engaging your people in the pursuit of growth, embracing their ideas and giving them the space and responsibility to grow their own parts of the business.

- Smart partnering – finding partners who can serve one need, for example in reaching a new segment, but from whom you could learn more, and work with in more ways too.

- Focusing resources – focusing on the markets and opportunities that matter most, doing fewer things better, with more resources and more commitment to the outcome.

- Organization agility – developing processes and culture that want and embrace continuous change rather than seeking consistency and sameness.

- Capital access – having faster and easier access to capital when it's needed, the mindset of venture capitalists being that they are ready to invest when they spot the right opportunity.

- Portfolio balance – ensuring that there is a good balance of strategic and operational initiatives underway, that investment and resources are suitably allocated.

- Dedicated management – making growth a clearly measured activity with dedicated responsibility and resources, focus and rewards.

The demands for growth will only get larger and faster. As global markets connect, as competition intensifies, as technology speeds up everything, and as customers get bored sooner, organizations will need to look at more significant and more accelerated growth strategies.

As Chris Zook says in *Unstoppable*:

> 'Over the next decades, two out of every three companies will face the challenge of
> their corporate lives: redefining their core businesses to stay competitive. Buffeted by
> ever-stiffening global competition, shifting global dynamics, and accelerating change,
> business leaders face an uncertain future. More and more, executives will realise that
> they must make fundamental changes in their companies' core to spur growth in the
> future – even as they continue to deliver the goods and services that keep their firms in
> business today.'

Insight 3: GE
Growing the world's most admired company

When Jeff Immelt became chairman and CEO in September 2001 he took control of an already
finely tuned machine. Whilst GE had always had an innovative culture, from its famous Blue
Book days of the Fifities, Jack Welch had instilled a formidable bottom line discipline on the
business too. Immelt turned to two of GE's strengths – process and execution – and set out in
pursuit of organic growth.

At GE's meeting of top managers at Baton Rouge in January 2006, Immelt told his leaders
that if they continued to grow existing businesses at current rates, the company would not
survive. 'Another decade of 4% growth and GE will cease to exist', he said. 'But if we can spur
our growth rate without losing our productivity edge, GE will keep being the most admired
company into the next century.

'We're now in a slow growth world. Things were different 25 years ago. Today's global markets
are driven by innovation, and stock market premiums are based on companies who can generate their own growth.'

Immelt described further, in a recent interview with *Harvard Business Review*, his belief that a culture of productivity, and relying on expansion and acquisitions for growth, is not enough. Innovation must be at the heart of organic growth and of value creation.

He believes this approach will enable GE to deliver average revenue growth of around 8%, double what it was in the last decade (and two to three times faster than the world's economy is growing), and that this will deliver 10%+ earnings and 20% returns.

To grow faster than the global economy, GE has turned organic growth into a process rather than just a goal.

> 'If you run a big multinational, multi-business company like GE, and if you are trying to lead transformative change, then that objective has to be linked to hitting levers across all businesses, and it must keep that up over time.'

In a letter to all his shareholders, Immelt illustrated the challenge and opportunity:

> 'A reliable growth company must have the courage to invest and the discipline to deliver. It took courage to invest over $1 billion in a new jet engine, such as the GE90, with minimal returns for more than 10 years. Today, because of these investments, GE enjoys exceptional success in commercial aviation. The GE90 engine should generate $40 billion of revenue over the next 30 years.'

He went on to encourage investors to 'think about the company over 10+ years the way an owner would think about it', and to get a sense of the strategic investments that are required to build the business, as demonstrated by those that are now delivering results rather than focusing on short-term returns. 'We are builders of businesses … we have a team that is focused on building a company that has enduring value and makes the world a better place.'

GE is now focused on establishing the capabilities that will create and sustain this organic growth – most crucially, a focus on customers, innovation and globalization.

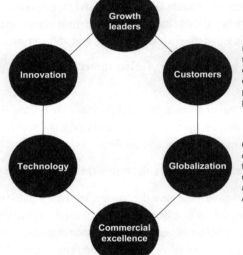

Inspiring and developing people
who know how to help customers
and are willing and able to work in
the new GE ways

Generating new ideas and
developing capabilities to
make them a reality, for
example through market-
driven opportunities and
imagination breakthroughs

Using processes excellence
to satisfy customers and
drive growth, measured for
example, through a 'net
promoter score' based on
positive recommendations

Having the best products,
content and services,
developed for example
through GE's
'Ecomagination' initiative

Creating new market
opportunities throughout
the world and expanding in
developing markets such
as Asia and South
America

Developing world class sales and
marketing talent, and demonstrating
the value of 'one GE', with integrated
branding and selling

GE'S FRAMEWORK FOR PROFITABLE GROWTH

The GE 'Execute for Growth' process is mapped out as a circle, with no clear start or finish. It
embraces new approaches and techniques, language and behaviour.

- *The 'Growth Playbook'* redefines the strategic planning process, recognizing that it should be a creative rather than financially-driven process, encouraging collaboration and rethinking, rather than incremental box-filling budgeting.

- *'Customer Dreaming Sessions'* bring together influential and creative people from across the industry to dream its future and through difference of perspective and opinion, to inspire new ideas and strategies.

- *'Imagination Breakthroughs'* focus senior management on the best ideas that will drive new revenue streams, irrelevant of where they come from.

- *'Innovation Labs'* support business strategy, product development and other initiatives with specialist resources and materials to drive and structure the innovation of products, businesses and markets.

- *'At the Customer, for the Customer'* is about opening up and transferring its own management approaches into customer companies to help them solve their own business problems, rather than just providing products and services

- *'CECOR Marketing Framework'* ensures that customers and market opportunities drive innovation and growth. It stands for 'calibrate, explore, create, organize and realize' strategic growth.

- *'Growth Traits'* are the attributes expected of future GE business leaders. There are five factors to get on in the company: external focus, clear thinking, imagination, inclusiveness and specialist expertise.

The new approach is not full of lengthy written proposals and PowerPoint slideshows; it's about people working together – people with diverse experiences, skills and perspectives (Immelt gets involved in around eight breakthrough sessions per month) – focusing on the best ideas and opportunities, capturing the essence of ideas in pictures and prototypes, communicated in short summaries and practical action.

The high-flying CEO reflects on his new, highly motivated, fast-growing GE:

> 'This is not a place for small times. Working at GE is the art of thinking and playing big. Our managers have to work cross function, region and company. And we have to be about big purposes.'

He reminds people that if they fail, the worst that can happen is that they will leave and find a bigger job somewhere else. But if you win at GE 'you get to be in the front seat of history, creating the future'.

The results are impressive. Since 2005, organic growth has averaged 8%, higher than competitors and twice GE's historical average. There is now a pipeline of 40 '$1 billion revenue products' to be introduced in coming years, and 60 'Imagination Breakthroughs' generating $25 billion, and many more on the way. Non-US revenue streams are now exceeding domestic figures and are predicted to grow at 15% annually, and more effective management of the installed base should generate decades of service-based growth.

Immelt, in an interview with CNN, believes that growth is ultimately a human challenge:

> 'Achieving this kind of growth depends on making it the personal mission of everyone here. If we want, we can cloak ourselves in the myth of the professional manager and hide any problem in the process flowchart. But if I want people to take more risks, solve bigger problems, and grow the business in a way that's never been done before, I have to make it personal.'

The best opportunities in a fast and fragile world

'The Chinese use two brush strokes to write the word "crisis". One brush stroke stands for danger; the other for opportunity. In a crisis, be aware of the danger – but recognize the opportunity'

John F. Kennedy

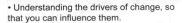

A more **intelligent** approach to **opportunities** that embraces stronger *left brain* thinking	A more **imaginative** approach to **opportunities** that embraces stronger *right brain* thinking
• Understanding the drivers of change, so that you can influence them.	• Having a better, bigger, broader vision of the world than others.
• Constantly tracking the business environment and how it changes.	• Seeing the world from new and interesting perspectives.
• Defining the context for your business, knowing what is relevant.	• Making sense of complexity, and learning to live with apparent paradox.
• Identifying new opportunities to drive profitable and sustained growth.	• Defining possibilities before they are shaped by existing conventions.
• Evaluating the short- and longer-term potential of emerging markets.	• Identifying unarticulated spaces that could be new markets.
• Identifying your best assets and how you can use them.	• Making unusual connections between markets, trends and opportunities.
• Connecting the best opportunities with the priorities of today.	• Engaging people in the future in a way that gives optimism and confidence.

We live, and do business, in an extraordinary time. We stand on the edge of two different worlds. One is smarter, richer and sophisticated. The other is divided, unbalanced and unsustainable.

If we get it wrong we will be faced with unthinkable, destructive consequences.

Our world has come an incredibly long way in a short time – when was it that we started driving and flying; how did we survive before telephones and emails? It seems rather dramatic to suggest that this could be humanity's last century or two – but the decisions we make in the next decade could also mark a new renaissance in the way we live, work and succeed.

Some statistics presented at the World Economic Forum might make you think:

- Every year we destroy 44 million acres of forest, creating an increasing imbalance in the way nature produces and absorbs carbon dioxide.

- Every year we lose 100 million acres of farmland, cutting down trees, diverting natural irrigation and creating 15 million acres of new desert around the world.

- Every year we use 160 billion tons more water each year than is being replenished by rain, enough to require a 450,000 km convoy of trucks.

- Every year our population rises towards 9 billion, mainly in poor countries, putting even greater demand on their diminishing supplies of food and water.

- Every year the rich get richer. If productivity continues to grow at 2.5%, within 100 years, society will be 12 times richer in real terms.

- Every year our consumption demands increase, particularly in rich countries, putting yet more demand on the overburdened factories and farmyards of poorer countries.

These may seem like statistics that we watch on TV or read in the newspapers, and they do concern us. But they seem disconnected from our world of work. Are they really going to stop you achieving your sales targets this year? Or driving new innovations? Do stock market analysts really care about them?

The reality is that they do – maybe not this quarter, but certainly in the mid- to longer-term future. And whilst it is easy to say big businesses, capitalism and a blind pursuit of wealth has caused many of these problems, it also offers the best solutions.

As businesses, we can have far more impact, make a larger, positive difference, than individuals can. We can probably make more of a difference than governments, too. Not through charity, but commercial solutions – doing business in better ways. Innovating in a way that also addresses some of these issues, engaging people in it so that they choose you for more reasons, and making money by doing the right thing.

As business leaders, we are the few individuals who really can change the world.

The list of challenges is long and scary. Yet many of the challenges are linked, and linked to the inputs and outputs of business too. The biggest problem of all is that we live beyond our means. Just consider some more of the factors:

- Global warming will lead to fundamental climate change; water shortages will increase as rivers dry up and crops die; the spread of deserts will accelerate as soil is eroded and warms; marine life destruction will reduce biodiversity and threaten food chains.

- Mass famines in the poorest countries will grow as crops fail and prices rise; there will be extreme poverty as the gap between the rich and poor gets larger; pandemics will spread further and faster than ever in a connected world; and there will be global migration to richer geographies, and the rise of poor and violent inner cities within them.

- Terrorism is increasingly unpredictable and the ringleaders cannot be located; religious extremism creates distrust and division between people; scientific and genetic experimentation will become increasingly unregulated; and ease of access to nuclear and bio-logical weapons will increase.

Al Gore has famously and fabulously documented how he sees some of these challenges in his Oscar-winning film *An Inconvenient Truth*. He focuses on the climate, and the implications of not acting on the rapid way that it is changing, largely due to the effects of business growth:

> 'Our climate crisis may at times appear to be happening slowly, but in fact it is happening very quickly – and become a true planetary emergency.
>
> The Chinese expression for crisis consists of two characters. The first is a symbol for danger; the second is a symbol for opportunity. In order to face down the danger that is stalking us and move through it we first have to recognize that we are facing a crisis.
>
> So why is it that our leaders seem not to hear such clarion warnings? Are they resisting the truth because they know that the moment they acknowledge it, they will face a moral imperative to act? Is it simply more convenient to ignore the warnings?
>
> Perhaps, but inconvenient truths do not go away just because they are not seen. Indeed when they are not responded to, their significant doesn't diminish, it grows ...
>
> We have everything we need to begin solving this crisis, with the possible exception of the will to act.'

In a fast-changing, complex and evolving world, the best opportunities to create and sustain growth are inextricably linked with the biggest challenges that we face in the world.

2.1 RIDING THE GROWTH WAVES
Changing markets require innovative solutions

Of course, it is incredibly hard for business to outgrow its market.

The median revenue of a Fortune 100 company is around $30 billion, therefore achieving 'double digit' growth (which you have probably noticed is the favourite phrase of any jargon-seeking IT executive) requires at least $3 billion new revenue to be found every year. No small task when the US economy itself is only growing at around 5% and therefore, by definition, so must the average business.

The averagely successful company is therefore unlikely to grow beyond 5% each year.

However, as we look all around us, the speed of growth is phenomenal. Looking back over the last 100 years we can see the continued rise of stock markets, through cycles with peaks and troughs, but rising overall.

If we map the emergence of some of the most familiar brands and innovations onto this trend line, then we can see how companies have constantly and rapidly innovated to ride the waves of change – and to grow rapidly to where they are today.

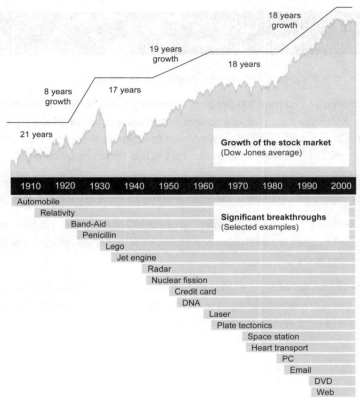

Growth of the stock market
(Dow Jones average)

18 years
growth

19 years
growth

18 years

8 years
growth

17 years

21 years

| 1910 | 1920 | 1930 | 1940 | 1950 | 1960 | 1970 | 1980 | 1990 | 2000 |

Automobile
Relativity
Band-Aid
Penicillin
Lego
Jet engine
Radar
Nuclear fission
Credit card
DNA
Laser
Plate tectonics
Space station
Heart transport
PC
Email
DVD
Web

Significant breakthroughs
(Selected examples)

100 YEARS OF INNOVATION AND GROWTH

Will the stock markets continue to rise and rise?

Probably during our lifetimes, with more bubbles – both booms and busts – along the way. The reality of our world is starting to work against us and it will take a new type of innovation, a more thoughtful business, to sustain growth into the future.

As the world innovates around us, people live and work in very different ways. We respect different types of authority – young rather than old, ideas rather than experience – and we attach ourselves to different loyalties – personal rather than collective, virtual rather than physical.

As business leaders and individual consumers we live in new ways: we want to learn rather be taught, we sense rather than believe in absolute knowledge, we turn to Google rather than our memories, we know that being street-smart gets us further than academic qualifications do.

As businesses we work differently too – at great speeds and distances thanks to instant technologies, as virtual organizations rather than feeling we need to do everything ourselves, as flat networks rather than hierarchical pyramids, and we maintain control by leadership and influence rather than management and power.

Insight 4: KIKKOMAN
The Japanese secret of a long life

According to Japanese folklore, the tortoise lives for 10,000 years and is the symbol of long life and prosperity. In the world of soy sauce, there is nothing older or more successful than Kikkoman, where 'kikko' means tortoise shell, and 'man' means ten thousand.

The Mogi and Takanashi families began soy sauce production along the banks of the Edo River in Noda, a small Japanese town. Since 1603, they created delicious, natural seasonings that were then transported down the river to Tokyo, where they became official suppliers to the Japanese imperial household.

In 1917, eight family companies merged to form Noda Shoyu Co. with capital of ¥7 million. The sauce first arrived in San Francisco in 1957 serving the large Oriental community, and local manufacturing began soon after in Wisconsin, the heart of American wheat and soya bean country.

The company became Kikkoman Shoyu Co. in 1964 and eventually Kikkoman Corporation in 1980. The business now has many affiliates and subsidiaries, together offering a diverse portfolio ranging from pharmaceuticals to food. JFC, for example, was acquired, offering 8500 Oriental food products, and brands such as Dynasty, Nishiki rice and Ozeki sake.

Kikkoman, according to its advertising line, is about 'flavours that bring people together'.

However, soy sauce remains at the heart of the business, made from soya beans, wheat and salt. Indeed the sauce has a legacy that goes back over 2500 years. Today it is an indispensable ingredient in Chinese and Japanese dishes, and the 'secret' ingredient of many chefs worldwide. It is now produced across the world, as well as on the banks of the Edo.

Kikkoman remains the global category leader, generating over $2 billion annual revenue, and is the subject of Ronald Yates' *The Kikkoman Chronicles: A Global Company with a Japanese Soul*.

The next time you sit down for Oriental food, look at the six-sided logo on your Kikkoman bottle, representing a tortoise shell with the Chinese character, or kanji, for ten thousand inside.

Kikkoman timeline

1603   Mogo and Takanashi start soy sauce production in Noda, Japan.

1873   Kikkoman wins international food award at World Fair in Vienna.

1917   Family firms merge to form Noda Shoyu Co. Ltd.

1925   Further merger of families to increase distribution reach.

1957   Kikkoman enters North American market in San Francisco.

1964   Company is renamed Kikkoman Shoyu Co. Ltd.

1969   Acquires JFC International Ltd, and wide range of foodstuffs.

1972   Starts US production in Wisconsin.

1980   Company is renamed Kikkoman Corporation.

2.2   BUSINESS HOTSPOTS
Learning to live in a new business world

The year 2000 was supposed to herald a new dawn, but at the time in the business world, it seemed like the crashing end of a brave new world, a glorious dream that became a nightmare: the 'dotcom bubble' had burst.

At the time, this new world seemed to be governed by new laws – Moore's Law predicting the doubling of computer power every 18 months, Gilder's Law saying that bandwidth triples every 12 months, and Metcalfe's Law saying that the value of a network is proportional to the square of the nodes.

Also in 2000, amidst the collapsing virtual structures and business confidence, a new book was published. *The Cluetrain Manifesto* was a seminal work but got a little lost in the fall-out of all the digital hype and over-expectations of the late Nineties. It articulated the real impacts of a fast and connected world, and perhaps now is the time to return to it:

'People of Earth

'A power global conversation has begun ...

'Networked markets are beginning to self-organize faster than the companies that have traditionally served them. Thanks to the web, markets are becoming better informed, smarter, and more demanding of qualities missing from most business organizations.

'The sky is open to the stars. Clouds roll over us night and day. Oceans rise and fall. Whatever you may have heard, this is our world, our place to be. Whatever you've been told, our flags fly free. Our heart goes on forever. People of Earth, remember.

'Through the Internet, people are discovering and inventing new ways to share relevant knowledge with blinding speed. As a direct result, markets are getting smarter – and getting smarter faster than most companies.

'These markets are conversations. Their members communicate in language that is natural, open, honest, direct, funny and often shocking. Whether explaining or complaining, joking or serious, the human voice is unmistakably genuine. It can't be faked.

'Most corporations, on the other hand, only know how to talk in the soothing, humourless monotone of the mission statement, marketing brochure, and your-call-is-important-to-us busy signal. Same old tone, same old lies. No wonder networked markets have no respect for companies unable or unwilling to speak as they do.

'But learning to speak in a human voice is not some trick, nor will corporations convince us they are human with lip service about 'listening to customers.' They will only sound human when they empower real human beings to speak on their behalf.

'While many such people already work for companies today, most companies ignore their ability to deliver genuine knowledge, opting instead to crank out sterile happytalk that insults the intelligence of markets literally too smart to buy it.

'However, employees are getting hyperlinked even as markets are. Companies need to listen carefully to both. Mostly, they need to get out of the way so intranetworked employees can converse directly with internetworked markets.

'Corporate firewalls have kept smart employees in and smart markets out. It's going to cause real pain to tear those walls down. But the result will be a new kind of conversation. And it will be the most exciting conversation business has ever engaged in.

'If you only have time for one clue this year, this is the one to get …

'We are not seats or eyeballs or end users or consumers. We are human beings – and our reach exceeds your grasp. Deal with it'

Source: www.cluetrain.com

Metcalfe is Robert Metcalfe, the senior technologist at 3Com. He was onto something but he was largely ignored in the rush online.

With Web 2.0, there has been a recent resurgence of interest and online businesses have taken it to their hearts – the rise of online exchanges like eBay and social networks like MySpace reflects the power which Metcalfe predicted, and really starts to use the Internet to its potential, and in a way that really does change the way that we do business and behave as real people.

With time to reflect and the emergence of the likes of Amazon and Google as admired twenty-first century business models, companies are at last starting to harness the power of networks to their real winning business models.

The new hotspots
The technologists flocked to Silicon Valley, the manufacturers grew rich in Japan and the Far East, the car industry converged on Detroit, the industrial revolutionaries focused on the English Midlands, and the gold hunters rushed to California in other moments of madness.

Today we are focused on the BRIC nations – the fast-growing, emerging markets of Brazil, Russia, India and China. But there are many other hot spots in the world of business too. The

Baltic countries are shrugging off a communist past and embracing the future – just visit the WiFi-enabled cities of Tallinn and Riga. The Gulf states are booming too, rich on their oil, but increasingly for broader business too.

If we were to consider the average growth in market capitalization by regions of the world, new names start to emerge. According to the World Federation of Exchange, the value of businesses in Shanghai grew by 320% during 2006/7. Shenzhen was not far behind on 180%, whilst some smaller countries followed with Peru and Slovenia on 120%. Compare this to the still impressive but dwarfed growth rates in New York of 9% and London of 18%.

So what creates a business hotspot? From Abu Dhabi to Bangalore, Macau to Sau Paulo, what are the secrets of these growth capitals? There are obvious factors, like a good communication and transport infrastructure, nearby technologies and research facilities, skilled workers and good living facilities, and access to capital markets. There is the support of governments – enterprise grants, fiscal concessions, and practical support.

However the biggest difference is probably who else is there. Whilst companies no longer need their suppliers on their doorstep, like the car makers once did, innovators feel more productive alongside other innovators. Maybe they share practical resources, even find ways to collaborate commercially, but sometimes it's just that they breathe the same creative air.

Scandinavia's Medicon Valley is the world's leading life sciences hotspot.

The area that spans from Copenhagen in Denmark and Skåne in Sweden contains probably the highest concentration of pharmaceutical companies in Europe – and the world's leading centre for developing treatments for diabetes, cancer and neurosciences. One hundred and fifteen companies can be found in 100 square kilometres. They are surrounded by 7 science parks, 12 universities, 26 hospitals, 5000 life science researchers, 41,000 people employed in the life science industry, 140,000 higher education students and the area has a population of 3.2 million. The region's product pipeline exceeds all other places, whilst there are more business/academic partnerships and clinic support resources there than anywhere else.

World's largest economic markets $bn	
1. USA	12980
2. China	10000
3. Japan	4220
4. India	4042
5. Germany	2585
6. UK	1903
7. France	1871
8. Italy	1727
9. Russia	1723
10. Brazil	1616
20. Argentina	599
30. Bangladesh	331
40. Greece	252
50. Venezuela	176

Source: CIA World Factbook 2007 (the gross domestic product or value of all final goods and services produced within a nation in year)

World's fastest growing markets	
1. Azerbaijan	32.5
2. Muaritania	19.4
3. Equitorial Guinea	18.6
4. Maldives	18.0
5. Angola	14.0
6. Cambodia	13.4
7. Armenia	13.4
8. Turkmenistan	13.0
9. Trinidad & Tobago	12.6
10. Liechenstein	11.0
20. Georgia	8.8
30. Malawi	7.6
40. Bahrain	7.0
50. Russia	6.6

Source: CIA World Factbook 2007 (based on GDP % growth adjusted for inflation)

THE WORLD'S HIGH GROWTH MARKETS

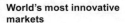

World's most innovative markets	
1. Japan	6.02
2. Switzerland	5.89
3. Germany	5.85
4. USA	5.75
5. Sweden	5.66
6. Finland	5.65
7. Denmark	5.40
8. Israel	5.40
9. Taiwan	5.38
10. UK	5.36
Australia	4.66
India	4.60
Brazil	4.09
China	3.75
Russia	3.55

Source: World Economic Forum Global Competitiveness Report 2006-2007 (based on business sophistication and innovativeness)

World's most friendly markets	
1. Denmark	8.77
2. Finland	8.72
3. Singapore	8.69
4. Canada	8.69
5. USA	8.68
6. Netherlands	8.64
7. UK	8.63
8. Switzerland	8.60
9. Hong Kong	8.60
10. Ireland	8.57
Australia	8.41
Japan	7.45
Brazil	6.78
China	6.36
Russia	6.06

Source: Economist Intelligence Unit 2006 (based on economic and political environment, foreign investment policy, tax, labour market and infrastructure).

THE WORLD'S INNOVATIVE MARKETS

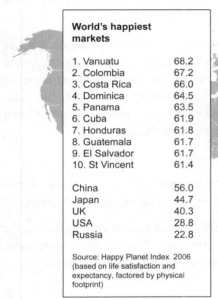

World's happiest markets

1. Vanuatu — 68.2
2. Colombia — 67.2
3. Costa Rica — 66.0
4. Dominica — 64.5
5. Panama — 63.5
6. Cuba — 61.9
7. Honduras — 61.8
8. Guatemala — 61.7
9. El Salvador — 61.7
10. St Vincent — 61.4

China — 56.0
Japan — 44.7
UK — 40.3
USA — 28.8
Russia — 22.8

Source: Happy Planet Index 2006 (based on life satisfaction and expectancy, factored by physical footprint)

World's most ethical markets

1. Finland — 9.6
2. Iceland — 9.6
3. New Zealand — 9.6
4. Denmark — 9.5
5. Singapore — 9.4
6. Sweden — 9.2
7. Switzerland — 9.1
8. Norway — 8.8
9. Australia — 8.7
10. Netherlands — 8.7

UK — 8.6
Japan — 7.6
USA — 7.3
China — 3.3
Russia — 2.5

Source: Corruption Perception Index 2006 (based on perception of business people and analysts, 10 = clean, 0= corrupt).

THE WORLD'S GOOD MARKETS

Insight 5: SECOND LIFE
Now you can be anybody you want to be

Snow Crash, a cyberpunk novel by Neal Stephenson, was the main inspiration behind the initial development of a virtual world by Philip Rosedale in 2002.

The book described a futuristic environment where people live and work virtually – they create the people they want to be and do anything they want. They work in this virtual world, setting up virtual companies that trade with other virtual people, creating a virtual economy. Their best friends are in this virtual world too. Not real friends, but people who other people want to be. Together this is where they hang out and increasingly spend their time.

Nothing was impossible in this world. There were no rules or conventions. A person who was old, fat and lacked confidence could live the life of their alter ego. They could be the cool, young dude who chatted up the babes, drove the fastest car and ran their own bar. The stressed out office worker could run their own business, or luxuriate on their own tropical island. If you were old you could be young, male could be female, red hair could be blonde hair. Of course it had a negative side too, with virtual crime, virtual bullying, and virtual terrorism.

Five million real people have now joined this virtual world.

Second Life is an Internet-based virtual world which hit the headlines in late 2006, and is one of a number of online communities that offer a more sophisticated form of social networking.

Founded by Philip Rosedale, a former CTO of RealNetworks, and his company Linden Lab, the initial version *LindenWorld* was a niche site for web developers. Beta versions soon followed introducing a virtual currency, the Linden Dollar, although at this time, the currency had no translatable value into US dollars.

The stated goal of Linden Lab is to create a world like the *Metaverse* described by Stephenson: a user-defined world of general use in which people can interact, play, do business, and otherwise communicate.

Second Life is a free, downloadable program that enables its users, called 'residents', to interact with each other through 'avatars' that they create themselves. Users can opt for different levels of interaction, the higher levels requiring an annual fee, but also providing greater initial funding of Linden Dollars. The currency is now exchangeable for US dollars, enabling people to acquire more, or to convert the virtual fortunes they make back into real money.

Just like in the real world, communities start to develop around the most convenient places, people start to interact in more formal ways, buying and selling, socializing and entertaining.

Property prices in the most popular towns rise, and if you were lucky enough to buy in the right place at the right time, you can sell for a significant profit. You can employ a (real) web designer to enhance your avatar further, or you can make money by opening a (virtual) coffee shop where the coolest people hang out.

As the virtual world grows, so does the economy; as the demand for Linden Dollars goes up, so does the exchange rate back to US dollars.

Many real world brands have entered the virtual world. Adidas was one of the first, offering virtual three-striped clothing for the sportiest avatars. From banks to beer, your avatar can now buy most of the things you like too. Remember: brands define people, and people pay more for them.

Music stars regularly perform in the virtual world, to enhance their hip credentials in the real world; Leo Burnett established a creative agency to tap into the ideas of people (so you can have a virtual job as well as a real one); and IBM regularly hold virtual seminars where delegates can explore and test new business concepts against the people's uninhibited aspirations rather than their convention-influenced needs in the real world.

Social networks with a distinctive idea can spread like wildfire. In October 2006, the site reached one million registered accounts; within two months this had doubled, and within another two months it had doubled again to four million. Around 10% of accounts are active at any time, most at 10pm in the evening (local time), fewest at 10am in the morning when most people are back in their real worlds.

Whilst *Second Life* and competitors such as *Active Worlds* and *Cyberpark* might be dismissed as online games by some, and by others as an environment that promotes unethical and even illegal practices, they also illustrate the rise of new forms of global community, and new economic models for business. A game, however, it is not. There are no points, scores, winners, losers or end-strategy in *Second Life*.

2.3 UNLOCKING THE GROWTH DRIVERS
Finding enduring growth, avoiding bubbles that burst

So what do CEOs see as the most important global trends for business over the next five years?

Importance to business ↑	
Increasingly global labour and talent markets	Growing number of consumers in emerging economies
Shifting of economic activity between and within regions	Increasing availability of knowledge and ability to exploit it
Increasing constrains on supply and use of natural resources	Development of technologies that empower consumers and communities
An ageing population in developed economies	A faster pace of technological innovation
Geopolitical instability	
Increasing sophistication of capital markets	Adoption of increasingly scientific management techniques
Shifting industry structures and emerging forms of organization	
Social backlash against corporate activity	
Growth of public sector	

Impact on profits ⟶

THE CEO AGENDA (SOURCE: MCKINSEY QUARTERLY, 2007)

Whilst most executives felt that emerging markets were a significant opportunity, only a minority had taken action to address it. Similarly, the majority of companies had also not addressed opportunities such as talent markets, resource constraints or ageing populations.

More generally, change in the business environment is largely driven by technology, but also sociological and economic factors. The drivers include:

- Rise of computing power, interactivity and virtual networks.

- Compression of distance and time, and the speed of change.

- Irrelevance of geography, borders and hierarchies.

- Rise of southern hemisphere and maturity of eastern markets.

- Frictionless economics and corporate transparency.

- Rapid imitation of new products and shortened lifecycles.

- Globalization of culture, alongside religious differences.

The changing business environment is accompanied by new practices, issues and regulations, presenting business and marketing with new challenges. The rise of more aggressive telemarketing approaches, such as the highly irritating recorded messages that interrupt your home at any hour of the day with the rather misleading suggestion that 'you have just won a major prize' has prompted a majority of US households to 'ban' such practices by registering at donotcall.com.

More general examples include:

- Demand for customer privacy and ownership of personal information.

- Customer backlash against the avalanche of and intrusion from direct marketing.

- Rise of social issues and ethics, from environment to transparency.

- Deficit of customer trust and prevalence of competitive promiscuity.

- Globalization of brands, leading to cultural sameness and classlessness.

- Increasing support for entrepreneurship in capital markets and from governments.

- Importance of intellectual properties and value of intangible assets.

Customers are more different and intelligent, their expectations are higher, and they are more powerful than ever. Research by Martin Lindstrom in *BRANDchild* for example shows that kids can cope with complexity far better than adults: they can do 5.4 things at the same time – watching, playing, talking, texting and eating simultaneously – whilst adults can manage 1.7 (men even less).

Some of the broader implications are:

- Western populations are more affluent but have less time to enjoy it.

- Older people are wealthier, with time, and want to travel the world.

- Kids grow up fast, quickly replacing baby toys with designer fashion.

- The rise of online communities, buying groups and political lobbies means individuals have more of a voice.

- We have concerns about health and obesity, including the falling standards in sports.

- There is a preference for small and local, rather than big and global brands.

- Many of us have everything we need; yet we still want more.

- We are in pursuit of happiness, improved lifestyle and wellbeing.

These structural and behavioural changes fundamentally reshape markets, making profitable ones unprofitable, requiring new ways to approach existing ones, and opening up completely new spaces to compete. Indeed it is useful to draw an illustrative map of your extended 'marketspace', your existing and adjacent markets, adjacent in terms of both business capabilities and customer applications.

Returning to where we started, this track leaves us with one important consideration.

We are standing at the crossroads between a richer, smarter civilization, and a new Dark Age. When we look beyond the conventions of industry reports, the short-term priorities of business, and the blinkers of capital markets, we will be reminded that we are living beyond our means.

Some of the historical economic bubbles that have burst include:

- Tulips – first introduced to Europe from Turkey in the sixteenth century; however with decades, the demand for new colours soared, a rare bulb selling for the same as an Amsterdam home.

- Mississippi – there was an eighteenth century rush by Europe, largely the French, for the riches of the West Indies and North America, but their investments were often found to be worthless.

- South Seas – soon after, rich pickings were believed to lie in the Spanish colonies of South America, but most investors found that their money had gone into fictional companies.

- Railways – overinvestment in the mid-nineteenth century railways soon led to overcapacity, as well as spiralling interest rates caused by the diversion of investment in other sectors.

- Wall Street – in the 1920s, stock prices rose by 400% in five years, totally unrelated to the worth of companies, leading to large debts, sharp falls and panic selling.

- Japan – relaxation of post-war controls led to a 1985 global buying spree funded by loans on property, but rising interest rates led to rising debts and economic stagnation.

- Dotcom – venture capitalists couldn't get enough of high-tech start-ups or anything else with a website, but by 2002 the Nasdaq had fallen by 70% and took many dreams with it.

It might be possible to sustain growth over a few more years, squeezing more out of existing markets, resources and tolerances.

However the enlightened business does not seek to squeeze a drying sponge. They look further afield. In many ways we are nearing the end of the industrial age. Whilst new technologies and service businesses have complemented product-creating businesses, we have still largely focused on making and selling things. What are the implications of the end of the industrial age?

It is possible that the whole of the last century has been an industrial age bubble – as we have raped the earth of its natural resources, without a care for the wider environment in which we work and live. Maybe it has been a bubble too, which, unless we take the right actions, is now about to burst. It will certainly be followed by a new age, but with new winners, and many old losers.

Our path of choice is not sustainable, and unless we make some new choices, finding better ways to achieve our dreams, then we could end up with unthinkable and unsurvivable consequences. It seems rather dramatic to suggest that this could be humanity's last century, but it could also mark a new renaissance in the way we live, work and succeed.

Insight 6: LI & FUNG
You can do anything in a 'flat' world

London. Paris. Sydney. New York. Walk through a shopping mall in any of the world's great cities, and 30 to 40% of the retailers and brand names that you see are likely to rely upon Li & Fung for their business success.

Li & Fung is the world's leading virtual supply chain. In a world where ideas and relationships are all you need to succeed, then this Hong-Kong based business can take care of the rest. Dream up your new fashion collection, and Li & Fung will sort out the sourcing, manufacturing, distribution, merchandising, and even your back office.

All you need is the good idea; everything else can be achieved through partners. You become an invisible business. Your value is in your intangible assets.

However, Li & Fung is not some enormous Asian factory churning out the world's clothes before branding. It is a smart, contemporary, invisible business too. It manages your supply chain, sourcing the best materials, finding the right manufacturers, planning the production, assuring quality, finding the most efficient distributors, packaging the items in your own brand too.

Li & Fung, as an invisible business, is all about ideas and connections, with $7 billion annual revenue and a market cap of $12 billion.

It offers companies like Levi's a virtual, customized supply chain. This is much more than out-sourcing your manufacturing: their offices in over 70 countries will identify the right place in the world to source any material or activity at any time. From clothing and furnishings, handicrafts and toys, gifts and promotional materials, it is your ultimate one-stop shop.

Old supply chains were driven by what factories made; now they are designed to match demand, driven by what people want to buy. In the past it was transactional; now it is a partnership with shared information and people, risk and reward. Old supply chains delivered goods to warehouses; now they package and put tags on them and deliver them directly to the store ready for sale.

In a 'flat world', distance and borders, economies and regulation, no longer shape what you can make or do. Li & Fung takes much of the cost, distraction, and risks out of being a global business. The vertically integrated model (where you sought to own and control your supply chain), and the cluster model (like the car manufacturers of Detroit, where suppliers were encouraged to locate themselves nearby) are both redundant in this new global workplace.

Founded in 1906 in Guangzhou, Li & Fung is now headquartered in Hong Kong, and was one of the original companies that made the island such an economic success. The island became the place for manufacturing, although through its success it became more expensive, and the trend moved to Taiwan, Korea, Bangladesh, India, and even back to Europe. Indeed, the whole idea of an item being 'made in' a country is increasingly meaningless. Imagine a new jacket, the shell made in Korea, the lining in Taiwan, filling in China, accessories in Hong Kong. So where was it made?

Since Li & Fung went public in 1992, the business had achieved a 22% compound annual growth rate, and whilst it took 93 years to get to $2 billion revenue, it has only taken 7 years to triple that.

Speaking at the 2007 Wharton Alumni Forum in Hong Kong, CEO Bruce Rockowitz said 'you learn from business school that when your numbers get big, your growth slows down, but we have seen the opposite in our business'. Having joined Li & Fung when his own business was acquired by them in 2000, he puts the phenomenal growth down to 'active entrepreneurship', strong planning and a clear vision of the new manufacturing world.

Rockowitz also describes the agility of Li & Fung, the ability to keep reinventing itself and its business model to meet the needs of its customers, and ahead of its competitors. 'Every three years we consider fundamental change. We spend much time thinking about what we can do better or different. We develop scenarios, anticipating how business will evolve, where will rise and who will struggle, then we jump into the future, and look back to see how our business can grow further and faster.'

From monks and magicians to leaders and managers

'The tail trails the head. If the head moves fast, the tail will keep up the same pace. If the head is sluggish, the tail will droop'

Konosuke Matsushita

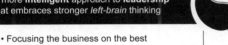

A more **intelligent** approach to **leadership** that embraces stronger *left-brain* thinking	A more **imaginative** approach to **leadership** that embraces stronger *right-brain* thinking
• Focusing the business on the best opportunities for value creation. • Developing the business strategies and defining priorities. • Managing people and processes, relationships and reputation. • Ensuring that budgets and resources are available where most effective. • Measuring operational delivery and performance improvement. • Managing assets and portfolios to maximize their long-term value. • Articulating commercial results and future potential to investors.	• Creating an inspiring vision of the future and the role of the business in it. • Engaging people in the purpose and strategy of the business. • Connecting the best people and best ideas inside and outside. • Driving innovation across the business and making ideas happen. • Supporting and coaching people in delivering their activities. • Energizing people to deliver great business performance • Building an organization for today and tomorrow.

In *The Monk and the Riddle*, digital entrepreneur Randy Komisar describes his journey from small company to larger companies, in his case in the start-up intense and growth-obsessed world of Silicon Valley. The metaphor of the monk, who rides off into the dessert on a motorbike, only to return much later back to where he started, is that working out is much less important than making the most of your journey.

Komisar reminds us that working simply to make money will leave us 'howling at the moon'. Instead, we should integrate our passions and values – the things that matter to us personally – into our working lives. 'Work hard, work passionately, but apply your most precious asset – time – to what is most meaningful to you,' he writes. 'What would you be willing to do for the rest of your life?'

To illustrate, Komisar takes the reader through a hypothetical Silicon Valley start-up, with an eager entrepreneur named Lenny trying to get funding for an online casket-selling business. As Komisar helps Lenny find the real purpose of the business, the passion behind the revenue projections, he reflects back on his life as an entrepreneur.

Komisar is not just an experienced entrepreneur but a great storyteller too, the kind of guy you'd feel honoured to share a bottle of wine with. And you believe his conclusion: 'When all is said and done, the journey is the reward.' It's great if you've made billions on the journey, but the important thing is that you do something you can truly throw yourself into.

The monk represents the subtle difference between *drive* and *passion*. (In short, 'passion *pulls* you toward something you cannot resist' and 'drive *pushes* you toward something you feel compelled or obligated to do'.)

In business we work because it pays a salary, to do a good job, to get a better job, and to come home before the kids go to bed. We care less about the grand visions of the organization, recognizing that we only play a small part in it. Komisar calls this the '*Deferred Life Plan*': step one, spending most of your life doing what you think you have to do; step two, spending your final years doing what you want to do, when it's usually too late.

Others of us take the entrepreneurial plunge, indulging our passion in a start-up business that pursues our dreams. Yet after a couple of years of big company formalities – managing cash-flow statements, keeping shareholders happy and being stuck in the logistical mire of supply chains – the shine of the dream starts to grow dimmer.

The lesson from the monk is that businesses grow and evolve in stages. And this has big implications for leaders too. Like the natural or human world, they require care and support, and these change as they develop. Recognizing the phases of the growth of a business – 'The Seven Lives of Business', with its particular challenges and opportunities at each stage, and indeed the most appropriate way to lead and manage it – is crucial to sustaining growth.

3.1 SEVEN LIVES, SEVEN LEADERS
Different challenges require different leaders

Many leaders of growth businesses ignore, or pretend to ignore, another inconvenient truth: that different types and style of leadership will be required at different points on the journey. The entrepreneur, with the obsessive focus to turn a concept into a new business, rarely has the skills or the patience to play the politics and etiquettes of larger organizations.

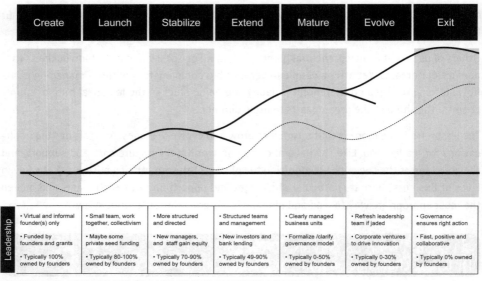

Leadership	Create	Launch	Stabilize	Extend	Mature	Evolve	Exit
	• Virtual and informal founder(s) only	• Small team, work together, collectivism	• More structured and directed	• Structured teams and management	• Clearly managed business units	• Refresh leadership team if jaded	• Governance ensures right action
	• Funded by founders and grants	• Maybe some private seed funding	• New managers, and staff gain equity	• New investors and bank lending	• Formalize /clarify governance model	• Corporate ventures to drive innovation	• Fast, positive and collaborative
	• Typically 100% owned by founders	• Typically 80-100% owned by founders	• Typically 70-90% owned by founders	• Typically 49-90% owned by founders	• Typically 0-50% owned by founders	• Typically 0-30% owned by founders	• Typically 0% owned by founders

LEADERSHIP CHALLENGES AT EACH OF THE BUSINESS LIFESTAGES

Perhaps the hardest point is to get beyond 'Stabilize', to move from one market model to the secondary one. The business stabilizes at a certain point – a successful 'small' business, maintaining revenue and profits that secure a comfortable lifestyle. But it fails to grow further. This is where the entrepreneur starts to struggle, and the more flexible leader can see new and better opportunities. Recognizing these limits, the entrepreneur is tempted to go for flotation, with the attendant demands of more disciplined management, or sell the organization to a larger player who can move to the next phase of growth with fresh ideas, complementary resources and experienced management.

Similarly, companies struggle to move beyond 'Optimize', by which time they have grown into a medium to large company, well established in their chosen sectors and geographies, and starting to feel that they have got as much of these markets as is realistic. They start to optimize their existing portfolios, making the most of their position, their brands and portfolios. To go further in a significant way needs new bold thinking. It requires existing or fresh leaders to fundamentally challenge strategies and assumptions, and to consider more radical steps, like completely new categories, new forms of partnership, refocusing on emerging markets and exiting old ones, or fundamentally shifting the core business.

Reaching 'Evolve' is some achievement, and most start-ups will have fallen long ago – stuck in an earlier phase, lost in the changing world, or formally deceased.

The journey has not been for the faint-hearted, and it will be a rare entrepreneur who has made the whole journey from concept to maturity. Those who have done, like Richard Branson or Bill Gates, will be wealthy and famous. They will have recognized that their role needed to change as their business changed, and like Randy Komisar's monk on a motorbike, will have gained much personal fulfilment from the journey as well as in what they have now achieved. For some, phase 7 will be exit, for some it will be time to start again, more like a lifecycle, and for the few with unlimited passion, there will be no finish line.

The journey requires continual attention and review, could span years or decades, and will frequently require change and sacrifice, investment and innovation. However the opportunities are great, exciting and incremental. Growth might seem obvious and easy, but sustaining it is much harder.

Insight 7: APPLE
iPods, iPhones and the reality distortion field

You are drawn to the white glow of the Apple logo suspended at the centre of the huge cube of glass, on the corner of Manhattan's Fifth Avenue and Central Park South.

Dazzling in clarity, a temple to technology, a showcase of desire – 'people haven't been willing to invest this much time and money in a store before,' said Steve Jobs at its opening, explaining how Apple has put as much effort into store innovation as it has into the products themselves.

And it doesn't just look good. It's a phenomenal commercial success too. Sales at stores down the road are impressive. Nearby electronics retailer Best Buy generates $930 per square foot per year, while Tiffany & Co. takes an impressive $2666. Apple, however, comes in at an extraordinary $4032 according to Bernstein analysis. And those numbers are just averages. Apple's 175 stores attract around 14,000 visitors every week, whilst the New York store is closer to 50,000 people.

- Humanizing technology.

- Revolutionizing music.

- Making phones desirable.

- The coolest stores in town.

- A brand to live your life by.

Apple does it all.

Steve Jobs started out as a physics and literature student but dropped out to found Apple Computer with his friend Steve Wozniak in 1976, based in his parent's garage and financed by the sale of his VW campervan. By the age of 23 he was worth over $1m, over $10m by 24, $100m by 25, and is now a fully-fledged billionaire.

He grew the business by focusing on niche markets, charging a premium for his novel products. However, 1985 saw him lose out in a power struggle with John Sculley as Apple began to crumble under the competitive might of Microsoft. This led him to Pixar animation studios, which has since created some of the most successful and loved animated films, from *Monsters Inc.* to *The Incredibles*, since the early days of Walt Disney.

Back at Apple Computer, with Jobs reinstalled as leader, Apple recognized that the computing world had changed. In the same way that Pixar had transformed movies, the likes of Dell had disrupted the computing world. But Jobs saw the future differently. He re-engaged his passion for well-designed computers, this time with open systems, and the launch of his bubble-gum coloured iMacs. More significantly, he recognized that the music industry was in desperate need of innovation.

Digital music formats were struggling to move beyond the CD and the retailer. Napster was the rogue, illegal download website. Everyone could see a market flex, but were uncertain where the future would go. Should record companies abandon physical formats? Should artists abandon record companies? Would network providers or phone companies seize the space?

Jobs saw the opportunity and quickly made the iPod a cultural phenomenon.

With its easy usability and translucent white casing, it quickly became an object of beauty and desire. The complementary iTunes download site quickly became the global leader in downloadable music, selling more than 70 million songs in its first year, and has quickly shaped the entire real and physical music industry. Upgrades and new models have rolled out at a frantic pace – and then came something transformational again.

This time, Jobs had his sights on the entire communications industry. MacWorld Expo 2007 in San Francisco saw the man in the black T-shirt back on stage as usual for what insiders call his annual 'Stevenotes'. This time he was introduced as CEO of Apple Inc. The 'Computer' name was no more.

Apple TV was launched without much stir, but what followed caused something close to global hysteria. The iPhone was launched. A revolution in yet another market, it immediately became the new globally most desired electronic gadget. Jobs and his team seemed to have done it again.

Apple is one of the most talked about brand on Kevin Roberts' Lovemarks website, where people rank their most passionate brands. Apple, not surprisingly ranks highly, with contributions such as:

> 'Apple enhances my life, and makes what I do possible in a way similar products by other makers never do. Apple's story, their myth, their mystery is unassailable. I never cease to be fascinated.'

Jobs as a CEO is no desk-bound executive. Nor is he a visionary, unafraid to make the hard decisions that are required to refocus and drive a large business forward in an ever-changing world. On his return in 1996 he decisively cut products and people, but only because he knew that Apple needed to move in a new direction.

He is the lowest paid CEO in the world – famously earning a one dollar annual salary – but making up for it handsomely in other rewards, even if some of his dealings have come under scrutiny. He is feared and loved, he is demanding and passionate, but always respected, and sometimes even imitated, as in the 'fakesteve' blog that kept Silicon Valley guessing about its real author in recent times. Was it a devious competitor, a fun-loving journalist or even Jobs himself?

Whilst some see him as an egomaniac, many others see him as a genius. Yet few cannot admire the success of Apple over recent years with Jobs at the helm. Indeed, his own staff call him 'a reality distortion field'.

'Genius sits in a glass house' wrote the Swiss artist Paul Klee. You will find it on the corner of Manhattan's Fifth Avenue and Central Park South.

3.2 ENTREPRENEURS, LEADERS AND MANAGERS
Seeing the road ahead or watching the car behind

The people at Virgin have a name for Richard Branson. They call him 'Dr Yes' because he generally won't say no. He finds more reasons to do things than not. His personal motto (and the title of his book) 'Screw it – let's do it' reflects the attitude that it is always worth giving ideas a go and a belief that the word 'can't' should never stop people.

'If you opt for a safe life, you will never know what its like to win,' reflects the man who started off a student magazine that became a mail-order business, that became a record label, that became an airline, a lifestyle brand, a multi-category retailer, a convergent communications business, and a pioneer of biofuels and space travel.

Entrepreneurs

Individual	Practical
Ambitious	Persuasive
Wealth-seeking	Temperamental
Obsessive	Whole brain
Rule breakers	Risk takers

Jean Baptiste Say, a French economist, first coined the phrase 'entrepreneur' in around the year 1800, saying, 'the entrepreneur shifts economic resources out of an area of lower and into an area of higher productivity and greater yield.' Are they born or can they be made? Previously the word conjured up an image of entrepreneurs born or bred, with money to finance their start-ups and the confidence to change the world.

Imagine that you are a venture capitalist (indeed it is often said that the best entrepreneurs also make the best investors) and that you had $50 million in cash. Which idea will you invest in? How would you choose a good investment? These are the factors that most commonly determine whether or not they believe in a business:

- Market with high potential, and can generate significant, sustainable demand.

- Management who are engaged and balanced in skills and experience.

- Proposition that is simple to understand, focused, practical and innovative.

- Clear way in which the VC firm can add value and enhance the ROI.

- Opportunity to make significant returns, profitable and with a clear exit strategy.

- Balanced portfolio of investments, large and small, high and lower risks.

As the chairman of a leading fund reflected, all of the other factors can be easily found or articulated with relative ease. He tends not to read the business cases. In deciding whether to invest, he looks primarily at the people – do they have the passion and dedication, the capabilities and maturity, the resilience and roundedness to throw themselves wholeheartedly into making a bright idea become a commercial success?

Entrepreneurs are typically self-starters – they need the motivation and discipline to get out of bed each morning and start work without anybody saying they must. They also have an obsessive energy which makes them hard to slow down. They strive every minute, every day, every week to move their idea forwards, mentally or physically, shaping it or selling it.

At the same time, they are not limitless fountains of ideas; indeed they tend to focus obsessively on a few things until they are accomplished. They drag people along with them, persuade and cajole, and eventually inspire once they succeed. They recognize they need people with different skills from their own in order to succeed.

They can often appear quite irrational, poor communicators, but at the same time they need to be able to live with paradox and complexity, as that is often the source of their future success. They can be difficult to get on with socially, because they have a focused vision that does not happily embrace everyone else's ideas and interests.

Their obsession sees them through the long hours and the early days of investment with little return. It also creates persistence, so that if they fail, as they probably initially will, they will keep trying until they succeed.

As their ventures grow, they do not see the need for the labels, structures and processes that more conventional mangers would expect. This starts to create confusion and conflict. Large teams expect more conventional management, particularly if they haven't shared the vision and the journey so far. Similarly at flotation, stock markets are concerned about the control and sustainability of entrepreneur-led businesses, shocked and dismayed by the apparent chaos.

For the entrepreneur, such chaos has never been a problem; indeed it is part of their way. For the conventional business executive it can be a nightmare. At the same time, large companies provide a structured environment that enable senior executives to perform, whilst for the entrepreneur who has grown the business from a start-up it can now seem like a hostile and frustrating world.

Leaders and managers

Whilst entrepreneurs have a passion to create and deliver great new things, management is much more about 'getting things done'. It is therefore a much more mechanical, linear and quantitative approach, driven by processes and controls, with clearly defined tasks and measurable outputs. It thrives on planning, organizing, delivering and controlling.

Managers break down a strategic vision into finite tasks, focusing on the detail and practicality of making things happen, step by step, day by day. It is a tactical mindset. It is about effective decision-making, effective delivery – on time, to cost, driving quarterly revenue.

Managers are much more likely to say no.

However a manager's success is by definition only achieved through others. Motivation is therefore a crucial attribute, as is understanding what makes people tick, understanding how to behave in a way that engages people – both those who they manage directly, but also peers across the organization, and their own managers.

'Middle management' often becomes an organization bottle neck – as it is these people who translate visions into reality, turn strategic priorities into daily tasks, communicate key messages up and down the organization, balance and connect the many different activities, and allocate scarce resources for most impact. Middle managers are the organization enablers, the politicians, and the engine room. In making change happen, in improving effectiveness, in making dreams come true, they are often the most important but frequently overlooked people in the business.

Leadership is the other side of management.

Management and leadership are the 'yin and yang' of large organizations. Whilst management is more heads down, focus and control, leadership is heads up, vision and connections. Leaders provide the inspiring vision that make people want to follow them. They pull rather than push, they engage and energize people, in a higher purpose, an inspiring vision, in seeing what is possible.

Leadership can be loud or quiet, rallying people from the podium, or influencing them personally.

Whilst management likes structure and process, hierarchies and boxes, leadership is more fluid. It brings people together, often from different parts and levels of the organization. It connects people and ideas who can do much more together than they could apart. A leader might be hands on, playing a specialist role, particularly in the early stages, or hands off, more of a facilitator and coach.

You will meet many types of leaders in business – some trying to live up to a certain style they believe is right, some adapting to what works for the organization, some doing what comes naturally to them.

Each leadership style has strengths and weaknesses:

Leadership style	Strength	Weakness
Charismatic	Inspiring change	Bored by sameness
Directive	Deciding quickly	Engaging senior people
Commander	Good in a crisis	Longer-term thinking
Aristocratic	Traditional and formal	Driving innovation or change
Guardian	Maintaining steady-state	Avoids necessary change
Intellectual	Strategic and visionary	Understanding normal people
Relaxed	Listening and facilitating	Avoids difficult decisions

There are no rights or wrongs, although a person who seeks to be anybody but themselves is inevitably going to be found as a fake, and will end up personally frustrated. Leaders of organizations today will need to embrace a number of these traits, even changing their style from time to time.

As individuals, leaders are the first to anticipate and respond to change – proactively and effectively – flexible and adaptive, open to alternatives, and willing to take risks. They are change agents rather than people who manage the status quo. And they don't just propose change, the make it happen. In many ways, therefore, entrepreneurs are the right people to lead organizations.

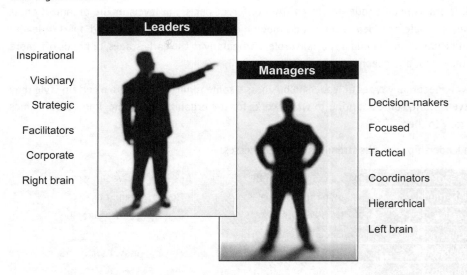

Inspirational

Visionary

Strategic

Facilitators

Corporate

Right brain

Decision-makers

Focused

Tactical

Coordinators

Hierarchical

Left brain

Managers and leaders are not necessarily different people, but can be complementary attributes of the same person. Whilst more senior managers will concentrate more on leadership aspects, they still need to provide focus and control. And whilst nobody is likely to have the perfect mix of all attributes, teams should be built so that they appreciate the differences that each member brings, and the collective strengths in combining those talents.

Insight 8: SHANGHAI TANG
The rise of Asia's first luxury fashion brand

Shanghai had the feel of exotic glamour, a spirit of limitless opportunity and a sense of danger too. The stars of the 1920s and 1930s, from Charlie Chaplin to Aldous Huxley, converged on the bustling Chinese port with its cruise liners, art deco hotels, film studios and opium dens. It was a cultural melting pot, where emigrating Russians met entrepreneurial Americans, Japanese jazz was enjoyed alongside the finest French champagnes.

One of the first truly international cities, it was variously known as the 'Paris of the East', the 'New York of the West' and sometimes 'the whore of the Orient'.

Almost a century later, Raphael Le Masne de Chermont, the new CEO of one of Asia's most glamorous luxury brands is watching the launch of his new collection. A crowd had gathered to view his latest examples of Chinese elegance in a contemporary style. With spotlights on, the music turned up, the stunning Asian models make their way down the red catwalk, oozing sensuality and the distinctive Shanghai style.

What would the ancient Chinese warriors have made of it? How would the Emperor have reacted to such female exhibitionism? Would the Communist Party have allowed such an event even a few years ago? Unlikely. But the modern, discerning audience loved every moment.

'Shanghai Tang is the best of 5000 years of Chinese tradition exploding into the twenty-first century,' says David Tang Wang Cheung, the British-educated son of a wealthy Chinese entrepreneur, who launched the brand in Hong Kong in 1994.

Whilst the fashion label certainly represents the new China – one in which style, creativity and wealth is quickly replacing an image of much tradition, cheap production and widespread poverty – it has not been an easy ride for Tang and the brand that bears his name.

In its first year, Tang's store attracted a million visitors, rising to four million within five years. The focus was on luxury, tailor-made clothing, employing some of the best Shanghai tailors, and he quickly expanded into ready-to-wear ranges targeting international visitors. The ranges were derived from traditional Chinese costumes and handicrafts – rows of vibrant *qipaos* ('Suzie Wong' dresses) to velvet-lined Mao jackets for men, silver rice bowls and painted lanterns.

In 1997 he sold a majority share in the business to Richemont, the Swiss-based luxury goods company that also owns Mont Blanc, Chloe, Dunhill and Cartier. Tang wanted the investment to take his brand into the Western capitals, and most urgently to take on the designer labels of Madison Avenue. He opened his store in typically flamboyant style. But America did not buy it. With low sales, high rents, the Asian financial crisis, SARS and demanding new owners, the founder was in trouble.

Le Masne de Chermont, with a classic French training in luxury brands, was brought in by Richemont in 2001 to set the business back on course. He scaled down the American ambitions and dropped many other international plans. He refocused the business back on China. Whilst the visitor market is growing rapidly, with American visitors there soon to outnumber those that visit Europe, the Chinese own luxury goods market is the real opportunity.

According to a recent Bain & Co. report, in 1980 there were no millionaires in China. Now there are over 250,000 of them, and their number is growing rapidly.

He also recruited a brash, self-confident Asian-American from Cincinnatti as his marketing and creative director. She immersed herself in Chinese history, culture and society. She was enthralled. She felt the existing ranges were overpriced, impractical and had little credibility with local people.

Joanne Ooi refashioned Shanghai Tang as modern and relevant. The brand needed more authenticity and depth. She dug deep into Chinese culture to find a theme for each season. She roamed art galleries, museums and antique markets to find inspiration. And she turned to pop culture for inspiration, too.

The clothes had to be luxurious and prestigious, but also wearable. She ditched all the tourist trinkets. Her designs were subtle and sophisticated, highlighted by mandarin collars or knotted buttons, borrowing designs from traditional dragons or even the emperors' robes. Yet every piece, she argued, should also be easy to wear with jeans.

Le Masne de Chermont and his team are on a high. The Chinese economy is booming, and its people are embracing designer fashion as if there were no tomorrow. David Tang is happy too, that he has created China's first significant luxury brand.

3.3 THE NEW BUSINESS LEADERS
Twenty-first century leaders for twenty-first century challenges

Can great entrepreneurs stay on at their organizations, manage teams of people and more complex organizations, conform to the rules of corporate governance, and play the games of boardroom politics?

Of course it helps if they are incredibly successful entrepreneurs like Branson and Jobs, who still own the majority of the companies. Who are you to argue with them? Surely they can do what the hell they like? Clearly John Sculley didn't think Steve Jobs could at Apple, although Jobs later came back to prove he could be an even better corporate leader.

Does becoming a business leader require entrepreneurs to swap their jeans and T-shirts for sharp suits and striped ties? Of course not, or at least not usually.

Warren Buffett, chairman of Berkshire Hathaway, says:

> 'In looking for people to hire, you look for people with three qualities: integrity, intelligence and energy. And if you don't have the first, the other two will kill you. You think about it; it's true. If you hire somebody without integrity, you really want them to be dumb and lazy.'

There are few dumb or lazy entrepreneurs around, even fewer who have been successful enough to build their companies into larger ones. The challenge for entrepreneurs is to play by the rules – the legal ones, obviously, but the unspoken etiquettes too of how people want to be managed, boards want to be served and shareholders want to be engaged.

If they can do this, then entrepreneurs will make mightily impressive business leaders.

The reality is that all business leaders need to embrace more of an entrepreneurial style in today's non-linear world. Playing the safe game, keeping your head down and maintaining the status quo is not good enough. As Ray Davis says in his book *Leading for Growth*, the story of how he transformed Umpqua Bank into the coolest financial services company on the planet:

> 'When I hear a business leader say "We want to stay right where we are – we don't need to change" then I would sell my stock in that company right away. Companies can never stay the same. Leading for growth is not optional. The simple fact is, you get better or you get worse. You cannot stay the same. There is no door number three.'

The successful business leader of the twenty-first century, in big companies and small, share some common characteristics – combining the passion and directness of the entrepreneur, with the rigour and discipline of the corporate executive.

The 5C Leader

The **Catalyst**

The **Communicator**

The **Connector**

The **Conscience**

The **Coach**

Driving change and innovation

Inspiring people to come with you

Facilitating better solutions

Doing the right thing

Getting the most our of people

They personify the 5Cs of the new business leader:

- *Catalyst* of change: constantly seeking new possibilities, challenging the business to think differently, to be more innovative and effective, faster and with more impact. This might be in the form of provocative ideas and disruptive challenges, being prepared to play devil's advocate rather than being a rule-maker.

- *Communicator* of vision: articulating a clear and inspiring direction for the business, living the values and personality of the brand, engaging all stakeholders in active dialogues. Externally they will be ambassadors of the brand – engaging stakeholders and partners, and the human face of the business to the media.

- ***Connector** of people*: bringing the best people and best ideas together – internally as well as from other companies and specialists – to generate bigger and better ideas and solutions. They will focus on building great teams, the right people in the right jobs for today, and planning for future succession.

- ***Conscience** of business:* deciding what is right and wrong, considering the big picture of the company and its role, and how it can help create a better world. Championing business ethics and corporate responsibility, cultural diversity equal opportunities, staying true to the business purpose and brand values.

- ***Coach** of high performance*: working with and supporting all levels across the organization, in their boardrooms and shop floors, and even with peers in other companies. The leader adds their own specialist skills to the business – their brains, technical knowledge, previous experiences, insights and instincts.

The new business leader will be a leader and manager, executive and entrepreneur. Look at the most successful CEOs of today and you immediately see these collective traits. From Ray Davis to Jeff Immelt, A.G. Lafley to Genentech's Arthur Levinson, Meg Whitman at eBay and Xerox's Anne Mulcahy – great leaders and managers, entrepreneurial and successful, at the top of the world's largest and most successful companies. They are role models of the new business leader:

From	To
Heads down	Heads up
Leading by control	Leading by inspiration
Managing the steady-state	Managing sustained growth
Ensuring consistency	Catalyst of change
Reserved and controlling	Passionate and energizing
Cautious and corporate	Open and personal
Overseeing work	Doing work
Managing hierarchically	Facilitating communities
Processes and tasks	Knowledge and innovation
Doing what has always been done	Embracing ideas from the outside
Enforcing regulations	Reinventing the rules
Products and transactions	People and relationships
Evaluating past performance	Supporting future performance
Generating more sales	Creating extraordinary value

The new business leader is different – growing a business is about business and personal growth. Growth is not possible without change, and sustained growth therefore requires continuous change. Organization change is rarely possible without the personal change of its leaders too.

Insight 9: UMPQUA BANK
Creating the greatest bank in the world

The River Umpqua weaves a lazy path through the green and golden forests, and the deep and rugged canyons of Oregon State.

This is the land of lumberjacks, and in 1953 the South Umpqua State Bank was founded to serve the people of Canyonville, population 900. It was a small, traditional bank, loved by locals and proud of its reputation for great service. It was also very conservative and only started to grow by acquiring one or two other small local banks.

In 40 years it grew to six branches, with a market cap of $18 million. Yet by the mid-1990s, the local logging business was now in decline, and the bank looked to be heading in a similar direction. The bank looked ready to be swallowed up by a national giant, but the Board were determined to maintain their independence. When the long-time president decided to retire, they thought about promoting from within, but something in their pioneering blood told them to look wider.

They took a big risk. They hired someone who was anything but your typical bank manager. He was energetic and dynamic, a banking consultant from Atlanta in his mid-thirties, who argued that his experience had allowed him to see many great ideas and others that were not so good. He wanted to bring the best of the best to Canyonville. At interview he told them directly, 'If you want things to stay the same, I am not your man. If you want wholesale change that will create shareholder value, I might be.'

Ray Davis set to work.

First was how to be different. Banks are notorious commodities – sterile, transactional, predictable and intimidating. Davis recognized that the opportunity to be different was in the 'how' rather than the banking products themselves. He focused on sales and service. He sought out those who did them best – people like Gap, Starbucks and Ritz Carlton.

He argued that Umpqua was in the retail business, and much more than a bank.

The 'store' concept was born. Employees were sent on field trips to experience life as a customer from the great deliverers of service. He started to rethink the whole concept of a bank branch. Why people go there, what for, what services it should offer, how it should look and feel, sound and smell.

The ambition of Umpqua Bank is simple:

> 'To create a unique and memorable banking environment in which our customers perceive the bank as an indispensable partner in achieving their financial goals; our people may achieve unparalleled personal and professional success; our shareholders achieve the exceptional rewards of ownership; and our communities benefit from our involvement and investment in their future.'

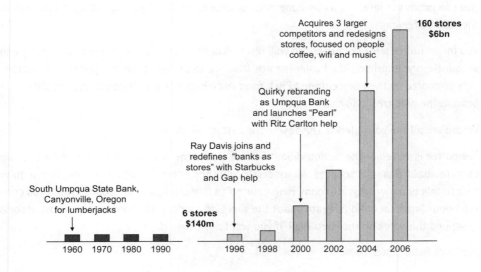

Within a year, and with $4 million investment, the first 'store' in West Roseburg opened. Twelve months later, Umpqua was named one of the best companies to work for. Another year later

Umpqua Holdings made its entry onto the stock market. With various acquisitions and mergers, the bank grew across the American West. With a simplified name of Umpqua Bank, it built a reputation for its funky store-concept banks that delivered a distinctive service experience.

By 2004 Umpqua had grown to 65 stores and a market cap of $600 million.

Today, the first clue that Umpqua is different is its huge fashion boutique-style windows. On entering you are greeted by a sign that says 'Welcome to the world's greatest bank'. How can this be? Now curious, you walk past people browsing their emails on bar stools, or sipping coffee on the huge leather sofas. Newspapers and lifestyle magazine hang on the walls, and you can catch the latest news on huge plasma screen TVs. Soft lighting and light funk add to the relaxed feeling.

You might notice large colour-coded wall displays of the latest financial services – 'your green account', 'in your prime', 'the business suite' (themed to the audience, not just standard products promoted on their percentage APRs). You can pick up a T-shirt, baseball cap or coffee mug bearing the pine tree logo too.

Where are all the bank clerks? The desks? The cashier windows?

The coffee is served at the 'Serious about Service' concierge desk, which is also where you can enquire about financial services. An associate will then come out and meet you, find a quiet sofa to talk or a more private room. Help yourself to free drinks and chocolate whilst you consider your financial options. Learn about the successful local restaurant owner, whose story is described this week on the Hero Wall, if you want more inspiration.

Sip. Surf. Read. Shop. Bank.

And when you are finished, you can read the paper, check your emails and tell your friends about the greatest bank in the world.

Future back, now forward

PART 2

▶ Future back, now forward

'It's your future. The only limits are the limits of your imagination. Dream up the kind of world you want to live in – dream out loud, at high volume'

Bono

Drive strategy and innovation more intelligently from **now forward** so that it is practical and delivers results short-term

Drive strategy and innovation more imaginatively from the **future back** to seize and shape the best opportunities long-term

Future back, now
forward

- ▶ The future is a much more inspiring place from which to lead a business, to see the best opportunities for growth, to define strategies and business priorities.

- ▶ Working from the future back allows you to work unrestricted by the conventions of today, developing solutions for the future mainstream market, not just the leading edge, and having a better vision of the future than others. Having a better view of the future than your competitors can itself be a competitive advantage.

- ▶ By connecting 'future back' with 'now forward', this better future can also become a practical reality. It enables us to pull off the trick of delivering today, whilst also creating tomorrow.

Finding the best markets of today and tomorrow

'No sensible decision can be made without taking into account not only the world as it is, but world as it will be'

Isaac Asimov

A more **intelligent** approach to **markets** that embraces a better *now forward* orientation	A more **imaginative** approach to **markets** that embraces a better *future back* orientation
• Finding the best existing markets and their value drivers.	• Exploring the new market spaces and how they will emerge.
• Analysing the current environment in terms of strategic fit and potential.	• Developing future scenario models based on trends, patterns and possibilities.
• Identifying the best opportunities to maximize profitability.	• Identifying the best opportunities for to sustain future growth.
• Defining markets physically, by geography and category.	• Defining markets in new ways, by customers and concepts.
• Recognizing defined market boundaries, to enable quantification.	• Realizing that many markets or borderless and blur with others.
• Evaluating existing market portfolios to decide which to focus on.	• Evaluating adjacent markets, and which offer the best opportunities.
• Understanding how to most effectively compete in chosen markets.	• Considering how to most effectively shape markets in your own vision.

Markets continually rise and fall, converge and fragment. They continually reshape. The most valuable markets in one year may well be different by next year. In the past, the markets were the constants, stable and predictable, and businesses jostled for the best positions within them.

Today, competitive advantage is more about making the smart choices of which markets to compete in, and which not.

Deciding which geographies, which categories, which customers you will serve is likely to have much more impact on your performance than a slightly better product, service or price. Economically, markets might seem good revenue sources, yet the capital investment and operating costs may quickly make them value-destroying rather than value-creating opportunities.

Of course it is tempting to want to serve everyone, to never say no to a customer, to be in ever more markets, to be a global player. But that is rarely the smart choice.

This of course requires knowledge: a deeper knowledge of your existing markets, the relative value of different customers; an understanding how they will evolve, particularly in relation to adjacent categories; and indeed a broad awareness of the opportunities and threats across geographies and sectors.

Markets themselves are unstable – constantly morphing in shape and size, as well as composition. They are borderless and blur with others. Technologies converge rapidly – communications and entertainment, fashion and media – whilst customers' needs diverge even faster – fads and trends, more individual and discerning. Together these create huge market spaces that are not easy to define.

Whilst the world has long been connected and fast-changing – witness the great explorers and global empires, the early communications and trade routes, migration of people and political instability that go back hundreds of years – it is fair to say that it is more complex and interdependent than ever before.

The always-on, 24/7, instant nature of communications means that we never switch off. The distributed and interactive role of the Internet means that our customers are anywhere, that the world is our locality. This creates enormous opportunity – and complexity. We could drown in the rush to do everything, or in our desire to serve even the most unprofitable customers.

Fast and fragmented, connected and interactive, transparent prices and rapid commoditization, high expectations and no loyalty: this is our business world.

Making sense of complexity requires intelligence. Bill Jenson wrote the book *Simplicity*, which seeks to interpret today's world into dimensions you can get your hands on. However, as the quantum physicists realized, complex problems require complex solutions. And whilst the result might look admirable, the derivation is not easy. Nothing is certain, everything has a level of ambiguity and risk.

We could do well to remember relativity and uncertainty into today's world. Not only do the old ways not work, but complexity also throws up many new opportunities if you have the right mindset. However the director who sits round the boardroom table and recites, 'In my day, we looked at these things simply' is probably missing the point, as is the marketer who seeks to apply simplistic, conventional models to the complex challenge.

Competing in fast-changing markets where borders have fallen and rules are broken can be a disorienting experience. Your perspective determines your competitors, your solution set, your customers and your potential for success.

The blurring of boundaries, of virtual and real worlds, and fusion of previously unrelated industries makes for a daunting challenge but also a fantastic opportunity. The creative possibilities within today's connected world are endless. Almost any brand can work with any other, or against each other, in markets that used to have no connection. Whether it is Time Warner bringing together the disparate worlds of magazines, movies and networks, or a single brand like Virgin reaching out into many seemingly unrelated service offerings, there is immense potential to be realized by those who have the dreams and brains, confidence and persistence to realize it.

4.1 FINDING NEW MARKETS FIRST
Exploring the hot spots, cool places and white spaces

'Ninety-seven per cent of growth in the next 25 years will come from emerging markets', says Michael White, Chairman and CEO of PepsiCo.

So where are the hotspots – the all-action markets of today, where growth is high, prices are premium, but competition is strong? Where are the cool places, with high potential but undiscovered by most of the competition? Where are the white spaces – the new opportunities, often borne out of merging borders or new technologies, which are there to be defined and shaped? And where are the black holes which are the markets of yesterday, maybe familiar and nostalgic, but now in terminal decline?

Within this extended space you can then plot where the best opportunities are likely to be, now and in the future, and where the competition is now and where it is likely to be. You can then begin to identify:

- *Hot Spots* where demand converges and all brands seek to play. For example, multimedia phones, the integrated computer and TV.

- *Cool Places* where lead users go in search of newness and difference, creating niches or the next big thing, e.g. Korean food, Smart cars.

- *White Spaces* where new opportunities emerge, often through convergence. They have not yet been exploited, such as interactive TV retailing or cashless wallets.

- **Black Holes** where traditional markets dry up and the lead players are blindsided and marginalized. For example, the photographic film industry or the car manufacturers.

Whilst this might sound impractical, far from the conventions of your own markets today, it actually describes the morphology of every market today. From sheep farming to corner shops, from industrial manufacturing to food restaurants, markets are more connected than ever, and influenced by outside change.

Some of today's high-growth markets worth exploring, perhaps requiring dedicated propositions and solutions, maybe in partnership with brands and distributors who have stronger existing connections with them, include:

- **Green markets** – the rise of conscience consumers who want to do the right thing. Whilst some care passionately about the future of the planet and its environment, many more are engaged in the issues concerning their locality such as security and education, and personal issues such as well-being.

- **Silver markets** – the 'baby boomers' are coming into their prime. From Bill Clinton to Paul McCartney, the jeans wearing, rock music loving shapers of the Sixties are now turning 60. They are wealthy and healthy, want to start new careers and travel the world. The last thing they want is a quiet retirement – at least, not yet.

- **Pink markets** – the gay markets are not new, but mainstream brands have been slow to address the large and wealthy market. Gays buy more premium technology products than anybody else. At the same time, there is a careful line to be drawn between serving and segregating audiences.

- **Red markets** – the former Soviet countries of eastern Europe may still have a suppressed image to some of us, but most of these countries – many now part of the EU – are booming, entrepreneurial economies. From Riga to Prague, Budapest to Warsaw, they want the hottest fashions.

- **Blue markets** – whilst the East might be the new West, the South is the new North. From South Africa to Brazil, India to Dubai, southern domains are stepping up from low-cost manufacturing economies into sophisticated, knowledge-driven, technological powers with high business and personal ambitions.

- **Grey markets** – the high-tech enthusiasts are suckers for any new gadget. Geoffrey Moore calls them the early adopters, but often they are simply different markets. The ones who want to do more with their everyday gadgets, either for personal productivity or because it looks cool.

- **Brown markets** – the fashion trend for 'retro' is enduring, riding on a recurring fashion cycle, but also reflecting a search for authenticity, for originality – from the earliest models of digital watches to the original 1972 Nike Cortez running shoe, from antique furniture to second-hand items.

- **White markets** – the low-cost markets, from airlines like Ryanair and Virgin Blue, to retailers like Aldi and TK Maxx – partly driven by the needs of the less wealthy, but also reflecting everybody's liking for a bargain. Even premium brands are developing low-cost, low-frills lines.

- **Gold markets** – the luxury goods market is perhaps the world's fastest growing market of all. The appetite for luxury brands across Asia is booming, as is the aspiration of main-stream markets throughout the western world too, even by those who shouldn't really be able to afford them.

These are not small pockets of opportunity. They are huge markets. Across eastern Europe, a survey by Boston Consulting Group identifies 350 million middle-income people who have a huge hunger for brands that define their progress and aspirations. The luxury goods market, for example, is worth $168 billion a year, and is growing at an annual rate of 7%, according to research by Bain & Co., with plenty of space and desire for more than the Gucci's and Versace's of the world.

Insight 10: NIKE
'There is no finish line' in the sports market

Eugene, Oregon. 1971.

Phil Knight was selling running shoes out the back of a van at the local university track meeting. The young business student had a passion for running, although he was never the most talented in his team. He therefore pursued his other passion, making money. He was creative too, importing Tiger running shoes from Japan, and became as well-known for his fast shoes as his own speed.

He trained hard all the same, seeking to get the best out of his talent, guided by the elderly University of Oregon track coach, Bill Bowerman. One day they were in Bill's kitchen making waffles after a hard morning training run. Phil took his shoes off, and by accident put one down on the hot waffle iron.

The smell of burning rubber caught everyone's attention.

It caught Knight and Bowerman's imagination, and soon they were making their own running shoes with a unique waffle-patterned sole. More traction, less weight, more speed. A few years later they added a swoosh logo, created overnight by a young designer called Carolyn Davidson for $35, and a sporting giant was born.

Nike. The ancient Greek goddess of victory.

Nike's mission is 'to bring inspiration and innovation to every athlete in the world'. Bowerman further qualified this definition with 'if you have a body, you are an athlete'.

For over 30 years, with Knight as CEO, Nike pursued its mission through 'the service of human potential', which in sporting terms means helping every person to achieve their potential in their chosen field.

Nike can now reasonably claim to be the world's leading sports and fitness company, a key player in every sport, in every corner of the world, employing around 30,000 people directly, and around one million more indirectly, all dedicated to the inspiration and innovation of athletes.

Of course its growth has not been all plain sailing. Most significantly, perhaps, were the negative perceptions of how it ran its Asian manufacturing operations, which Nike has since addressed, and because of its concern is perhaps now one of the world's leading sustainable businesses and ethical employers.

Nike's brand has grown to represent attitude and excellence in the world of sport, standing alone as a brand identifier in recent years. Nike also deploys a wide range of sub-brands to be more relevant to specific audiences – such as Nike Jordan, Nike Golf, Nike Running, Nike Football and Nike Woman.

Perhaps the masterstroke of Phil Knight was when he signed up basketball superstar Michael Jordan. Celebrity endorsement was a new concept, certainly for sports, yet the power of the sports star in reflecting excellence and aspiration is unmatched. This was not simply a cosmetic agreement: Nike works closely with their endorsed athletes to help them achieve their best performances, and in return the athletes work with Nike to develop new products and promote the brand.

However Nike has also recognized that its brand cannot be all things to all people, and has both acquired and grown its own portfolio of brands in recent years. Kids are unlikely to label anything cool that their parents think is cool, therefore Nike uses the Hurley surf and skatewear brand to reach the teen lifestyle.

Similarly, to be taken seriously in the office or upmarket leisure markets, Nike uses Cole Haan as a more formal footwear brand, alongside G Series and Bragano. More recently, Converse, the legendary US brand, joined the Nike stable, whilst the Exeter Brands Group was created to develop low-cost lines such as Starter and Shaq to be sold through large retailers.

Nike's hometown is in Beaverton, not far from the University campus where Knight first gained his thirst for sporting excellence. When you walk up the road to their World Campus, you are shadowed by god-like statues of their most famous athletes – from Michael Jordan to Tiger Woods, Alberto Salazar to Joan Benoit, Carl Lewis to Sebastian Coe – leading to the Mia Hamm building.

Nike is constantly searching for the edge, to move forwards, to evolve, or as it states in its book of *Nike Maxims* issued to all Nike people, to 'amplify what's good, change what isn't':

From	To
Elite sports	Active life
Big	Big and strong
Resource hoarding	Resource sharing
Slow	Fast
Process quicksand	Process agility
Innovation	Innovation (cubed)
Athlete icons	Athletic heroes
Exploitive	Supportive
No and maybe	Maybe and yes
Advertising	Communicating
Isolation	Alliance
Brand awareness	Brand respect
Complacent	Aggressive
Consensus	Courage

THE NIKE MAXIMS (SOURCE: *BOOK OF NIKE MAXIMS*)

Nike's annual report to shareholders captures the essence of a genius brand. Rather than being dominated by figures and graphs, the report is articulated in pictures and stories. The goal itself is not to make the sportswear or deliver the best returns to shareholders (Nike has more than doubled the S&P growth over the last decade), although these might well be the result. There is a bigger, more inspiring and more relentless goal.

business
genius

> 'Speed: our idea of a good investment ... The margin between first and fourth in modern 100m races has been as little as .005 of a second ... Our calculations tell us that Nike Swift apparel can deliver a 1.13% improvement in times.

> 'Nike Swift technology took us 36,000 hours to develop. So it wasn't all that fast in development. But it's fast everywhere else. And its only one of the many, many things we do to help athletes go faster. To a lot of athletes, 1.13% more speed could be the difference of a lifetime.

> 'To us it's just good business.'

The report describes the performance of a genius brand, one that is driven from the outside in, one that has a disciplined focus on what matters most for customers and shareholders, but with a creative spirit to do it differently and better.

The 2004 report was Knight's last, handing over the role of CEO after 40 years building a $12 billion business. His protégé, Mike Parker, who grew with Nike over many years, has now taken over the reins, whilst he remains chairman. (He now devotes as much time to his fledgling animation business, Laika, working with his son, Travis.) He signed off at Nike with the following anecdote:

> 'Nike remains a kid at heart. Just a few weeks back, on the Michael Johnson Track at World Headquarters, we celebrated the fiftieth anniversary of Roger Bannister and his royal performance as the first to crack the four-minute mile.

> 'Providence was ours that day. The mile race was won with 3:59.4 – matching exactly the good doctor's time set 50 years earlier ... It was a magical day for more than 2000 screaming Nike employees crowding the track. This is the Nike that will always be.'

4.2 GROWING WITH ADJACENCY
The best opportunities are often close to home

When looking to grow, adjacent markets can offer the easiest, fastest and lowest-risk opportunities. How can you create a broader solution for your customers – food with drinks, insurance with travel, shoes with clothes – or how can you collaborate with partners who have complementary capabilities – production and distribution, hardware and software, chocolate and ice cream?

It might seem obvious, but even when considering geographical markets, people tend to look far before they look near. Before trying to conquer the United States, or China, consider entering a market nearby, with a similar culture, language or climate.

Managers tend to see opportunities with blinkered vision, rather looking around them to see what is nearby. Rather than investing billions in new technological developments, consider easier options such as adapting a men's product for women, or a gift version of an everyday object.

There are three primary types of adjacent markets:

- *Adjacent categories* – defined by business types (e.g. drinks), product types (e.g. juices) or applications (e.g. meal times).

  If you produce soft drinks, could you also make beer? If it's a complement to meals, how about extending the brand as a thirst quencher after sport?

- *Adjacent customers* – defined by segments (e.g. teenage girls), geographies (e.g. southern Europe), or channels (e.g. supermarkets).

  Who is the most adjacent audience, older females or same-aged males? Which channels are most similar to supermarkets, small shops or online retailing?

- *Adjacent capabilities* – defined by capabilities (e.g. brand management), processes (e.g. retailing) or assets (e.g. distribution rights).

    If you are good at brand management, you could be good at managing other properties, or licensing them. If you are a retailer, you could also be a wholesaler.

Growth opportunities exist in 360-degree directions from your existing core business, and rather than just working harder to sell more of the same thing, it might be far easier and more effective to do other things, in other ways, or in other markets.

Of course some of the adjacent opportunities might be so attractive that you want to focus on that rather than your core business. IBM's move from computer manufacturing to service provision is a great example of a business having the guts to move with the market, to focus its resources on what was initially an adjacent market but became its new core.

There are many examples of companies sustaining growth over many years by continually entering adjacent markets and then further adjacent markets to them. With lower effort and risk, they built their franchise with existing audiences, and reached new ones:

- Disney created animated characters that children loved. It was not hard to translate that affection into movies, TV shows and theme parks. A capability in running theme parks was easily applicable to running hotels, vacation clubs and a cruise line.

- Tchibo built a chain of coffee shops across Germany. It then started selling other everyday items through the stores. With an expertise in coffee, there were many other consumer and business-to-business opportunities to reach new audiences.

Google, whilst clearly the world's pre-eminent search engine, might also seem like a complicated, thoughtless mash-up of many other services – from maps to mail, shopping to blogging. However, clustering them into themes, they reflect an emerging vision of an individual and democratic, connected and information-driven view of the world:

- *Searching:* Google spends more time improving the speed and accuracy of its search engines than anything else, developing bespoke versions for businesses, and specialist applications and appliances to integrate within a company's infrastructure.

- *Communicating:* Gmail is now a well-established challenger to other free email services like Hotmail, whilst the Internet-based telephony service Google Talk is taking on Skype in a world where cities are increasingly and freely Wi-Fi enabled.

- *Shopping:* Google Base is a comprehensive classified advertising site that will soon rival eBay and Craigslist, whilst Google Checkout is a new online payment sysyem to compete against PayPal, for which eBay paid $1.5 billion.

- *Entertaining:* YouTube, another $1.5 billion acquisition, is now being integrated into the Google fold, addressing the huge amounts of commercial and user-generated music and video that is in need of ordering and easier access. Apple's iTunes should be worried.

- *Navigating:* People are amazed by Google Earth and increasingly depend on Google Maps, but this is just the beginning. Imagine instant local directories where the best shops, services and restaurants are ranked by users and located by your phone.

Whilst you might think of Google as a search engine, with competitors such as Yahoo!, its competitive landscape embraces everyone from Apple to Microsoft, eBay to Blockbuster, Amazon to Michelin Guides.

Nike's adjacent market is even more pronounced. From the personal passion for running of founder Phil Knight, it quickly moved from shoes into apparel, from running into basketball, from men's gear into specialist women's wear, from clothing into accessories, from sportswear into casualwear and workwear. Nike's 'market map' shows how the business has grown along each of the adjacent axes – customers, categories and capabilities.

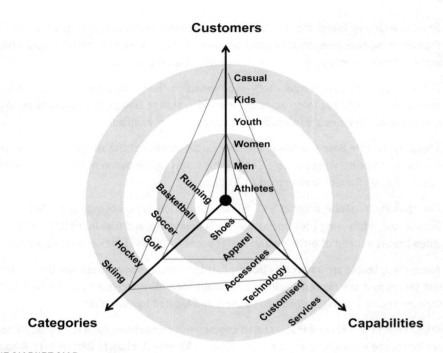

NIKE MARKET MAP

The 'swoosh' extended across most of these categories, although in some cases, where the audience or concept changed, an alternative brand was created. Nike Women required a different personality from the adrenalin pumpyness of 'Just do it'. A calmer, softer, more pastel-based brand was developed, and the dedicated stores features water fountains, candles and Zen-like music. Similarly, brands like Hurley and Cole Haan were more appropriate to other segments.

Insight 11: DISNEY
Dreams go digital at the magic kingdom

Since 1923 The Walt Disney Company has remained faithful in its commitment to delivering the best entertainment based on its rich legacy of creative content and storytelling.

From the early days when Roy and Walt Disney created the likes of Donald and Mickey, the company has become the master of growth through adjacent markets, constantly developing the business into new but related businesses, using its characters, audiences and capabilities as springboards. If you can make animated film, you can make TV shows. If you engage customers with characters they love, they want to go see them. If you can run theme parks, then you can run cruise liners.

Today Disney and its 133,000 employees are divided into four major business areas, each bringing together a range of famous and integrated brands and activities, but linking together across the group in order to maximize their exposure, engagement and impact.

Since Bob Iger replaced the embattled Michael Eisner in 2005, Disney has been firing on all cylinders. The share price has climbed almost 50% since Iger took the hot seat. According to investment analysts, this is partly because Eisner invested wisely, and part through Iger's more effective management style.

He has ensured that Disney has brought together its diverse assets for real impact. Most crucially he has ensured that content works harder in a multimedia, digitally enabled world. With so many different platforms, Disney can take a film, show or character and make it work in many formats, taking it to many more people, and creating an enduring revenue stream.

Record-breaking revenue of $34 billion was due to an impressive string of hits – from *Pirates of the Caribbean: Dead Man's Chest* (the world's best-selling film and DVD) to *Cars* (the best-selling animated film), top TV shows such as *Lost* and *Desperate Housewives*, and Disney Channel's *High School Musical* also delivered a best-selling album.

Indeed, Disney as a brand has been so consistent and successful in its marketing over the years that it has gained 'ownership' of a handful of emotive words that perhaps define its brand better than any slogan. Disney words (words which over 80% of people associate with Disney, according to Martin Lindstom's *BrandSense*) include:

- Fantasy.

- Dreams.

- Magic.

- Creativity.

- Smile.

The four businesses that make these words come to life are:

Disney Studio Entertainment

The studios are the foundation of the company. From Mickey Mouse to *Snow White and the Seven Dwarfs*, the world's first full-length animated film, they entertain the whole family. The productions are distributed in the form of movies and music, recorded and for hire through well-known subsidiary brands such as Touchstone Pictures, Miramax and Buena Vista.

Disney Parks and Resorts

This is where the magic lives, home to Disney's beloved characters. In 1952 Disneyland first started to develop in Arnheim, California, and has since spread across the world with 11 parks, 35 hotels and 2 luxury cruise ships. From the Magic Kingdom to the Epcot Centre, Disney creates a series of fantasy environments that build on its studio productions and sell yet more of its consumer products.

Disney Consumer Products

The brand extends into every form of merchandising – toys and clothing, interactive games and fine arts, home décor, food and drink. Indeed Disney is one of the largest licensors in the world. Its publishing arm is the world's largest children's publisher, and Baby Einstein is the leader in developmental toys, whilst Disney Stores and its online and direct marketing are never far away.

Disney Media Networks

Disney has brought together a vast array of television, cable, radio and Internet brands. ABC brings together a broad portfolio of TV stations, whilst ESPN, Disney Channel and Fox Kids are some of its cable properties. Also in the media networks business are Beuna Vista television, a leader in syndicated programming and Disney Internet Group that brings together the online activities of all its businesses.

The timeline of growth in Disney's portfolio demonstrates the gradual acquisition of multiple content sources and their integration, and the ways in which subsidiary brands have evolved to stand alongside the Disney master brand.

DISNEY GROWTH THROUGH ADJACENT MARKETS (SOURCE: DISNEY.COM)

Disney is also benefiting from the boardroom arrival of Steve Jobs. When Disney acquired his Pixar animation studios for $7.4 billion, Jobs joined the board and also became the company's largest individual shareholder. Whilst Pixar is breathing new life into Disney's movie-making business, Jobs is having an even greater impact in encouraging the use of digital platforms.

In late 2005, Disney's ABC became the first supplier of TV programmes to the iTunes store, selling at $1.99 an episode. In 2006 they were the first to stream full episodes for free onto the ABC website, upgrading the site's video player to something close to cinema standard. Viewers can vote online to shape the plot of TV programmes, and engage in it much more deeply.

Whilst other media companies might be concerned about free content taking customers away from its TV audiences, and therefore from its sponsors and advertisers, Disney sees it as incremental. Reaching new audiences, or deepening relationships with them, creates new opportunities. With advertisers, it can partner to create co-branded web versions of shows, which have proved to have more impact than traditional TV format advertising.

The results are impressive. By 2007, iTunes had delivered 21 million downloads of Disney ABC shows, generating $41,790,000 of additional revenue to be shared between Apple and Disney, with the majority to the content supplier. Meanwhile, in the first year of free online downloads, 90 million episodes of Disney Channel shows have been viewed on disneychannel.com, and 76 million episodes of ABC television viewed on abc.com.

4.3   THE BEST MARKETS
Choosing the markets for profitable, sustainable growth

New markets can be evaluated in terms of their performance in terms of market attractiveness – the most profitable and the highest growth.

This is demonstrated with the example of Coca-Cola. Whilst it was a leader in the narrowly defined carbonated soft drinks category, it found that by extending its 'market map' wider, there were adjacent categories that offered much more significant growth and profit potential.

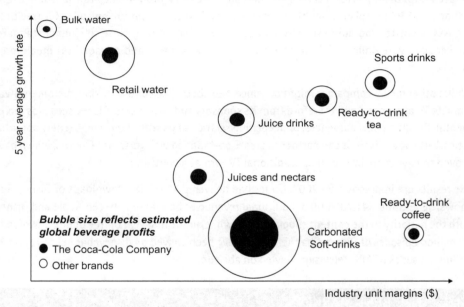

COCA-COLA MARKET MAP (SOURCE: THE COCA-COLA COMPANY)

In addition to strategic fit, a market should also be evaluated in terms of its fit with the strategic direction of the business.

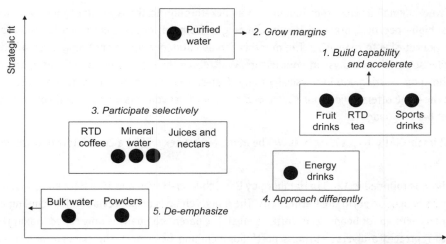

COCA-COLA MARKET STRATEGY (SOURCE: THE COCA-COLA COMPANY)

Whilst the business should not restrain itself from new markets because of lack of capabilities – which can quickly be sourced through partnership – the new opportunities do need to support the purpose and strategy of the business.

Priorities can then be identified and activities defined to seize these new market opportunities, playing to your strengths, and to your agenda.

Insight 12: TCHIBO
Much more than a German coffee shop

'Captain's log: 082007. Humanity is preparing itself for its biggest mission yet: to clear the moon of all its dust and restore its former shine. Advanced household equipment from Tchibo is just the thing for this particular job. May the force of Tchibo be with you!'

The weekly email arrives from Tchibo, and a click-through to the website engages you in its latest high-spec, own-branded, low-priced range – from clothing to electronics, for adults and kids, pocket-size to room-size. The monthly Tchibo catalogue arrives not long after, offering a wider selection to browse at your leisure. Walk down the main street a little later, and the Tchibo shop is luring you in physically too. A fast-service coffee shop format showcases and sells the same offers. Enjoy your *Kaffee und Kuchen* whilst you persuade yourself you need the latest bargain gadgets.

Most importantly, buy it now, or it will be gone. Next week will be a completely new range of offers.

Tchibo was founded in 1949 in Hamburg by Carl Tchilling-Hiryan and Max Herz and still maintains its headquarters in the German city. The name Tchibo is an abbreviation for Tchilling and Bohnen (German for beans, as in coffee beans). The parent company is now called Maxingvest AG to represent a diverse business portfolio, including Beiersdorf, the skincare and beauty products business that includes brands such as Nivea.

During the early years Tchibo focused on selling freshly roasted coffee beans by mail order, and today Tchibo's Gold Mocca is Germany's leading coffee brand. The company then started to open coffee shops, initially as tasting bars, but then as stand-up coffee shops where you can have a quick drink in the middle of your shopping trip. The coffee bars quickly became a feature of towns throughout Germany and beyond.

Tchibo is now best known for its weekly-changing range of consumer goods, 30–40 products each week, selling in huge volumes at low prices, themed by season or special interest – everything for an outdoor summer, everything to take the family skiing, everything for a new school term. The goods are all own-branded, well designed but at incredibly low prices. Nothing lasts for much longer than a week, so buy it now or never.

'At Tchibo, customers are our guests. Here, they can buy the best coffee, enjoy a variety of coffee drinks and snacks away from the hustle and bustle of everyday life, and let themselves be inspired by our wide range of attractive consumer goods in a pleasant atmosphere.'

The business is a fantastic example of gradual diversification – by adjacent category, channel, segment and geography – whilst also retaining a distinctive core purpose and unique business model. As a private company, Maxingvest is dedicated to a long-term approach to value creation, one that creates enduring value for its customers, employees and owners.

'Jede Woche eine neue Welt' remains the Tchibo slogan. Every week a new world.

Tchibo timeline

1949   Max Herz and Carl Tchilling-Hiryan launch their roasted coffee by mail business.

1955   First coffee shop opens in the centre of Hamburg, as a specialist coffee tasting bar.

1961   Tchibo Man debuts and becomes one of Germany's best-known advertising icons.

1963   Launches shop-in-shop format, a coffee bar inside local bakeries or Konditorei.

1973   Starts selling weekly-changing ranges of consumer goods through coffee shops.

1973   Tchibo Coffee Service supplies coffee and machines to catering trade and businesses.

1980   Acquires Reemstsma cigarettes (but eventually sells it as non-core to strategy)

1987   Shop-in-shop format is extended to national supermarket and store chains.

1992   International expansion, particularly in post-Soviet, eastern European markets.

1996   Establishes catalogue and mail-order business to sell consumer goods beyond stores.

1996   *Tchibo Reisen* travel magazine launched, rapidly followed by a full travel business.

1997   Acquires Eduscho, its main coffee shop competitor, and establishes online business.

2000   *Tchibo Magazine* with gossip, TV listings and weekly offers distributed through shops.

2004   Acquires majority stake in Beiersdorf AG, and French mail order firm l'Homme Moderne.

2004   Tchibophone is launched with O2, offering low-cost handsets and calling plans.

2005   Intelligent Cafissimo coffee machines launched, and Arena flexible store format systems.

2007   Maxingvest AG is new name for holding company – a diverse, international business.

Shaping your future, not shaped by others

'Wherever you see a successful business, someone once made a courageous decision'

Peter Drucker

A more **intelligent** approach to **strategy** that embraces a better *now forward* orientation	A more **imaginative** approach to **strategy** that embraces a better *future back* orientation
• Defining a clear strategy for the business, where and how to compete.	• Defining an enduring purpose for the business, its role in the world.
• Making strategic choices about what to do, and what not to do.	• Developing a vision of the future and the business's mission it.
• Matching the most valuable business assets with the best market opportunities.	• Mapping strategic horizons as stages of achieving the strategic goals.
• Quantifying the goals, metrics and targets for high performance.	• Capturing the values and principles that the business will live by.
• Developing a financial plan for the business, the targeted budget.	• Developing an operational plan for the business, the priority actions.
• Choosing the market position of the business, its value discipline.	• Choosing the market posture of the business, how it will shape markets.
• Establishing a regular planning cycle that builds in thinking and collaboration.	• Establishing a rhythm for the business that builds speed and agility.

Strategy is about making choices.

Deciding where and how to compete, and how you will make money out of it. Strategy gives people clarity of direction, where to focus, and connects all the small fragmented and functional activities into a coherent canvas.

Can you put your business strategy on one sheet of paper?

If not, it is unlikely that your people, including your most senior managers, will really grasp the direction and focus of the business, what matters most, and what doesn't. If managers don't get it, then their actions quickly become unfocused, dispersed and tactical.

Worse still is the strategic pursuit of money – 'to maximize the returns to our shareholders', as so many mission statements proudly proclaim.

Putting aside the lack of inspired thinking in this statement, it does not relate in any way to the market, or indeed to any difference. It is a commoditizing, internalizing statement that drives a blind, thoughtless, money-making machine. Yes, absolutely, commercial organizations typically have an important requirement to deliver good returns to their owners, but they should have a higher purpose.

What is the higher purpose of your business?

And then there is the most negative aspect of strategy and planning. Strategic planning typically becomes viewed as a slow and painful, financially driven, spreadsheet-dominated negotiation that delivers a financial plan and a budget. The choices and activities that will spend and deliver these numbers becomes a footnote, a supporting argument, or just forgotten.

And why do we develop the plan we do? We need more money to compete better, and by selling more we will grow the top line, we argue. This, of course, assumes that markets and customers, competition and propositions will be exactly the same as last year. Not a bright idea.

Can strategic planning be a faster, more positive activity?

Most organizations will spend three to six months in their planning cycles, with their senior managers distracted and demotivated by the endless paper chain. This is hardly a way to deliver great results. It is not an environment for innovative thinking, making smart or bold choices, for seeing the bigger picture, the opportunities and threats in a changing world, or to energize people.

So what is a better approach to strategy?

Strategy must start with a clarity of business purpose – why does the business exist, how does it really add value to its world, and what would be missed if it wasn't here? It must be a more imaginative thinking opportunity – to engage managers quickly and collaboratively in evaluating changing markets, new opportunities, smarter ways of working.

Strategy must be a more intelligent decision-making process – evaluating the bigger and best market opportunities, strategically and financially – and need only last 3–4 weeks. It must deliver a clarity of business priorities: where you will compete, how you will be different and what will drive financial performance, and you must be able to summarize it on one page.

5.1 BUSINESS WITH A HIGH PURPOSE
Looking beyond the pursuit of profits

Businesses need to look beyond mission and vision statements to a 'higher purpose', one that gives an organization more meaning and personality, and articulates its role in the world.

- *The why* – the higher purpose why you exist.

- *The what* – ambition or mission and vision.

- *The way* – values or principles and practices.

Peter Senge, author of *The Fifth Discipline*, recently argued that the ultimate test of an organization that really knows itself is when 'there is a clear articulation of what the world would miss if that organization did not exist'.

Whilst every organization clamours for its 'how we will be great' mission statements, they are usually incredibly internal – to be the best at, to be the number one, to beat the others, to be the most profitable, most innovative, first choice, and create more value than others in your sector. Whilst such slogans make great CEO rally cries, they fail to say much. They fail to articulate what the company does for the world, for its customers, how it adds value to people's lives in some way.

Companies today need an overriding purpose, beyond the pursuit of profits, one that justifies their existence and that anchors their personality, evolving strategies and diverse activities. As Goethe said, 'One must be something in order to do something.'

AN ENDURING PURPOSE THAT SUSTAINS THE BUSINESS

A purpose is like a moral compass for business – it's why we come to work each morning, it's why investors come to us when it might not make pure financial logic, it's why customers might choose us when everything else about us is the same as our competitor.

A purpose is enduring, makes sense, and makes a difference to the world. Some companies, by design or default, do articulate a purpose, what it does for the world:

- Disney – 'making people happy'.

- Ford – 'machines to improve the world'.

- M&S – 'making aspirational ideas accessible to everyone'.

- Nike – 'enabling people to achieve their personal best'.

- Sony – 'to innovate in useful way'.

- Wal-Mart – 'to give the customer a good deal'.

More generally, companies tend to align around one of a number of types of purpose – some that are strongly action oriented – implying that they will indeed focus on innovation, or quality, or service to do more for people – and others that are more internal reasons, to do with behaviour and values:

- *Explorer companies* – they seek to go where nobody has gone before, to civilize a new market, to define the new technical age, to enable people to do something new. IBM, creating a world of computers or 3M, constantly seeking better solutions.

- *Challenger companies* – they play the underdog, challenging bigger or more established brands and practices, taking the customer's side, and provoking authorities and publics to rise up and join them. Virgin is the ultimate challenger, although it too is challenged by Ryanair.

- *Servant companies* – they believe in putting customers first, and that all customers are equal, and in universalism, fairness, equality and human rights. Google succeeds through democracy online, Wal-Mart seeks to give everyone a good deal.

- *Quality companies* – they strive for perfection, they set the technical standards, they believe that product excellence comes first. *The Economist* portrays itself as the highest quality business publication. BMW as the 'ultimate driving machine'.

- *Hero companies* – they seek to change the world, to pioneer a better way for everyone, to dare to be different and deliver a better life. Ford revolutionised the way we travel, whilst Bill Gates and 1985 are regarded as the reference points for 'BG' and 'AG' in modern society.

- *Conscience companies* – they believe that business must be a force for good, putting their ethical, community and environmental responsibilities first, as the platform from which to also make money. From BP to Innocent Drinks they put principles before profits.

- *People companies* – they put people first, caring for their employees, for their customers, and for the local communities in which they work. They define their offer through people serving people, be they the John Lewis Partnership or Starbucks Coffee Company.

A business purpose might sound rather like a brand statement; indeed, it could be derived from the same idea. The business purpose is clear and enduring, and exists for the company. Brands should be clear and enduring too, how they are devices that must also engage external audiences, and indeed should reflect their aspirations rationally and emotionally. The brand is a broader, richer, more energising reflection of the business purpose.

Insight 13: DIAGEO
The drinks company that wants to be adored

Diageo is quite clear on who it is, what it wants to achieve and how it will get there. Whilst many corporate missions and strategies are reduced to generic phrases that are so undecipherable as to be irrelevant, or so bland as to be a commodity, Diageo has worked hard to articulate itself.

DIAGEO STRATEGIC FRAMEWORK (SOURCE: DIAGEO.COM)

There are seven components to defining Diageo:

- *Purpose*: Diageo is clear on who it is today, '*the world's leading premium drinks* business', with the broadest and most recognized collection of premium drinks brands globally.

- *Vision*: There is a compelling customer-oriented vision, '*celebrating life, every day, everywhere*'. Indeed the word Diageo comes from the Latin for 'day' and Greek for 'world'.

- *Goal*: Diageo has a single-minded goal, similar to a mission statement in other companies, that '*every adult adores at least one of our brands*'.

- *Strategy*: It has a clear strategy too, represented in its strategic triangle, defining the imperatives that will achieve the goal, recognizing the needs of all its stakeholders, from employees to customers, investors and society.

- *Plans*: Diageo recognizes that it is made of many parts, and leaves the bottom two layers of the triangle – initiatives and enablers – to be defined by each business in the most relevant way.

- *Values*: It articulates the four underpinning values that will make this happen – being '*passionate about customers*', giving people '*freedom to succeed*', being '*proud of what we do*', and '*we will be the best*'.

- *Reputation*: Diageo reminds us of what it wants to be famous for:

  - People. 'Releasing the potential of every employee'.

  - Brands. 'Using great consumer insight to power our brands'.

  - Performance. 'Winning where we compete'.

Diageo began a strategic realignment behind its premium drinks brands in 2000, which included the uncoupling of its previous interests in non-drinks activities such as a partnership with General Mills. Organic growth of core, premium brands is seen as key to its success, whilst the company recognizes that it has to take a lead in responsible marketing, particularly with regard to health and the youth market.

> 'Our brands help people mark big events and brighten small ones. Enjoyed responsibly, they enable people to celebrate life, every day, everywhere.'

As well as being the home of Guiness, Diageo also manages 17 of the top 100 premium spirits brands in the world – from Smirnoff, the world's number one premium vodka, to Johnny Walker, the leading Scotch whisky. Baileys is the world's top selling liquor whilst José Cuervo is the global leader in tequila.

Innovation has also been key, focusing on the specific opportunities to do more in high value-creating markets, and with high value-creating brands. These have typically been a combination of new drinks formats, particularly reflecting the shift to lighter, smoother drinks. Baileys Glide, Guiness Extra Smooth, and Smirnoff Cranbury Twist are some examples.

Packaging can equally be important, not just in enhancing the visual appeal, but introducing more effective materials, or smaller, multiple formats where margins are even greater, for example, Baileys Miniatures, Smirnoff Icon and Johnnie Walker Red Label.

Indeed the financial benefits of such moves are obvious. Mixer drinks contain far less alcohol, and when promoted as a funky drink to be seen with in lifestyle bars, can quickly command a price ten times more than the same quantity of drink could be purchased for off trade. Spirits can also become dated, associated with an older generation – the difference an ice cube and more youthful context can make to advertising representation can be enormous in terms of its impact.

However market leadership is not Diageo's measure of success. It very publicly ranks itself (in its annual report and on its website) against a broader peer group, against a more meaningful measure of shareowner return: the total return through capital growth and dividends delivered to them over recent years. The table gives a far more insightful view into the true performance of their business, and others, rather than looking at any more transient or narrow-focused metric.

TSR RANKING WITHIN DIAGEO'S DEFINED PEER GROUP (TOTAL SHAREOWNER RETURN IN PERIOD 1 JULY 2002 TO 30 JUNE 2005):

Pernod Ricard	142%
SABMiller	128%
Allied Domecq	89%
Brown-Forman	57%
Cadbury Schweppes	47%
P&G	44%
Diageo	35%
Interbrew	33%
Nestlé	27%
Carlsberg	25%
Unilever	24%
Scottish & Newcastle	23%

5.2 MAKING THE RIGHT CHOICES
The essence of a smart business strategy

A strategy is not a plan or tactic – it must be the commitment to an enduring course of action. 'What is our strategy to win this sale?' involves a misuse of the word, as does, 'What is our strategy for next year?' Strategies require a sustained approach: commitment to a course of action which may take investment and time to deliver results.

A 'corporate' strategy defines the organization's overall purpose, and its vision of the future and the mission for achievement within this. It sets the context for business, defining which business areas it will focus on, which are then typically represented by business units in the organization structure. The corporate goals and values, brand and culture align to this overall strategy.

The components of the corporate strategy are:

- *Purpose*: why we exist, and our enduring role in the world around us – the value we add to society, by enriching people's lives or making the world a better place.

- *Vision and mission*: deciding how we see the future of our particular world, what it will be like and what people will want; and then defining our business success in that world.

- *Strategic goals*: defining our objectives and goals for each stakeholder group – mainly customers, employees and shareholders – and the measures of success.

- *Business definition*: the businesses in which we will operate, their cohesion whilst also being different, and how they support the purpose, mission and goals.

COMPONENTS OF A BUSINESS STRATEGY

A 'business' strategy, or business unit strategy, makes the more specific choices within a chosen business unit about where and how to compete, and the ways this will be achieved. It therefore specifies which markets the business will focus on, and how it will be distinctively positioned in these markets. It also specifies how the business will make money: the business model.

The components of the business strategy are:

1   ***Where to compete***. The choice of markets, defined by geography and category, customer, or otherwise, will reflect the best market opportunities for profitable growth. These are evaluated against the strategic fit of the business, supporting the direction, and effectively utilizing the business assets. These assets, or distinctive strengths, will be increasingly intangible, such as brand and reputation, knowledge and skills, relationships and networks. Focus can be further clarified by defining where not to compete, particularly when prioritization reduces market scope.

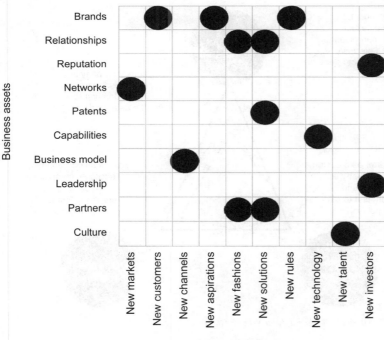

MATCHING ASSETS AND OPPORTUNITIES

2   ***How to compete***. The competitive advantage should be articulated in a clear market 'position' relative to the key competitors (more expensive, higher quality, more personal, etc.) and eventually through differentiated propositions. Whilst different products and services might have diverse reasons to be different, what ideally comes together is a 'value discipline' for the business. These are best articulated in the model where an organization should be 'good at all three disciplines, but chooses to be the best at one of them'. Again, it requires a choice.

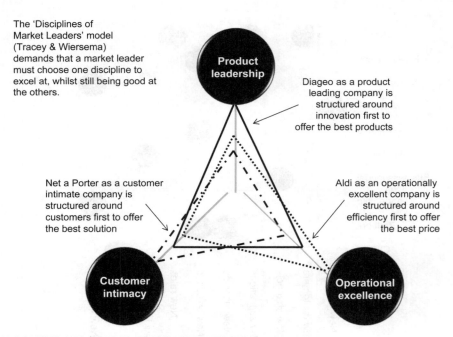

The 'Disciplines of Market Leaders' model (Tracey & Wiersema) demands that a market leader must choose one discipline to excel at, whilst still being good at the others.

Diageo as a product leading company is structured around innovation first to offer the best products

Net a Porter as a customer intimate company is structured around customers first to offer the best solution

Aldi as an operationally excellent company is structured around efficiency first to offer the best price

VALUE DISCIPLINES (SOURCE: TRACEY AND WIERSEMA)

3 **What to do**. The business model defines the way the organization will sell its products and services, who pays what, and the partners involved. These are not always obvious, and may require prioritization and selection from within a broader portfolio of existing activities. Equally the choice of partners (for example, to franchise rather than sell directly, to outsource customer service rather than do it personally, to sell or lease) will affect the business and resources required. Again this requires choice – from a portfolio of products, from a range of distribution techniques, from a range of pricing models.

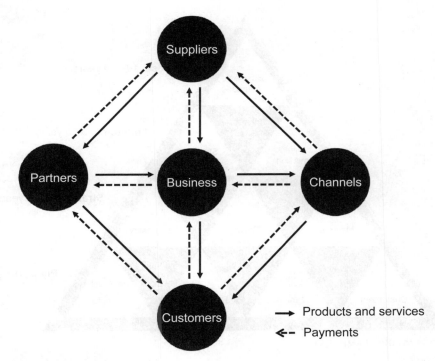

THE BUSINESS MODEL

Once the business unit strategy is established, then the rest of the organization and specific functional areas can develop their strategies and plans. Indeed this should ideally be an iterative process, so that functional managers help shape the business strategy, but not in return for compromise or delay. Strategies can and should be developed collaboratively, and quickly. At the end, the organization should not just have the sum of constituent parts, but a clear and agreed agenda for the business.

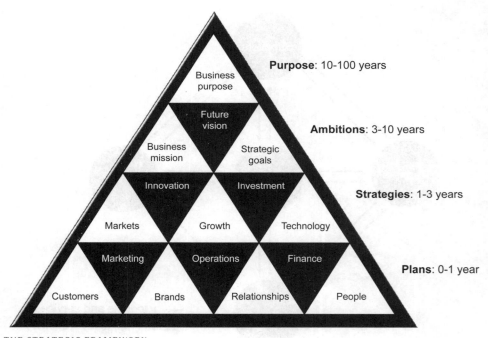

THE STRATEGIC FRAMEWORK

The 'strategic framework' shows a number of cross-functional 'strategies' to support the business strategy. They represent the longer-term decisions that will be required over the same timeframe, requiring longer-term approaches, such as building brands in certain markets, or investment in new areas of innovation.

Supporting these strategies are the operational plans of the business – the operational side of the strategy – typically developed on anything from a quarterly (three-monthly) to annual basis. These are more functional plans, developed within specific areas, and requiring budget and resource over a one-year period.

Insight 14: NATURA
The secret of the girls from Brazil

Walk along the beaches of Rio de Janeiro or visit the nightclubs of São Paulo and the Brazilian girls will be only too keen to tell you the secrets of their beauty. However, you are unlikely to be able to buy it in a shop. Instead they are more likely to invite you along to one of their Natura parties. In their homes your will find their secrets laid out in front of you, ready to buy.

Natura is Brazil's leading cosmetics company, selling a comprehensive range of cosmetics, fragrances and toiletries directly to consumers through around 500,000 sales representatives in Brazil and 100,000 more across Latin America.

The business has come a long way since it was founded by Luiz Seabra at a small laboratory and store in São Paulo in 1969. He came from a poor background, not attending university until his mid-twenties. After some years of experimentation, Seabra was keen to adopt the network selling model that he had seen so successfully used by Avon around the world.

In 2005, after an IPO the previous year, Natura became Brazil's largest cosmetics company with revenue of $1.5 billion. It is one of South America's most loved brands, according to Interbrand, and also wins many awards for its environmental performance.

Whilst 97% of revenue currently comes from the home market, Natura has a strategy to take its secret to the rest of the world too. Recently, CEO Pedro Passos announced plans to build on his strong position in the Brazilian market by targeting neighbouring Latin American markets first, eastern Europe second, and then North America. He has also opened a flagshop store in Paris, right under the noses of the likes of L'Oréal.

Natura has delivered average 26% revenue growth per year for the last six years, well above Brazil's national growth rate of 13%, and enabling it to treble its revenue from 2001 to 2006. Three major factors have been driving Natura's performance: firstly, the ability to grow with consistency amidst Brazil's recent financial stability; secondly, its strong networked distribution model; and thirdly, continuous innovation of its product portfolio.

International growth is important now, both because of the opportunities globally, and to diversify its business, and so become less dependent on the local economy. In addressing his shareholders, Passos defined his three strategic priorities to sustain the remarkable success of the business:

1   To sustain growth in the Brazilian market

Sales growth has recently started to slow, although it's still highly profitable, as competitors such as Avon improve their performance. Improving marketing and brand differentiation will be crucial, as well improving operational effectiveness. Improving stock inventories through better forecasting and enhancing the effectiveness of sales consultants will also be priorities.

Natura will also look at ways to defend their direct channel leadership, improving the quality of sales consultancies, providing more coaching and information, building closer relationships with regular consumers, and working with other companies to form more integrated cosmetics and broader 'bundled' solutions for consumers.

2   To enter high-growth international markets

This will be in carefully chosen markets, based on their growth rates, competitiveness and adjacency in terms of language, culture and capabilities. Developing new direct channel networks will take time. Therefore new channel models and forms of franchising will be explored, and also possible acquisitions.

In each new market Natura will need to develop an appropriate infrastructure (such as manufacturing, warehousing and logistics) in multiple markets, which could quickly absorb significant capital and place new risks on the business. Therefore effective partnering and outsourcing will become important to the international growth.

3   To develop more adaptive management

A more diverse Natura, in terms of geography and markets, one which seeks to seize the best opportunities first, to protect its position from new entrants and drive innovation, must be prepared to change. Subsidiaries and more distant franchisees will require more autonomy and flexibility. This will require a different, more adaptive management style.

The best way to select new markets is to get into them, to test the market and learn from it, to adapt and evolve. Indeed the only way to continue driving growth at around 30% will be to continuously adapt and innovate the business.

A strategy for global growth has required Natura to make hard choices. They could stay focused on Brazil with its booming economy and high profitability, at least for now. Or they could consider the fashionable new markets, such as India and China, where everyone else is headed, which is perhaps in itself a reason not to. Or they could take a middle path, taking their strengths and distinctiveness to markets that will most appreciate them.

Maybe it won't be too long until the secrets of the girls from Brazil will be available for purchase from a party in your local neighbourhood too.

5.3   BUSINESS JAZZ
Learning to improvise with a strategy

Jack Welch argues, 'When the rate of change inside the business is exceeded by the rate of change outside the company, the end is near.'

Today's markets can evolve incredibly quickly. New ideas and structures, standards and expectations can spread in a way that was previously reserved for fads and fashions. Speed is driven by the connectivity of people through technology, the rise of non-locational communities, and the constant desire of consumers to have the latest, best, coolest, smallest, fastest devices.

Whether it is the latest multi-disciplinary mobile phone, a new range of Puma shoes or the latest interactive game, as soon as it enters one market, it enters all markets. In the past, movies were shown in North America up to six months before Europe. Within weeks of release in LA, they will now be bootlegged in the shops of Bangkok or available online to people anywhere.

Similarly with products, the rapid and repetitive disruption of the data storage market shows how large floppy disks were displaced by smaller disks; they in turn were displaced by CD-ROMs, and then they by USB devices. The benefits of each new device were huge – scaling up storage capacity many times, shrinking in size, cheaper and more convenient. Once the new device hits the market, everybody wants it everywhere. And one click of amazon.com can deliver it within days.

Rapid market entry, particularly into emerging or newly defined markets, requires you to create a 'market vortex' – establishing your position before others, engaging customers before others – enticing people in like a whirlpool in the market, building momentum that keeps the process going and to blow down physical and mental blocks, learning and evolving as you go. The vortex ensures that you own the space you want, and that the impact is rapid.

Think iPod, iTunes and the transformation of the music industry.

1. Market making
Finding the best new opportunities
And using innovation to awaken
untapped potential demand

2. Game changing
Redefining the market context,
the boundaries and rules, the
customers and competitors

3. Market shaping
Developing the new market in
your vision, with new business
models and perceived value

THE MARKET VORTEX

The market-driving vortex will also affect the wider markets and emerging competition. Isolated and maybe unnoticed at first, the vortex starts to influence competitors and other new entrants, it conditions consumer behaviour and with new expectations. The vortex moves from a market entry role to establishing new standards and conventions. It changes the game. Eventually new market conditions start to form, and the business must actively shape these new structures as it normalizes.

Speed and agility are therefore crucial in dynamic markets.

Whilst some business leaders might argue that strategy is too bureaucratic and restricting in a dynamic market, they might look like entrepreneurial heroes in the short term, but will fail to make the choices that will deliver profitable and sustainable growth in the longer term.

Agility can be built into the organization in many ways:

- **Strategy within limits** – where the rules are simple: 'This is where we want to get, with these as essentials and priorities, and these are the things we will not do – but otherwise it's up to you...'. This is empowering and flexible, but makes resource planning harder and requires greater management capability and accountability.

- **Building a strategic rhythm** – whilst most strategies cover a three-year period, they are reviewed and updated annually. This creates a 12-month rhythm in your organization that typically ends up driving the rhythm of sales and innovation. Shortening your 12-month cycle to 11 months would give you an extra month each year on your competitors.

- **Accelerating the strategy process** – rather than making strategic planning a long, time-consuming, box-filling and distracting task, take all your key people away for two weeks – we call them 'business accelerators', involving some pre-work and post-finessing – to design your business future in a way that is focused, energetic and collaborative.

- **Accelerating the strategy execution** – ensuring that strategies are implemented through faster processes in the organisation, for example by ring fencing key initiatives so that they are not distracted by conventional rules, by reducing sign-offs and phasing, parallel processing, then learning and evolving a concept – test, learn, test – when it's in the market.

Your market 'posture' becomes important. Speed of execution is good, but it's also about constantly sensing and responding, evolving the strategy as the market evolves, shaping rather than being shaped by others, being on the front foot rather than the back foot.

Of course it is good to be market-driven, responding to competitive actions. It's even better to be customer-driven, responding to their changing needs and wants. These are prerequisites.

However, succeeding in new markets requires a market-shaping approach – defining the agenda, establishing the rules, setting the rules to suit your business, to play to your strengths, shaping the market in your vision rather than others.

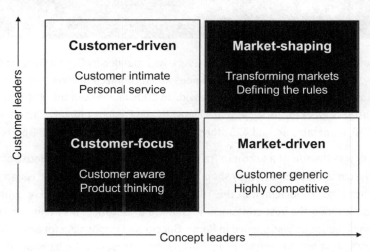

BUSINESS POSTURE

Think back to life before the iPod – the music industry was in turmoil, counterfeiting was rife, new formats were competing for position, and Napster, a then-illegal MP3 download site, was starting to get noticed. Jobs and the team at Apple didn't rush in with another, similar offering; they sat back and said, 'How can we do this better, different, and in our vision, rather having to live by somebody else's?'

When Jobs did eventually take the stage at MacWorld, and launch his solution to a U2 'Vertigo' fanfare, the industry was quickly transformed. Whilst the gleaming iPods drove desire, it was the accompanying download site and business model, iTunes, that redefined the rules of the music business and reshaped the market in Jobs' vision.

Insight 15: GUCCI
Less sex please, we're Italian

The House of Gucci, better known as simply Gucci, was founded by Guccio Gucci in Florence in 1906. Today, Gucci is one of the most prestigious and recognized fashion brands in the world, generating over US$7 billion revenue worldwide in 2006 and ranked the 46th most valuable brand by *Business Week* in the same year. Owned by the French company Pinault-Printemps-Redoute (PPR), it operates around 425 stores worldwide, responsible for 70% of its revenue.

Guccio Gucci was the son of a northern Italian merchant. He started the House of Gucci as a small, family-owned leather saddlery shop. Guccio was an exceptional craftsman and began selling leather bags to horsemen in the 1920s. As a young man, he quickly built a reputation for quality, hiring the best craftsmen he could find to work in his atelier. In 1938, Gucci expanded and a boutique was opened in Rome. Guccio was responsible for designing many of the company's most notable products. In 1947, Gucci introduced the bamboo handle handbag, which is still a company mainstay. During the 1950s, Gucci also developed the trademark striped webbing, which was derived from the saddle girth, and the suede moccasin with a metal bit.

In 1953, his son Aldo helped lead the company to a position of international prominence, opening the company's first boutiques in London, Paris and New York. He then targeted the Far East for further expansion in the late 1960s, opening stores in Hong Kong, Tokyo, and Korea. At that time, the company also developed its famous GG logo (Guccio Gucci's initials), the Flora silk scarf (worn prominently by Hollywood actress Grace Kelly), and the Jackie O shoulder bag, made famous by Jackie Onassis.

Gucci remained one of the premier luxury goods establishments in the world until the late 1970s, when a series of disastrous business decisions and family quarrels brought the company to the verge of bankruptcy. 'In the 1960s and 1970s,' wrote *Vanity Fair* editor Graydon Carter, 'Gucci had been at the pinnacle of chic, thanks to icons such as Audrey Hepburn. But by the 1980s, Gucci had lost its appeal, becoming a tacky airport brand.'

A turnaround of the company in the late 1980s made Gucci one of the world's most influential fashion houses and a highly profitable business operation. In October of 1995, Gucci went public and had its first initial public offering. The firm was named 'European Company of the Year 1998' by the European Business Press Federation for its economic and financial perform- ance and its strategic vision as well as the management quality.

In 1989, Maurizio Gucci managed to persuade Dawn Mello, who had revived New York's Berg- dorf Goodman to join as creative director, who subsequently hired a young, unknown Texan designer named Tom Ford.

However the early 1990s were another poor time for the business, and Maurizio eventually recognized he was incapable of running the business, handing over to the then-head of Gucci America, Domenico De Sole, who also replaced Mello with Ford, recognizing that the brand needed a radically new image, and investment. PPR took a 40% stake in the business, later rising to 68%.

Tom Ford's Gucci was an orgy of sex and eroticism, celebrity and glamour.

With his permanent tan and designer stubble, ripped jeans and jackets, the Texan was larger than life. His women stepped out of stretch limousines with dark shades, high heels and half- naked. Gucci was accused of embracing 'porno chic' which is probably justified given that one of Ford's advertisements featured the Gucci 'G' shaved into a female model's pubic hair. He was charismatic and creative in an 'in your face' kind of way, but also responsible for getting Gucci back on track, much anticipated at every fashion show, and back at the cutting edge of designer fashion.

However Gucci was now part of a larger business whose French owners didn't see the future of the brand in a man who they felt put his own ego before one of the most valuable luxury brands in the world. De Sole and Ford were replaced eventually by the more down to earth Mark Lee as CEO and Frida Giannni as head designer.

Lee describes Ford's vision as a low point for the Gucci brand, when it swapped its cosmopolitan home on the glamorous streets of Rome for the dark and aggressive nightclubs of LA.

Gianni, meanwhile, says that she is much more interested in the brain than the body, keen to get back to the Gucci glamour of the fifties, to its Italian roots, optimistic and a little eccentric, sensual rather than sexy, more Isabella Rossellini than Paris Hilton.

Business performance is improving too. Revenue exceeded $3 billion for the first time in 2006, with the strongest growth in North America and Asia, and profits over $800 million. The online business is growing rapidly, as is its stores portfolio, particularly in China.

More sense and sensuality is selling much better than sex.

Seeing things differently, doing different things

'Business is a continual dealing with the future; an instinctive exercise in foresight'

Henry Luce

A more intelligent approach to innovation that embraces a better *now-forward* orientation

- Defining the most plausible solutions to deliver more distinctive solutions.

- Converging all the best ideas through practical and commercial filters.

- Identifying business assets and exploring how they could be used in new way.

- Focusing on solutions with strategic fit, and better utilize business assets.

- Developing new business model – people, process and performance.

- Developing better products and services, processes and solutions.

- Accelerating solutions to maximize their commercial potential.

A more imaginative approach to innovation that embraces a better *future-back* orientation

- Exploring all the possible solutions by seeing things differently.

- Diverging to explore unlimited ideas through disruption and creativity.

- Rethinking the context for innovation by seeing things from different perspectives.

- Creatively fusing the best ideas to create more powerful and compelling ones.

- Shaping new market models – customers, channels and competitively.

- Creating distinctive concepts that engage people and improve their lives.

- Evolving solutions through continuous market testing and learning.

Innovation is the driving force of competitiveness and differentiation, profitability and growth. Whilst it can easily be put into the rather narrow box of product development or technology, it is a fundamental challenge for the whole business. Whilst it can quickly become a buzzword of the times and then quickly be forgotten when times get harder, it must be an ever present, continuous process. It can energize, improve and transform every aspect of business internally and externally.

In a world of intense competition and instant imitation, innovation needs to be on a big scale – only then will it be difficult to copy, be differentiated, sustain a price premium and shape markets. Whilst many of the disciplines of new product development can be applied to strategic innovation – research, creativity, evaluating, testing, launching – they are applied within a much broader context.

- '*Business innovation*' addresses the business holistically – products and services, channels and relationships, processes and supply chains, business models and organizational culture.

- '*Market innovation*' addresses the potential markets – more by influence and impact, it explores how to transform structures and practices, challenge rules and conventions, change behaviours and expectations.

- '*Value innovation*' captures both aspects of business and market innovation, challenging and creating them in a way that delivers the strategy and creates win-wins in terms of value creation for all stakeholders.

Innovation should be driven by and engage all business leaders, embracing cross-functional teams to ensure that big ideas can be delivered across the business. This requires participation in the whole process, not just the final stages. Strategic forms of innovation demand a more conceptual approach that will embrace many functional areas. And it requires clear management, a disciplined process, delivering a portfolio of opportunities that will have commercial impact over time.

Surprisingly – given that it came top of the CEO agenda at the World Economic Forum – innovation is one of the most badly managed aspects of business. How many organizations have innovation strategies? Innovation leaders? Innovation processes? Innovation budgets? A separate innovation department is rarely appropriate (and might be counter-productive).

Innovation needs more about organizational brainpower and effort than anything else – to out-think the competition, to engage the customer in new ways and to out-grow the market. When breaking new ground, you are limited only by your imagination.

6.1   GETTING A NEW WORLDVIEW
Seeing your world from different perspectives

Innovation requires new perspectives – seeing things differently, thinking different things. Finding new insights, better ideas and the best opportunities. 'The Innovation Compass' considers eight different worldviews, separately and then collectively considering the viewpoints of customers, business, competitors, parallel markets, technology, responsibility, finance and the future.

Having clearly defined an issue or opportunity – an emerging customer need, declining share in key markets, a new technological application, a convergence of markets, an underperforming distribution channel or the need for a new style of service – then consider the possible ways of addressing them from the different perspectives. What would Virgin do? What would customers love? What would Einstein have done? What might it look like in the future? What new technologies could help?

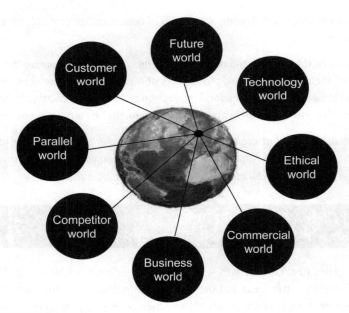

THE EIGHT WORLDVIEWS

The eight 'worldviews' to drive strategic innovation are:

- *Customer world* – exploring the needs and wants of diverse individuals, their experience of you and your competitors, their frustrations and aspirations, trust and loyalty.

- *Business world* – exploring the drivers of business performance, key issues and opportunities, assets and capabilities, assumptions and employee ideas.

- *Competitor world* – exploring the strengths and weaknesses, postures and differences, strategies and potential actions of direct and indirect competitors.

- *Parallel world* – exploring how companies in different markets address, or have addressed, similar issues; who won and who lost, and what they did; and even extreme situations.

- *Technology world* – exploring the emerging fields such as networking technologies, computing, mobile technologies, artificial intelligence, biotechnology and nanotechnology.

- *Ethical world* – exploring the increasingly vital issues of the environment, ethical practices, fair trading, human rights, local communities, well-being and transparency.

- *Commercial world* – exploring the consequences of changing price, costs, profits, market share and the wider implications of changing regulations, governance and competition.

- *Future world* – exploring future scenarios based on emerging trends, pattern recognition and random possibilities that might be driven from science or sci-fi.

These perspectives provide a wealth of discontinuous and complementary insights.

They can also be fused with existing knowledge: customer behaviour, market research, employee surveys, boardroom thinking, business performance, industry reports, technological insights, analyst reports, and catalytic thinkers.

Collectively, they synthesize to provide the basis for rich insights: new viewpoints about the future, patterns that start to reoccur across the different perspectives, synthesized into scenarios for what it might be like, identifying the trends that will be most influential, and the business value drivers that will be key to turning innovations into commercial performance.

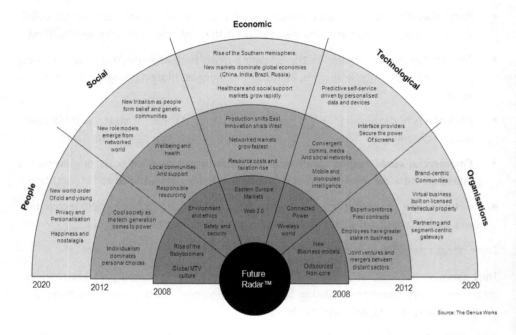

Economic

Social

Technological

Rise of the Southern Hemisphere

New markets dominate global economies
(China, India, Brazil, Russia)

Healthcare and social support
markets grow rapidly

Predictive self-service
driven by personalised
data and devices

New tribalism as people
form belief and genetic
communities

Production shifts East
Innovation shifts West

Interface providers
Secure the power
Of screens

New role models
emerge from
networked
world

Networked markets
grow fastest

Convergent
comms, media
And social networks

Wellbeing and
health

Resource costs and
taxation rise

Brand-centric
Communities

Local communities
And support

Mobile and
distriputed
intelligence

Organisations

People

New world order
Of old and young

Responsible
resourcing

Eastern Europe
Markets

Virtual business
built on licensed
Intellectual property

Privacy and
Personalisation

Cool society as
the tech generation
comes to power

Environment
and ethics

Web 2.0

Connected
Power

Expert workforce
Flexi contracts

Partnering and
segment-centric
gateways

Happiness and
nostalgia

Safety and
security

Wireless
world

Employees have greater
stake in business

Individualism
dominates
personal choices

Rise of the
Babyboomers

New
Business models

Joint ventures and
mergers between
distant sectors

Global MTV
culture

Future
Radar™

Outsourced
Non-core

2020   2012   2012   2020
                    2008   2008

Source: The Genius Works

'Market radar' is one way in which we can map out the key factors that will influence our future, structured by relevant themes and timeframes, and identify the likely impacts of environmental change, and the best opportunities for innovation and growth. The radar will be different for every market, and indeed for every company, given their strategic priorities, assets and ambitions.

Insight 16: CIRQUE DU SOLEIL
Reinventing the world of entertainment

In 1987 Cirque du Soleil took the biggest risk of its brief life, by putting on a show called *We Reinvent the Circus* at the Los Angeles Festival and agreeing to underwrite the entire costs in return for the gate proceeds.

It gave the USA its first taste of Cirque's innovative approach to circus arts, a unique and awe-inspiring blend of acrobatics, theatre, dance and live music. It was the Canadian company's big attempt to break into the American market and succeeded not only in doing that, but in reinventing the whole concept of a circus too.

In *Blue Ocean Strategy* Renee Mauborgne argues that Cirque has completely redefined its market, and therefore its competitors and audiences too. Is it a show? Is it art? Is it entertainment? Mauborgne argues that Cirque has defined its own space by fusing the thrill of the circus with the intellectual sophistication of the theatre and ballet to create a new form of performing art.

From its Quebec origins of 1984, the accordion-playing, stilt-walking, fire-breathing CEO, Guy Laliberte, has turned a group of street performers calling themselves 'Le Club des Talons Hauts' (the high-heels club) into a world leading act. Cirque is now a multi-million dollar entertainment company, with over 50% brand awareness in the USA, and has produced 15 completely different shows that have been performed to around 40 million people worldwide.

Innovation has been a constant feature of Cirque's performances, and a driver of its rapid growth and global reputation. As one enthusiast describes it on the Lovemarks website:

> 'Cirque du Soleil's creative vision fills me with wonder and enchantment. I'm transported by their music, costumes, characters, and performances to a magical place, somewhere amazing. It feeds my soul and excites my senses. Whenever I see a show, I am inspired by what the human body can do and what the human mind can create. The highly imaginative performances enrich and transform me.'

In the early 1990s, Cirque secured long-term partnerships for resident performances for MGM Mirage in Las Vegas and at Walt Disney World in Orlando. This gave it the financial platform to move internationally – into Europe, Japan, and Australia. The shows continued to grow in their creativity and risk-taking too, always accompanied by their original music and handmade costumes that also drove a large licensing and merchandising business.

In 2001, Cirque won an Emmy for the Outstanding Non-Fiction Program, a reality TV series called *Fire Within*. In 2003, they got even more adventurous with a sexy and provocative new show called *Zumanity* for adults only, whilst Cirque's website has won many awards too.

Selling the Cirque shows seems almost unnecessary, such is the level of customer advocacy and media interest that it has built up.

In each location, the company selects media partners who then jointly fund and deliver the promotional messages. Over 15% of all tickets are sold to members of the Cirque Club, which you can join online and receive regular newsletters and invitations to exclusive events. There are now over 750,000 club members. This is upmarket entertainment, so attracting the sponsorship of prestige brands such as IBM, American Express or BMW is no problem, driving corporate hospitality, and further enhancing Cirque's own premium brand credentials.

Another Cirque fan summarizes her experience:

'My first show was their first show in NYC. I was instantly mesmerized by the advertising, and purchased tickets right after the commercial. I wanted to be in that world
... NOW ... Once you enter the yellow tents you are a part of their world. The clowns
come out before the show as you are sitting down, they serve as almost like an appe-
tizer, cleansing and preparing your palette and mind as they instantly usher out your
concerns, stress or whatever you might have brought in with you in order to prepare
you for the main course, the show. Since that time, I have seen almost every show and
they have yet to disappoint. They have changed what we call a circus by their non-use
of animals and have made us, the human form, the most fascinating, funny, sensuous,
mesmerizing, inspiring instrument to admire and be in awe of. They continue to push the
limits of human entertainment on every level.'

Like the high wire artist, Cirque has to continue to tread carefully to balance its need to generate
profits with the significant investments required in an artistic and creative business. It is this
balance that enables the brand to continually surprise and delight its audiences worldwide.

6.2   THE POWER OF CONCEPTS
Applying innovation to a bigger idea

Innovation is about the commercial implementation of the best ideas, be they new products
and services, new ways of working, or even the fundamental business model by which you do
business.

Innovation might take a broad or narrow scope:

- *Concepts* – new business ideas that address customers aspirations in new ways, that
  redefine the way things are done and the business model to support them. Consider the
  way IKEA has transformed the world of home furnishings with its flat-packed, democrati-
  cally designed furniture. Or Nike's creation of flagship brand experiences as Niketown.

- **Solutions** – product and service ideas that are more functional and tangible, that individually or collectively serve customers better. Examples might include Dyson's bagless vacuum cleaner, the iPod as a digital photo album, Virgin Mobile's pay as you go phone tariffs and Ritz Carlton hotels developing a more personal style of service.

- **Markets** – ideas that reshape markets, change people's behaviours, drive new aspirations, and create new commercial dynamics. Imagine coffee before Starbucks essentially created the modern-day coffee shop, the diversity of offering and the premium experience. Similarly Apple, and in particular iTunes, has transformed the dynamics of music purchasing, listening and storage.

In fact all three of these forms of innovation can coexist – a 'concept' might remain as a new way of doing business, or might be translated into products, that then require customers to behave in new ways once it reaches market. For example, the concept of personal home entertainment was productized in the form of Tivo and Sky+, carbon neutral travel was manifest as the G-Wiz.

Similarly a straight product idea might be enhanced to thinking of broader applications, perhaps more aesthetic than functional. Such a product might still need to influence its market structure in some way, in order to be accepted. The Gucci handbag is much more than a functional bag – to some people it might be a fashion accessory equal to a designer coat, or an object of desire like a new car.

Innovation differs in scale as well as scope.

Look at your toothbrush or your shampoo. It is hardly innovative. If one brand angles the head, the others do. If another adds funky colours, everyone follows. If one has special ingredient x, the others will soon add formula y. It doesn't break new ground, it merely levels the game. Moving forwards to stand still.

Market shaping companies most fundamentally innovate their markets – the needs of customers, the structure of competition, the channels that connect them, the rules by which they work. Indeed business and product innovation will rarely have the dramatic impact that they seek unless they are associated by fundamental market innovation too.

And not least, the business itself must be innovative in its structure and funding, design and delivery of brands and propositions, in its use of channels and media, pricing and service, promotions and rewards.

Geoffrey Moore's *Crossing the Chasm* is a fabulous reminder as to why so many innovative products and services fail, not just in tech markets but in all categories. The 'chasm' which so many great ideas fall into and never get out of is the gap between the early adopters and the mass market.

Whilst the geeks in the know will queue up waiting for the new product with blind faith in its quality, there are many more consumers who will not rush to your door. It will take them many more months to become aware, convinced and persuaded to join those early adopters. If companies can't move from the initial niche to the mainstream, they will rarely secure the critical mass and just won't see the volumes of sales that are often essential to pay back the initial investments in product development and market entry.

Consider the limited success of Apple's early Macintosh, and even its more recent iMac. Even if they were fantastic innovations, they never quite managed to make it to the mainstream. In comparison, the iPod and its derivatives have leaped over the chasm onto every high street – a must-have fashion accessory as well as a great innovation.

Moore argues that new solutions should be carefully and differently marketed at each stage of their maturity – to engage the early adopter will require very different messages, channels and pricing to what will eventually engage the populace. Yet so many marketers switch off once a product is launched, hoping that it will ride on its launch hype, and that the one message, one proposition, even one form of the product will engage everyone.

Insight 17: 3M
'Bootlegging' at the innovation company

In 1969, Neil Armstrong took man's first steps on the moon wearing space boots with soles made of synthetic material from 3M. In 2000, Michael Johnson sprinted to an Olympic 400m title wearing shoes made from 24-carat gold 3M Scotchlite Reflective Fabric, developed by 3M.

3M describes itself as 'an innovation company'. Formerly known as the Minnesota Mining and Manufacturing company, it is now an $18 billion global leader with an unrelenting focus is on sustained profitable growth. Its 55,000 products are in areas as diverse as healthcare and safety equipment, electronics and industrial markets.

The company's 67,000 employees remain focused on creating 'practical and ingenious solutions that help customers succeed', and are encouraged to continuously seek innovation through a wide range of techniques. These include giving every employee 10% of their weekly time to 'bootleg' on crazy ideas, to insisting that at least 30% of revenue come from new products.

3M has a long history of innovation – not only investing in new solutions, but also transforming markets and customer behaviours too. In this way it ensures that its creations – everything from sandpaper to adhesive tape – become practical and profitable too. Its innovation process consists of an integrated and parallel approach to concept, product and market innovation.

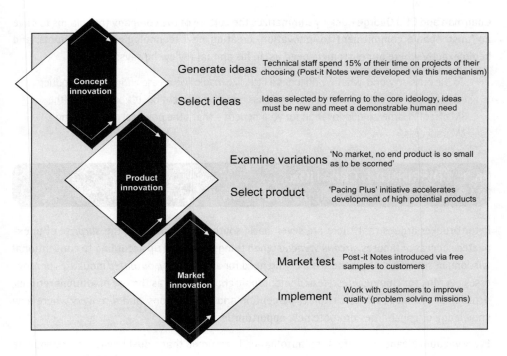

Generate ideas — Technical staff spend 15% of their time on projects of their choosing (Post-it Notes were developed via this mechanism)

Select ideas — Ideas selected by referring to the core ideology, ideas must be new and meet a demonstrable human need

Examine variations — 'No market, no end product is so small as to be scorned'

Select product — 'Pacing Plus' initiative accelerates development of high potential products

Market test — Post-it Notes introduced via free samples to customers

Implement — Work with customers to improve quality (problem solving missions)

Concept innovation

Product innovation

Market innovation

INNOVATION AT 3M

Perhaps most famous is the story of the choirboy who dropped his hymnbook during a church service and with it all the loose bits of paper that marked the important pages for him. The observation led to the creation of the Post-it note, now an essential part of any office desk, and available in a bewildering range of colours, sizes and formats.

Chairman and CEO George Buckley summarizes the culture of the company that claims to have an 'unstoppable commitment to innovation, creating new technologies and products, and being exactly where our customers need us'. In his annual review he says:

> 'To the outside world, what we do looks a little like magic. We create entirely new product categories and breathe new life into markets crying for reinvention. It's been called "the 3M effect". Harnessing innovation for your benefit – that's the practical magic behind 3M's success.'

6.3 DISRUPTIVE CREATION
Making the best ideas happen profitably

Peter Drucker argues that there are seven basic sources of innovation: the *surprise* of unexpected success or failures, *inconsistencies* when things don't add up according to conventional wisdom, *desperation* where there is a crying need for a better way, *outdated* industries or processes overdue for change, *lifestyle* or demographic changes such as the rise of affluent retirees, *attitudinal* changes such as customer perception and expectations, and *discovery* where new knowledge or capabilities promote new opportunities.

Every vacuum cleaner manufacturer automatically assumed that a dust bag was a prerequisite within their designs. Until James Dyson came along. Every airline thought it unrealistic to put a bed on a transatlantic aircraft. Until British Airways met a yacht designer. Every analyst thought it was impossible to make money out of free information online. Until Google created a fundamentally different business model.

Innovations disrupt conventions.

The disruption might be a challenge or even a reversal in the received wisdom of the market – in the ways in which companies make money, in the assumed needs of customers, and the types of solutions that most effectively fulfil them. Hotbeds of disruption might come from something that creates a high level of customer frustration (e.g. how to remortgage your home), complexity (e.g. how to integrate your many computing devices) or a paradox (e.g. how to shop in bulk when you have no space in your home to store it).

Clay Christensen, Harvard professor and author of *The Innovator's Dilemma,* describes the frequent appearance of 'disruptive innovation' in today's markets where a market leader – until then usually well-respected and profitable – is quickly humbled by a lower cost-entrant offering an inferior but perfectly acceptable product. The new entrant has typically paid much closer attention to the priorities of customers, and found ways to deliver against them at lower cost, rather than seeking to do more than is necessary as the incumbent (and indeed most brand leaders) is so tempted to do.

Imagine your DVD player, your phone, your camera, your PC – it has far more functionality than you will ever need. What if we removed all the non-essentials and thereby significantly reduced production costs, and offered a much lower price?

Prior to 1960 handheld electric tools were heavy and cumbersome, designed for heavy-duty professionals, and very expensive. Black & Decker then created plastic encased tools with universal motors that only lasted 25 to 30 hours, long enough for the lifetime of the occasional hobbyist or gardener and, at a tenth of the price, far more affordable too.

Technological innovation can often get the better of companies. Once the macho focus on product specifications takes over, the business can become blinkered by the competitive race for ever-more sophisticated solutions – bigger, stronger, faster – and can easily lose focus on what matters to customers.

Technology can quickly distract us and with its constant ability to do more – faster processors, smaller components, more memory capacity – simply urges companies to embrace them in its next generation. Yet customers will only use technology up to a point: most electronic devices do far more than you ever do, most software on a PC remains largely unutilized, most new gizmos are reflections of aesthetic aspirations rather than functional need.

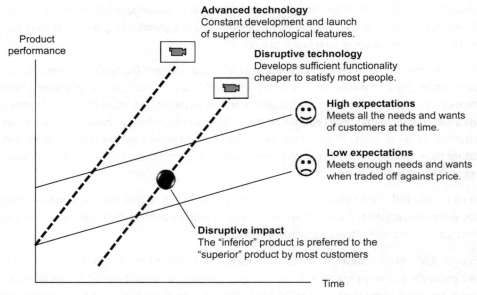

Advanced technology
Constant development and launch
of superior technological features.

Disruptive technology
Develops sufficient functionality
cheaper to satisfy most people.

High expectations
Meets all the needs and wants
of customers at the time.

Low expectations
Meets enough needs and wants
when traded off against price.

Disruptive impact
The "inferior" product is preferred to the
"superior" product by most customers

Product
performance

Time

DISRUPTIVE INNOVATION (ADAPTED FROM PROF. CLAYTON CHRISTENSEN).

'Disruption', as Christensen describes it, happens when this tech progress is far ahead of what customers need and can use. This overshoot creates the opportunity for a new entrant to come in with something that is cheaper, simpler and 'good enough' for a significant number of customers.

Once this new entrant has carved out a niche at the lower end of the market, they can rapidly persuade more customers that they are good enough for them too. The disruption might be product related as in Dell's disruption of the PC market, or market related as in eBay creating an entirely new marketplace.

The phenomenon can be seen in everything from complex data storage devices being 'disrupted' by small, cheaper ones, to doctors often being displaced by nurses, and similarly in markets as diverse as airlines and insurance.

Commercially, it is not really about technology, but about the business model. Small agile companies can succeed with business models unattractive to larger companies. An existing company may need to deliver a 40% margin in order for a new product to be attractive, yet to a smaller company, a 20% margin might make them extremely profitable.

Larger companies don't only have financial blind spots to such opportunities. Capabilities and culture are also limiting factors. If BMW prides itself on its design and manufacturing excellence, it is difficult for it to accept that it should make 'inferior' products, not because they don't work but because they are not the best they can be. Similarly British Airways struggled to compete against the new low-cost entrants such as Ryanair and easyJet partly because, culturally, a full-service airline that prides itself on its customer service finds limited service a difficult concept to grasp.

Yet larger companies who do embrace disruptive thinking can be successful too. The rise in corporate venturing and 'intrapreneurship' is as much focused on replacing the existing paradigms of the core business as it is in utilizing existing capabilities or IP in new ways. Jack Welch's parting gift to GE was a programme known as 'destroy your business' where he encouraged staff across the monolith to think like Internet entrepreneurs would – and probably are thinking – to disrupt its own business before somebody else blows them out the water.

Disruption enables more radical creativity. Once you have disrupted the status quo, a better, more creative solution is required in its place.

Of course creating a disruption is only the starting point, as it then requires creativity to exploit it in some useful and different way. Thinking radically about why markets exist like they do, and what they shouldn't become like. Thinking radically about future market models, and how they should work. Pure creativity is fun and energizing, but must be structured in order to deliver meaningful results.

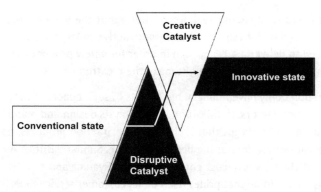

DISRUPTION AND CREATIVITY

There are many different creative techniques, some of them high-tech, requiring significant preparation and equipment; others requiring none at all. However creativity needs effective facilitation and structure. The development of long lists of ideas might be useful, but can fragment and annoy people if they are not quickly grasped, distilled, connected and taken forwards. The worst scenario is that, because of a lack of 'getting to the answer', executives compromise on easy options or do nothing.

Most importantly, innovation needs both disruptive and creative catalysts to break the conventions as well as explore the possibilities. Creative thinker Edward de Bono might in some situations encourage a group to use his coloured 'thinking hats' through which they each take different perspectives on a problem, or might simply say, 'Take an object out of your pocket'. The team is then encouraged to generate as many solutions to a problem based on the attributes of the object. 'How would you solve the problems of retail stock-outs by comparing it to a matchstick?'

Disruptive catalysts	
Value mapping	Where is business and customer value created and destroyed? How is it created? Who, what, when and why?
Hot spotting	Identifying overlaps and waste, sites and sources of complexity, confusion. Where are the cost/time 'basins'?
Heritage hunt	What made you great? What are, or were you famous for? How was it earned? Could you create a new 'heritage'?
Rule breaking	What are the explicit/implicit rules, inside/outside the business? There are no others? Test/stretch to limits
New perspectives	Taking different perspectives, from stakeholders, competitors, unrelated viewpoints. What if you use inversions?
Reduction filters	Reduce to components? What are the commonalities? What if we eliminated aspects at random? Is it vital? Better?
Sacred beliefs	What do you value and treasure? What does this enable and restrain? What if you adopted a new faith?
Disruptive technologies	How could emerging technologies challenge, replace, change or enhance how you currently do business?
Thinking dimensions	Changing the thinking tracks (the parameters, the blocks) in which you currently think, plan or work
Corporate fool	Asking the unaskable, challenging logic and assumptions, dismissing evidence, artistic, lateral, always asking 'why?'

Creative catalysts	
Trend architects	Extrapolating, applying, building on available trends of social, economic, political and technological changes.
Futurist visions	What are the possible visions of the future state – what do they have in common and what is different?
New horizons	Designing an inspiring future in words, pictures and multidimensional forms. Simulating the journey over the horizon
Parallel tracking	Learning from other places, e.g. different sectors or markets, and from beyond business (education, law, nature etc.)
Creative fusions	Combining new ideas and conventions in highly unusual ways. Harnessing positive tensions and dualism
Perfect day	Bringing together the best of the best, from across companies, within the company, and over time/location
Creativity techniques	Exploiting established creative tools such as lateral thinking, de Bono's hats, brainstorming, mindmaps, etc.
Collective genius	Harnessing the ideas of the best minds available to develop creative ideas Interactively, e.g. realtime brain writing
Extreme sports	Applying your approach in to extreme Situations, e.g. car brakes to space shuttle to stretch performance and application
Thriving on paradox	Accepting what convention said was unacceptable – recognizing paradox, and how to 'have your cake and eat it'

There are many other techniques to be selected and sometimes combined, depending on the nature of the problem, the group of people who are seeking to solve it, and some of the broader objectives which people seek to achieve whilst solving it, such as team-building, or engaging decision-makers.

The development process by which radical ideas become innovations and practical reality will differ depending on the challenge; however, a classic product development process will most importantly have a series of stages in which the concept is increasingly filtered, tested and shaped until it is right for the customer and commercially viable. Of course these filters must be designed in a way that facilitates non-conventional solutions rather than only supporting the convention – that recognizes unarticulated customer needs, or new sources of value creation.

Breakthrough

Harnessing one or more of these sources helps us to challenge our thinking and explore new approaches, and then to think more about how we can smartly turn the best opportunities into commercial reality.

Einstein argued, 'It is impossible to solve a problem by using the same thinking that created it.' Similarly, Tom Kelley of IDEO, one of the world's leading product developers argues that product development is 'part creativity, part logic and part golf swing'. New solutions need radical visions in order to break through convention, and to appeal to sponsors and customers. As Kelley argues, this vision will be part creative – the new idea – but also based on strategic alignment, customer analysis and commercial logic.

The starting point is to be clear on the business issue or market opportunity to be addressed, ensuring that sponsors and other stakeholders agree with the purpose of innovation. This should then be built on by an 'immersion' into the context for innovation – looking at what research already exists; talking to real customers about their needs and wants, frustrations and aspirations, and more broadly about how they live or work; and talking to innovative companies in other markets who have overcome similar situations.

Innovation is then an 'opening up' and 'closing' down process.

1   **Creative divergence**: Creativity enables us to stretch our domain of thinking, to consider
    what's possible – even if it doesn't yet seem practical or profitable – and to generate many
    diverse ideas. The more effectively we can diverge, the greater the range of possibilities
    we then have from which to combine and select the best ideas. Anything is possible; don't
    judge or filter at this stage. You should use a wide range of creative techniques, not be
    limited by the inadequacies of brainstorming!

2   **Concept fusion**: The clustering, connection and combination of different ideas drives the
    formation of distinctive new concepts – still a creative approach, the combination of ideas
    that might previously have seemed inconsistent, unconventional or unrealistic is how we
    start to drive more significant solutions. Using parallels, you might imagine the IKEA of
    your industry, what it would take to do an iPod/iTunes, or how Branson could reinvent your
    world. Explore ways in which you could apply your best assets in the best opportunities.
    Shape the strongest concepts, perhaps 8 to 12 of them, with theme names and illustra-
    tions of how they would work. Still don't judge or filter them.

3   **Commercial convergence**: The concepts are then filtered to ensure that they are strategi-
    cally, practically and commercially viable – the strategic and portfolio fit; development
    and operating costs; time to market; risks involved; and the potential differentiation and
    symbolism that the solution offers. The concepts that make it through might then offer
    further opportunities for connection, to strengthen them, or need a little tweaking to
    improve their viability. At the same time, it is important to avoid just adding in everything
    and losing the clarity of concept.

The best solution emerges, supported by a business case and implementation plan. Once approved,
the solution development process should be mapped out, working backwards from when and how
you would achieve maximum impact in the market. When would people be most open to buying

it? When, where and how should it be launched? What are the implications, therefore, working further back in terms of design, testing, prototyping – in terms of the product or service itself, but also in terms of systems and processes, training and support, channels and trade promotions, packaging and communication?

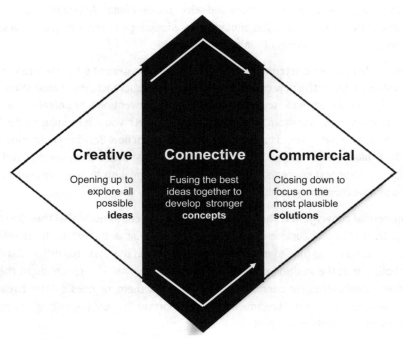

Creative

Opening up to explore all possible **ideas**

Connective

Fusing the best ideas together to develop stronger **concepts**

Commercial

Closing down to focus on the most plausible **solutions**

THE 3C INNOVATION PROCESS

In fast-changing markets, launch is often just the beginning of a successful development. Firstly, the early adopters of a solution are always the most challenging to satisfy, and can often provide lessons for improvement, although they may require quite different solutions to the mainstream. Secondly, it is the applications of solutions that really matter to customers, and where a new product or service can often have the most impact, therefore requiring specific development. Thirdly, markets themselves must be developed to embrace new entrants – in their knowledge and capabilities, distribution and support structures, with related products and service – if the innovation is to be successful.

Innovation should live in the organization, as a fundamental practice, and a constant source of energy and opportunity for people across the business. The innovation strategy drives a portfolio of initiatives from large 'big bet' concepts through to small 'no brainer' improvements. The portfolio mix of initiatives should balance risk and reward, working on some long-term, market-shaping, value-creating projects, whilst also keeping products and services sharp and distinctive in the short term. Convention-busting innovations may require 'ring fencing' to protect them from the short-term priorities or existing culture of the business, but also to establish faster, more creative, more collaborative ways of working that can then spread across the business.

Unlocking the power of creativity and innovation – through more radical strategies and concepts, ideas and insights, processes and cultures – is addressed in more detailed in Peter Fisk's new book *Creative Genius* (also published by Capstone in 2008).

Insight 18: ZARA
The Spanish 'ready-baked' business model

It was in a shop window in the northern Spanish port of La Coruña that Amancio Ortega and his girlfriend spotted a beautiful silk negligee, but with a price tag well out of reach of the shirt maker's budget.

That night, he went back to his workshop and reproduced what he had seen for a fraction of the price, and with the approval of his girlfriend launched his own fashionable but affordable nightwear and lingerie business. The public reaction was so positive that he quickly moved into broader fashion and opened his first shop in the quiet, slightly dull fishing town in 1975.

Ortega pursued his vision of 'ready-baked' clothes, as he called them, translating the latest ideas from the catwalk and trends on the street into new ranges faster than anyone else.

The business grew rapidly through the Eighties, and in 1989 he opened his first international stores in Paris and New York. Perhaps one of the more interesting approaches has been the different competitive positions that Zara has adopted in different markets – in Spain, Zara is low-cost, high-fashion; in the USA it is more premium-priced; and in the UK, mid-priced.

Zara is now the largest brand within the Inditex group, which, with a turnover of $8 billion, 32,000 employees and 3100 stores in 70 countries, also includes brands such as Pull and Bear, Massimo Dutti, Stradivarius and Bershka. With Ortega still very much at the helm, the group's headquarters is only a short ride from La Coruña, with its large and minimalist campus, full of designers deeply immersed in their market research and fashion magazines or back from the catwalks and yarn mills, ready to take the latest ideas to the high street in record time.

Zara was described by Louis Vuitton fashion director Daniel Piette as 'possibly the most innovative and devastating retailer in the world'.

Speed and efficiency are the real source of Zara's success. Everything is streamlined to ensure that Zara can be the first to market with the latest fashions at affordable prices. The concept depends on the continuous creation and rapid replenishment of new designs. Zara's 'sense and respond' approach enables them to occupy the leading edge of the fashion cycle, when demand and prices are highest, and, coupled with their highly efficient supply chain, margins are greatest.

Visit any one of the 1050 Zara stores in 55 countries and the same fashions are unlikely to be in store for more than a few weeks. With new products arriving every day and around 10,000 product designs a year, there is no wonder that customers are impulsive buyers and regular visitors to their stores. Indeed, on average, customers each visit Zara stores 17 times a year.

The Zara in-store experience is also the primary marketing platform, rejecting the typical fashion approach of image-based TV and press advertising. The company believes that there is more value to be gained in finding the best retail locations, spacious and contemporary interiors and the impact from its stylish navy carrier bags than there would be from a few seconds of over-crowded, two-dimensional airtime. Indeed, Zara spends around 0.3% of its revenue on marketing, yet has still managed to build one of the most desirable and talked-about brands on the high street.

Similarly, Amancio Ortega, the old shirt maker from Galicia, may not be the best-known name in the fashion world or often compared to the likes of Armani, Klein, or Dolce and Gabbana; however, he is one of the wealthiest. With a personal fortune of over $9bn, only Bernard Arnault of luxury goods firm LVMH outranks him in the Forbes rich list, which also makes him Spain's wealthiest man.

Zara timeline

1963   Ortega begins his career as a shirt maker.

1975   He opens the first Zara store in his local town of La Coruña.

1980   Zara extends its store network across Spain.

1985   Inditex SA becomes the name of the corporate group.

1988   Zara goes international, to Oporto, then New York and Paris.

1991   Inditex launches Pull and Bear, a more family-oriented brand.

1995   It acquires menswear fashion chain Massimo Dutti.

1998   Inditex launches Berksha, targeting younger females.

1999   Inditex acquires the Stradivarius chain, a more upmarket brand.

2001   Inditex launches the Oysho lingerie brand and the corporation goes public.

2003   Zara Home stores begin to open across Europe.

2007   Ortega ranked by Forbes as Spain's wealthiest individual.

Outside in, inside out

PART 3

Outside in, inside out

'What if I should fall right through the centre of the earth ... oh, and come out the other side, where people walk upside down?'

Lewis Carroll

Engage your customers more intelligently from the **inside out** to be more distinctive focused and effective.

Engage your customers more imaginatively from the **outside in** to be more responsive, appropriate and personal.

▶ We go to work with blinkers on.

▶ At home we are just like our customers – human beings living in a complicated world, trying to do the right thing, but often forced to make compromises, whilst still hoping to achieve our broader dreams. At work we live in the black and white – defining the boundaries of what matters to us, seeking finite problems that fit our predefined solutions. We limit ourselves by our conventions, processes and laziness.

▶ Seeing business from the 'outside in' opens up a richer, broader perspective from which to compete.

▶ Power has fundamentally shifted from suppliers to customers. In markets of infinite choice and excess supply, customers are in control. They expect companies to do business where, when and how they want. They don't expect to be thwarted by internal processes or bureaucracy; they don't appreciate the pursuit of profits being put before their own needs.

▶ Starting outside in, then responding inside out, is a more focused and enlightened way to do business.

Doing business on customer's terms

'I see a fundamental shift in power to the consumer, to the people. That requires us to engage, to create and connect with consumers on a scale that we've never seen before'

Mark Parker

A more **intelligent** approach to **customers** that embraces a better *inside out* orientation		A more **imaginative** approach to **customers** that embraces a better *outside in* orientation
• Taking a market perspective, the best markets and segments.		• Taking a customer perspective, selecting the best, more individually.
• Segmenting the market by physicality, motivations and potential value.		• Customizing solutions and relationships to individual high-value customers.
• Using broad research techniques, to understand broad priorities.		• Using individual research techniques to understand customers more deeply.
• Quantifying articulated needs, priorities and preferences by segment.		• Uncovering unarticulated needs, aspirations and energizers.
• Organized by products, focused on sales and transactional delivery.		• Organized by customers, focused on solutions and relationships.
• Doing business in the context of defined products and competitors.		• Doing business in the broader context of customers and their applications.
• Doing business on your terms – what, when, where and how you want.		• Doing business on customer terms – what, when, where and how they want.

Customers are more different and individual, more discerning and demanding than ever. Whilst 100 years ago, a new car buyer would be more than happy to buy a Ford Model T, a model that hardly changed in decades in 'any colour as long as it's black', today customers are intelligent, expectant and pedantic. Their stated needs may well be true, but their unstated needs and wants often matter even more.

They can appear ambiguous and inconsistent too, particularly when we seek to understand them in simple, high-level ways. Consider the BMW parked outside whilst the driver secures the best prices at Aldi, or the Gucci bag found on the discounted shelves of TK Maxx. Their motivations and aspirations are complex and personal, and it can take a highly skilled psychoanthropologist to decipher them.

Indeed, it's increasingly difficult to make sense of such markets using classic techniques such as segmentation. Customers no longer fit into simple boxes with homogeneity within each box and differences between them. Some companies find that they need to break their customers down into around 500 clusters before they can get any relevant segmentation. And such groups rarely follow simple physical or demographic descriptors – postcodes, socio-economic groups and occupations are less relevant than ever in describing who we are.

Added to this, the increasing complexity of our lives means that we are probably in different segments for different activities – prepared to pay a premium for the best car, but wanting to save every penny on our weekly shopping; too lazy to change energy supplier, but ready to travel double the distance to get a lower cost flight – and even depending on our mood when doing such activities.

Our life patterns are less predictable too. With 500 channels of TV broadcasting 24 hours a day, it is hard to tell who will be watching what when, how to target advertising, or schedule programmes. We move house frequently, we marry more often and change job every few years. The baby-boomer over-60s probably have more in common with gap year students than they do with the previous generation of pensioners. We can no longer be stereotyped. Consider some more attitudinal shifts:

- We value products less than ever before; instead, how we engage with brands through service and support is far more important.

- We respect youth more than age and we aspire to be youthful at every age, rather than looking up to our elders.

- We value life more than money, preferring to deal in currencies such as knowledge, friendship or well-being than cash.

- We seek to enhance the things we enjoy or value, and to minimize the things that we don't enjoy or are not important to us.

We live in the age of the intelligent customer where, prior to a transaction, the consumer has probably done far more product research and price comparison than the sales assistant. We can buy anything from anywhere and expect it to be delivered next day. Ethical issues suddenly matter much more too, not as an option – fairtrade, food miles, packaging – but as a basic requirement.

Transparency means that promises have to be realized. Indeed, trust in companies and their brands has suffered as a result. Few companies manage to be whiter than white. Trust, however, is a relative concept. According to research by the Henley Centre:

- A US consumer has on average 69% trust in Starbucks, whilst a UK consumer has 36% and a French consumer 12%.

- We trust our banks more than we trust lawyers, despite the fact that banks lock us into accounts with incredibly low returns.

- We trust global brands more than local brands in developing countries, but trust local brands more than global brands in developed countries.

The challenge is as it has always been: to understand customers, to develop solutions to their needs and to connect with them in appropriate ways that result in their satisfaction, maybe even their loyalty and advocacy, and deliver a profit for the business. It is just a million times more complicated than it was for Henry Ford.

7.1 DEEP DIVING FOR INSIGHTS
Finding what really drives and energizes people

Customers are real people with a diversity of motivations and aspirations. They cannot be neatly summarized as the averages of a regression analysis. Learning that 52% of people like apples rather than oranges hardly means that we should abandon one for the other, or that we should create some kind of combination of the two. It might sound silly, but that is what so often happens. Companies would do much better spending their huge research and analytical budgets on understanding a smaller number of customers deeply, rather than seeking the meaningless averages of large samples.

However, before jumping into the customer world, it is useful to focus our effort on the customers who are likely to be most relevant and ultimately most valuable to us. Segmentation is a fundamental requirement of addressing any market. Customers are not all equal, in motivation or value. No company can seek to be all things to all people. Few brands are likely to get beyond a 30–40% market share; therefore, it's far better to work out which 30–40% you would ultimately like before trying to engage them.

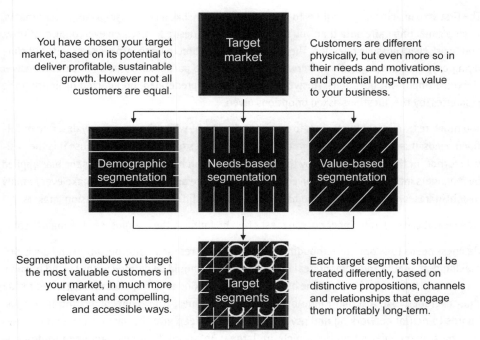

You have chosen your target market, based on its potential to deliver profitable, sustainable growth. However not all customers are equal.

Target market

Customers are different physically, but even more so in their needs and motivations, and potential long-term value to your business.

Demographic segmentation

Needs-based segmentation

Value-based segmentation

Segmentation enables you target the most valuable customers in your market, in much more relevant and compelling, and accessible ways.

Target segments

Each target segment should be treated differently, based on distinctive propositions, channels and relationships that engage them profitably long-term.

SEGMENTING AND TARGETING THE BEST MARKETS

So with a clearer target audience, how do you understand them more deeply? How do you gain real insight?

Insight is more than research findings, it is more profound. It tells you something new and useful, it considers aspects that you have not thought about before, which are not described within the conventions of markets. It puts knowledge into context. It describes why and how, as well as who and what.

The first step in achieving insight is to stop using research 'like a drunk uses a lamp post'; that is, to stop collecting more data than you need, resisting the desire to research everyone constantly, and to ask every possible question. There is also a temptation to jump into research without clarifying objectives, often finding afterwards that it has no particular purpose, or cannot answer the most important questions. Answers are then often predefined, prejudicing or limiting the responses, by the questions asked or options given.

Too much research asks customers to say what they want when they can rarely describe unfulfilled needs. It is also tempting to use the same techniques for everything, because it is the easiest method, or the most preferred by the incumbent research agency. Add to this the bias applied by managers internally – preconceived wisdom, prejudice and laziness often make every mildly insightful research result bland and banal by the time it filters through to decision-makers.

Newness, it is worth remembering, can most often be found in the margins, not the mainstream.

Business needs to adopt more thoughtful approaches to research, interpretation and decision-making that enable and demand real insight. Research should be defined with the end in mind, focused on learning more about the best customers, looking for anomalies and extremes rather than averages. Use a broad range of research techniques, from concept testing and mood boards to neural networking and psychographics. Dig deep into the vast customer databases that most companies sit on but which are largely untapped. Find new language to describe insights, metaphors and analogies.

Neuroscience can now offer business an even more scientific approach to understanding human responses – often utilizing brain imaging techniques, such as functional magnetic resonance imaging (fMRI), a non-invasive scanning technique – to understand consumer behaviours.

The 'Pepsi Challenge' was conducted whilst scanning the reactions of customer brains. When given Coke and Pepsi, separately, as unlabelled drinks, the response to Pepsi was five times stronger – most significantly seen in the ventral putamen, one of the brain's reward centres.

However when the brands were revealed, nearly all volunteers preferred Coke. Coke stimulated a different part of the brain – the medial prefrontal cortex, an area more associated with thinking and judging, and with our 'sense of self'. The brand, or at least some aspect of it, was clearly resonating with people at a much higher level and overriding more functional responses.

Most important of all, however, is to simply get out there, and be with customers.

Walk in the customers' shoes, see the world as they see it, try out competitors, or solving their problems in different ways. Observe how customers behave: what is difficult, what frustrates them, how they use and store things, all the irrational things we all do. Talk to them too. Not 'Hi, I'm from X, what do you think of my great product?' Instead, learn about their broader needs and wants, frustrations and ambitions. Go deeper into areas that you know, from more standard research, matters more to people. Dig for ideas. Listen to the language they use. Keep your ears and mind open. Capture the quirky findings; don't disregard them as the craze of one person.

'Energizer pyramids' are a simple way to reflect what matters most – rationally and emotionally – to real customers. For each person you meet, as well as some of the actual facts and stories you learn, seek to identify the following:

- '*Essentials*' that were absolute prerequisites for any brand to deliver in their eyes, both the hygiene factors (like safety and security) but also basic expectations – even a low-cost flight is expected to serve drinks on board, although they may come at a price.

- '*Enablers*' that practically helped them to do more, which might be offered by some brands but not others, and became part of a rational trade-off against brands and price – faster delivery, 24-hour support, range of colour options.

- '*Energizers*' that might seem small and trivial but can emotionally make a big difference – the biscuit served with your coffee, the free newspapers, the choice of music, the free toy for the kids, the buzz of sales staff.

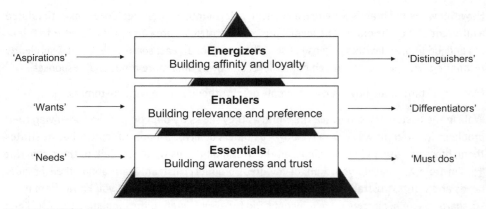

THE ENERGIZER PYRAMID

The pyramid can be completed from the customer perspective – what they need, want and would love to have; and also from the brand perspective – the products and services offered that address the customer at each level. Of course responding to customer desires is about choices, deciding which of their motivations you will address and how they will combine to create your differentiation – your source of competitive advantage.

Insight 19: DIESEL
Designer fuel for the cool generation

'Diesel is not my company – it is my life', proclaims the driving force behind some of the coolest jeans on the planet. He sips his espresso as he looks out over the vines and olive trees of Diesel Farm in the Marostica Hills of Northern Italy, with a passion and imagination that has created one of the world's fast-growing brands.

Renzo Rosso is a lifestyle entrepreneur.

His fans include Kate Moss and Keira Knightley. His 320 stores reach across 80 countries, and his holding company, Only The Brave, generates sales of over €1.5 billion. Not only does Diesel make jeans, but it extends into everything from jewellery, watches and fragrances to organic wines and olive oils. His farm is not only a working vineyard, but the venue for some of the most eye-catching fashion shoots you will see,

Everything, as the brand proclaims, for 'successful living'.

In a small, beautiful town not far from his farm you will find the engine of Diesel, the people who are inspired by the latter-day winemaker. Designers and marketers mix a more laid-back lifestyle with the next fashion ideas. Rather than the trendy studios of Milan, they prefer the ancient walled town of Bassano del Grappa. With its terracotta roofs, narrow cobbled streets, you might be surprised to find the town full of youthful, trendy creative types.

The streets are quiet by day but liven up beyond recognition when the Diesel crowd emerges from their work. Youth and laughter, ideas and energy. Look closely and you will notice their designer, vintage jeans and tailored shorts. They might even occasionally sample a bottle of his Rosso di Rosso, which can be found in the most fashionable restaurants at €350 per bottle.

Diesel was created as a jeans label by Rosso and the older Adriano Goldsmith in 1978. Within seven years Rosso had taken sole control, and started about building a lifestyle beyond a product. However, it is not just about marketing. Diesel developed innovative denim dye techniques, innovative washes and treatments, cuts and detailing. Within two years it had established a chain of stores throughout Italy, and was ready to take its high-octane, cool lifestyle to the rest of the world.

Rosso recognized that the brand could easily reach into other lifestyle accessories too – the core 'D-Diesel' brand quickly supported a full wardrobe of shirts, jackets and shoes. To stay cool for youth, whilst reaching older, wealthier audiences, he recognized a different brand was necessary and introduced the up-market Style Lab label, and 55DSL for the urban youth. Most recently, jewellery, watches and fragrances were added in partnership with the likes of L'Oréal.

Whilst diversifying its range, Diesel stayed focused on its core product and nurturing its brand. Establishing brand personalities that engaged each audience was particularly important. 'Cool' is a subtle thing to get right. It had to move with the times: like music and celebrities, last year's cool can suddenly become this year's naff, requiring the brand to constantly evolve to stay at the cutting edge.

Diesel brand	Era 1 **'Greasy rockability'** 1978–1993	Era 2 **'Quirky fashionistas'** 1993–2000	Era 3 **'Conscious hedonism'** 2000–present
Reason for being	Dress the tough guys and their smoking girls	Make people feel different and provocative	Help people carry a more pleasant existence
Audience	Tough guy wannabes	Intelligent urban fashionistas	Hedonistic hipsters
Value proposition	Stylish jeans and workwear with a used worn-out look	Affordable fashionable urban street wear	Fun, imaginative and colourful fashiion
Differentiation	Worn-out style	Risky and experimental hard urban style	Stimulating happy clothing
Persona	Tough, wild, adventurous, living on the edge	Provocative, polemical, sarcastic, extravagant	Wit, culture aware, conscious, ironic, naive
Associations	Rebels, hot chicks, bikes, gas stations, 60s	Political issues, social conventions, sexuality	Youth, vitality, happiness, hedonism, sex
Range of authority	Jeans and workwear	Jeans, clothing, shoes, fragrances	Jeans, clothing, watches, sunglasses, shoes, bags, fragrances, hotels, fashion

EVOLUTION OF THE DIESEL BRAND (SOURCE: ENRIC GILL FORT, INSTITUTE OF DESIGN, IIT)

Thirty years on, Rosso is still the driving force behind the brand, remaining passionate as it grows across markets and categories. His smart deals and creative flair have turned Diesel into a major fashion player. Read the label on his unusual blend of Cabernet Sauvignon and Merlot as you sit back and enjoy the taste of a lifestyle brand:

'... My origins, the land that I love, the rural traditions of my father, the old custom of homemade wine, with his charm and secret touches, together now with the more modern techniques, they have given life to a unique product... Enjoy.'

Diesel timeline

1955   Renzo Rosso, born in Padua, studied textiles and manufacturing.

1978   Formed the Genesis Group, brands included Hamnett and Diesel.

1985   Rosso acquires 100% of the company; it moves from jeans label to fashion brand.

1987   Turnover reaches €250 million with growing range and national store chain.

1991   Launches global strategy with ironic, quirky ads, and 'for successful living' slogan.

1995   Establishes Diesel Farm in the Marostica Hills, producing own branded wines and oils.

1996   Receives the 'Premio Risultati' for the best Italian company of the year.

1997   Named as one of the world's 100 most important people by *Select* magazine.

1998   Launches upmarket Style Lab label and wins advertisement of the year at Cannes.

2004   Diesel Denim Gallery limited edition range is launched in NY and Tokyo.

2005   Debuts on the catwalk at New York Fashion Week.

2005   Celebrates 50th birthday with a book, *Fifty*, telling the Diesel story and its future.

2006   Launches jewellery and fragrance collections in partnership with Fossil and L'Oreal.

2006   Turnover exceeds €1.2 billion with 3500 employees, 320 stores in 80 countries.

7.2   GETTING A CUSTOMER PERSPECTIVE
Taking off your blinkers and seeing the customer's world

Apple Store should by now be familiar to most of us. But when a group of senior managers from one of the world's premier retailers were encouraged to visit, they struggled to understand the unconventional approach. The open space and low tables, products free to use by any teenager or backpacker, jarred with their own retail beliefs. Why wasn't there shelving stacked high with as many products on display as possible? Why wasn't it maximizing the use of prime retail space? Why weren't there sales assistants seeking to close sales? The point is not to maximize sales per square metre, but to showcase the brand, engage people in it, change attitudes not simply drive sales. The managers went away challenging their own conventions and beliefs.

We are all customers in our everyday lives, yet when we go to work we put these incredibly narrow blinkers on. We limit ourselves in so many ways – to our own definitions of the markets in which we compete, to all the real and perceived conventions of the market, to our narrow functional roles, to the products we sell and the short-term priorities we set ourselves for results.

This is not how customers think.

Customers have a much larger and more interesting view of the world, unlimited by definitions of 'what sector are you in?', or the rules, or functions, or time. You might sell them a drink, but they want to party, to meet people, to celebrate a birthday, or whatever. You might sell them a loan to buy a new car, but what they really want is to treat themselves, to look the cool cat amongst their mates, or go on a family holiday with enough space to breathe.

In these bigger, broader consumer contexts, brand choices are based on a different set of alternatives from your own defined competitors – how else they can party or transform their image – and their perceived value of this could be completely different from a product-based price. Changing the context gives you an incredibly simple opportunity to do more, to better meet needs and wants – and at the same time, sell more, charge more, sell other things – and drive profitable growth.

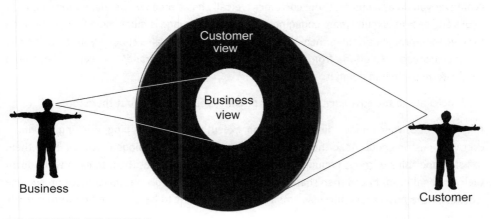

THE CUSTOMER PERSPECTIVE

In the business world, we define our sectors – 'we work in insurance' – and conventions – 'prices are based on business risk', or 'our stores are open Monday to Friday, 9 until 5pm', or 'the contract is always 12 months in duration'. Where do they conventions come from? Why do we use this language? What if we did things differently?

In the customer world, we use real language: 'I want peace of mind', 'I think that my peace of mind is worth this much' or 'I'd like to sort out that stuff on a Sunday evening'. But we also see a bigger world. One person's car is status symbol, for another it's part of a family holiday. One person's phone is a social facilitator, for another it's a business tool. One person's loan is a debt repayment, for another it's the enabler of their dreams.

It's not so much the product but what customers do with it that matters.

You could think of this simply as the '-ing' ... BMW doesn't sell cars, it sells driving experiences; IKEA doesn't sell furniture, it sells living solutions.

Whatever you do as a business, the customer typically has a broader agenda. Addressing their issues and desires is much more engaging. Using their language is much more human. Seeking to solve their problems or help them to achieve their ambitions also enables you to potentially sell much broader solutions from your own range, and other brands, as well as become a longer-term partner in doing it.

Don't delegate to the customer; as a CEO or director, you should get out there too.

Take your CEO, your finance director, the non-executive team, shopping, drinking, or whatever your customers do. Take them to extreme competitors or analogous worlds. Help them to listen and think without prejudice, to see things differently. Get them to each write down their personal insights and then share them. You will be amazed what incidents soon become legends in the boardroom and how small insights will start to be discussed more frequently than financial results.

Engaging senior executives in a 'deep dive' into the real world of customers is an incredibly simple yet powerful way of sparking new ideas, support for new initiatives and commitment to their delivery. These people usually live incredibly busy, isolated and pampered lives. Immersing them in the customer world in a structured, facilitated way should be the starting point to any significant decision.

Executives like to sit back and wait for proposals to be presented by their hard-working people. However, an ivory tower is the worst place to make decisions. At P&G, every manager, including A.G. Lafley, the transforming CEO, spends time each week in shops and people's homes – not shaking hands and being corporate, but learning what it's like to do a weekly shop in 30 minutes with a crying baby, or the passion with which Chinese people view a clean and tidy kitchen.

Indeed, one multinational oil company argues that when it comes to major investment decisions, intuitive choices of senior managers are far better than those based on arbitrary projections of future cash flows. The challenge is to ensure that the intuition of these decision-makers is based on the real world around them.

'Reframing' the context for doing business is perhaps the most powerful way of transforming a company's culture, driving radical innovation and finding sustained competitive advantage. By reframing the context you redefine your boundaries, challenge every convention and can engage customers in far more relevant, compelling and profitable ways.

Insight 20: FC BARCELONA
Join the passion of the Catalans

'Mas que un club' is its motto, Spanish for 'more than a club'.

Futbol Club Barcelona, or Barça as it is more fondly known, was founded in 1899 by Hans Gamper. Today it is one of the world's wealthiest football clubs and, unusually in an age of billionaire owners, it is entirely owned by its supporters – or at least 130,000 of them. It is also a club of many sports, a leading player in at least 10 disciplines from swimming to basketball.

However, Barça is more than even a sports club. For millions of people all around the world, it is a symbol of their identity, in terms of society, politics and culture. Throughout the most difficult of times, Barça was the standard that represented Catalonia and the Catalan people's desire for freedom, recognition and success. Indeed the club's flag was used as an expression of local pride when the Catalan flag was banned by Franco.

This is much more than a football club.

Barça's home is the magnificent Camp Nou, Europe's largest football stadium, built in 1957 and extended in 1982 so that it can now seat 100,000 spectators, although with an average of 73,400 attendees. However the club has a much wider following – with an estimated 13 million fans, of which 60% are international, 61% are over 30 and 70% are male.

Each week, the *blau-grana* walk out with expectations on their shoulders more fitting for gladiators than footballers. Superstar Brazilian striker (and former world player of the year), Ronaldinho leads a collection of global stars who are attracted to the unique atmosphere of the club.

Winning is everything at Camp Nou. To fail to win the Spanish La Liga is one thing; to come in behind Real Madrid is a complete disaster. In 2006 the Catalans were not only champions of Spain, but of Europe too. In 2007, they finished equal on points to their great rivals, but lost out because of an inferior head-to-head record during the season.

However Barça is a club with a difference.

This is where the fans, and particular the club's paid-up members become so important. As a member they have a vote, and together they run the club. The club's president is decided by membership votes, with elections typically based on manifestos to bring certain managers and players to the club, to play more attacking football, to win the UEFA Champions' League.

Players, too, must be acquired out of the funding from members, or other commercial revenue generated by the club. This is in sharp contrast to the sugar-daddies of most other top clubs, who willingly plunge their clubs into significant debt in order to buy the best players, thereby creating a difficult economic model for a club like Barça, which knows it must break even, to compete against.

In recent years, the soccer world has changed enormously. Whilst the loyalty of fans can be leveraged through branded merchanidise and licensing deals – everything from the sale of club strips, to hospitality facilities, international tours and mobile phones – the cost of competing has grown astronomically as players' fees and wages have rocketed.

Football	1980's	1990's	2000's
What matters	Match results Local support TV income Sponsorship	Match results National support Broadcast rights Licensing partners Brand management	Match results Global support
Business model	Matchday Circus event	Match related Media business eg MTV	Media business Entertainment Brand experience eg Disneyworld
Performance	Low revenues Low costs No profit	Rising revenues Rising costs Volatile profits	High revenues High costs Consistent profits

CHANGING BUSINESS OF FOOTBALL

Barça needed money, new ideas and more members.

In 2004 the newly elected president Joan Laporta, a charismatic lawyer, set about transforming the club. Whilst splashing out €100 million on new players, he introduced a new commercial rigour behind the scenes. He put together a new management team, recruited from the likes of Nike and Tiscali, with backgrounds in marketing and digital technologies.

He then launched a new membership drive – the 'Big Challenge' – developing and articulating the benefits and involvement of members in the club. It played on the Catalan pride of its supporters. It focused on the ability of supporters to directly influence the running of the club. And it offered a broad range of benefits, from preferred seating to discounts on partner brands to Barça TV.

The result was an almost 20% increase in members to 135,000. Revenue grew by 23% to €208 million in 2005 and €240 the following season, with record profits of €15 million. Their aspirations, however, are much higher – perhaps not unreasonable in a country where football generates more than €8 billion, around 1.7% of Spain's GDP.

The Catalans are flying high again, on and off the pitch.

With new players and even greater crowds, Barça is heading in the right direction, to be the best as well as the best supported football club in the world. Its huge fan base enables it to negotiate huge broadcasting deals, including a €54 million from Televisió de Catalunya. Meanwhile Havas have been asked to coordinate sponsorship and Telefónica Móviles has formed an innovative mobile phone partnership. Nike has licensing rights to the Barça brand worldwide and runs the club shop, La Botiga, sharing all profits equally with the club.

Surprisingly, Barcelona is the only major European club not to have a shirt sponsor, deals which can easily be worth around €80m, the fee AIG paid to feature on the shirts of Manchester United. Sometimes the club's supporter members are not happy to compromise their beloved club for money. Which brand could possibly be worthy of adorning their beloved shirts, they questioned?

Instead they gave the prime advertising space at no charge to Unicef as part of a wider charitable initiative around the world by its players and supporters.

Barça is a club with a difference, a club of the people.

7.3   BEING A CUSTOMER BUSINESS
What it means to be a customer-centred business

Putting customer thinking into practice is far more than research, ideas generation or even a service culture. It can affect every aspect of your business. Tesco and Toyota are two market leading examples of companies that have embraced a 'lean' approach to their businesses. In simple terms this means that they redesigned their business from the outside in: only doing the things that matter to customers; designing processes that work from the customer backwards; doing business on their customer's terms. This results in both greater customer intimacy and greater business efficiency.

'Outside in' rather than 'inside out' thinking starts with opportunities rather than capabilities – finding the best markets, then developing the capabilities to win in them; finding the best customers, then bringing together the right products and solutions that enable them to achieve their goals. It applies to every aspect of your business – doing what, when, where and how customers want, not when, where or how you necessarily do.

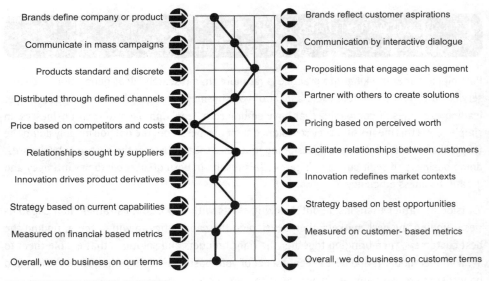

Brands define company or product		Brands reflect customer aspirations
Communicate in mass campaigns		Communication by interactive dialogue
Products standard and discrete		Propositions that engage each segment
Distributed through defined channels		Partner with others to create solutions
Price based on competitors and costs		Pricing based on perceived worth
Relationships sought by suppliers		Facilitate relationships between customers
Innovation drives product derivatives		Innovation redefines market contexts
Strategy based on current capabilities		Strategy based on best opportunities
Measured on financial based metrics		Measured on customer- based metrics
Overall, we do business on our terms		Overall, we do business on customer terms

THE CUSTOMER POWER PROFILER

Ask yourself these questions:

- Does your brand define your target customers and their ambitions – or arrogantly talk about your business or product and what it does?

- Is your research still centred on average statistics or existing prejudices – or does it listen to and explore more deeply the real needs and wants of individuals?

- Do you still subject all customers to blanket communication campaigns – trying to sell what you want, when and how you choose, not what they want on their terms?

- Are your distribution channels chosen for your convenience and efficiency, rather than who and where your consumers want?

- Is your pricing model playing at the margins of your direct competitors, rather than based on the perceived value relative to your customers' view of their alternatives?

- Do you still try to persuade customers to have 'relationships' with your company, when they'd thank you much more for connecting them with other people like them?

- Are you brave enough to take a lead in your market, take risks and set new rules, to shape your own destiny, or are you happy to live by that of others?

Profile yourself and see how customer-centric your business is. Whilst it is obviously important to find a balance, the balance should start from the outside not the inside. The challenges of designing and implementing a customer-centric business are explored more deeply in *Customer Genius* by Peter Fisk (published by Capstone in 2008).

Insight 21: BANG & OLUFSEN
Perfect sound for discerning customers

Some 350 km north-west of Copenhagen you arrive in the small town of Struer, the world's capital of designer hi-fi, and in a nearby glass and concrete building is the headquarters of Bang & Olufsen. Here they create the world's most stylish music systems and televisions – perfect lines, darkened glass and brushed stainless steel is everywhere.

Even the smallest, lowest priced item exhibits beautiful styling and intelligent design. A tiny spherical key ring with which you can open your door, switch on the lights to your home, turn on your TV, DVD player and music. It will even sort through music and computer files, the magic key to an integrated home information and entertainment system. (There is a spare if you ever lose it.)

New York's Museum of Modern Art describes B&O as creating 'the largest and most consistent design portfolio amongst the world's industrial companies'.

B&O's customers are obsessive. Whilst relatively small in number they are loyal, passionate and addicted to the brand. They will build their own B&O collection over decades, gradually adding more pieces to their bespoke systems.

In the US, for example, around 1000 customers account for 80% of revenue. However, they spend around $250,000 each on their B&O set-ups. Another 10,000 customers might have bought one or two items – perhaps aspirational customers just starting their collections. In total, 300,000 customers are tracked by database and account for at least 30% of revenue.

In 1952 B&O was created for perfection by audio engineers Peter Bang and Svend Olufsen, seeking to create a better quality radio than any other. They set the exceptionally high standards and design principles and developed the unique production techniques that now create the most advanced home audio and cinema systems around.

The enigmatic pursuit of truly distinctive solutions and eye-catching design runs in the blood of the Scandinavian business. However design has always been the starting point – its designers and anthropologists spend hours in people's homes observing how they live, and how they could make it better. The technology then follows.

In the Struer museum you will find designs from thirty or forty years ago that still look futuristic.

However B&O has not always succeeded in turning its design leadership into commercial success. In recent years, the rise of Asian electronics manufacturers changed the market dynamics, requiring European firms to rely on their quality to compete. Dutch electronic company Philips recognized this and acquired a 25% stake in B&O in 1993, allowing it to invest in specialist boutiques, more personalized service and customer lifetime support.

As the mass market turned East, B&O became more and more niche.

In 2001, Torben Ballegaard Sørensen joined from Lego as new CEO. He set out on a transforming agenda to reinterpret the iconic brand for a new century and once again help it to become a home entertainment powerhouse, albeit a very specialist one.

He focused B&O on these rare, discerning and sophisticated customers. Who they are, what they really want from the designer brand and what role it plays in their lives. He found that people typically discover the brand in their thirties. Yes, they want quality sound and vision, but each piece is also like a prestigious artefact of uncompromising quality and aesthetics; one that gives them pride and symbolizes achievement.

Customers didn't compare B&O to Sony, Samsung or Panasonic. They compared the brand to high-end luxury furniture, to designer boutique hotels. They said, 'Shall I buy a new piece of B&O equipment or a new Mercedes SLK?'

Each product has to make sense on its own, as that might be all the customer will ever be able to afford, or be easily integrated with other pieces to create home solutions. These solutions were not only hardware. In a world of iPod and iTunes, integrated and intelligent software and appliances are also important, helping customers to source and store their music more effectively as well as listen to it and share it.

Customers want a relationship, not a transaction; and so dealers have become 'service portals', physically and virtually supporting users to get the most out of their personal systems. Increasingly, people are mobile – wanting to access their favourite music and movies anywhere in the world, in the car, in a hotel, at their friends' homes.

B&O realized that it must do more than design objects of desire: they had to become part of people's lives.

Sorensen has transformed the organization's culture – introducing goals that support long-term relationships rather than market share, beliefs that start outside with customers rather than inside with products, processes that embrace digital as well as mechanical engineering, results that that do not depend on retail alone.

B&O Idealab was created to develop new customer visions and embrace scenario planning and virtual design techniques. It has even resulted in some outsourcing of basic manufacturing as the business focuses even more on innovation and design.

In the lab you will discover the latest BeoLab 5 speakers being developed to 'listen' and analyse the sound of the room in order to customize their performance accordingly. Not the cheapest speakers at around $20,000, but certainly delivering one of the best listening experiences.

B&O not only develops the in-car entertainment systems for the likes of BMW and Audi, but also utilizes its precision techniques to develop other car interior parts, cameras for other brands and even medical equipment that benefits from the company's expert processes.

Its top of the range equipment can also be found in the best designer hotels of Stark and Shraeger, adorning the latest properties for sale in Dubai, and onboard the most luxury jets and yachts.

Sorensen's changes are having an impact financially. In 2006, revenue was up 8% and profits up 29%, as he targets making B&O a $1 billion company by 2010.

Engaging customers in more relevant ways

'Don't sell customer goods they are attracted to. Sell them goods that will benefit them'

Konosuke Matsushita

A more intelligent approach to propositions that embraces a better *inside out* orientation

• Brands reflect the big idea of a business in a simple and compelling way.

• Brands reflect a promise to the customer that becomes trusted and memorable.

• Brand identities create a short-hand for customers, driving trial and affinity.

• Propositions to each target segment collectively support the brand.

• Propositions are customer themes that introduce products and services.

• Distinctive benefits and price combine to offer superior 'value to customers'.

• Communication articulates brands and propositions in compelling ways.

A more imaginative approach to propositions that embraces a better *outside in* orientation

• Brands capture the dreams and aspirations of customers.

• Brands capture the distinctive values and personality of a business.

• Brand reputations exist in the customer's heads, influenced not controlled.

• Propositions capture tangible differentiation and relevance.

• Propositions engage customers in a broader dialogue and relationships.

• Broader solutions and greater loyalty drive greater 'value of customers'.

• Experiences deliver brands and propositions in personal ways.

Most purchase decisions are made in 2.6 seconds, according to the latest neurological studies. Indeed Malcolm Gladwell, author of *Blink,* argues that the quicker we make decisions, the better they often are, arguing that more information often confuses rather than enhances our judgements. He calls its thin slicing – how a little information can go a long way.

As you pause in the supermarket aisle, or sign off on purchase orders between meetings, when it comes to the moment of decision, does all that marketing science really work? Yes, most of it has had some impact, but long before that moment of truth. The secret is to ensure that your brand is already lodged firmly in the decision-maker's mind – in their 'ROM', if you like. The challenge is to get it there, ensure that it is sticky enough to stay there, quick to recall and powerful to persuade when the moment comes.

The brand works at a high level, creating an icon, a memory of a particular brand idea for customers. However propositions – or, more formally, 'customer value propositions' – turn the brand idea into something far more tangible, specific and relevant for each target segment of customers. Propositions describe the value to the customer, the combination of distinctive benefits for a price, that will hopefully create net value superior to that offered by competitors.

Propositions are, therefore, about targeting, benefits, differentiation and relevance. Strong and distinctive customer benefits help you to justify a higher price. However, propositions are not products. They are the themes that sit above products, engaging customers in the issues or aspirations that really matter to them, and then introducing a range of products and services that meet those goals. Propositions, therefore, help you sell a broader solution, cross-sell adjacent products, and build more active dialogues and relationships.

Propositions are like a bridge connecting the big conceptual ideas of brands with the real issues and objectives of individual customers. Their theme then acts as a basis for more targeted, relevant and engaging communication, and delivery of customer experiences.

8.1 BRANDS THAT DEFINE YOU
Brands are about customers, not about companies

Brands are about you, not me. Brands are about people, not products. Brands are about customers, not companies.

A great brand is one you want to live your life by, one you trust and hang on to whilst everything around you is changing, one that articulates the type of person you are or want to be, one that enables to you to do what you couldn't otherwise achieve.

Brands were originally developed as labels of ownership. However, today it is what they do for people that matters much more: how they reflect and engage them, how they define their aspirations and enable them to do more. Powerful brands can drive success in competitive and financial markets, and indeed become the organization's most valuable assets.

Yet there are few great brands around. Most brands are still labels, relying too strongly on brand names and logos, and focused too heavily on the companies and products that they help identify. They are articulated through superficial straplines and delivered through generic service. They make promises that the organization struggles to deliver, often failing to even attract attention, and rarely gaining the trust of sceptical customers.

Powerful brands have the ability to cut through the noise and competitiveness of markets, and to engage and retain the best customers in a way that delivers superior financial results in both the short and long term. A powerful brand is one that:

- Defines a compelling purpose, a big idea that stands out from the crowd, that goes beyond the product or industry, and really matters to people.

- Reflects the customer, building an image and reputation in the mind of the customer that has personal relevance, even if it alienates others.

- Engages customers in achieving the big idea together, delivered in a style which has people saying, 'This is my kind of company'.

- Enables customers to do more, reinforcing the benefits and supporting their application, but also enabling them, physically or emotionally, to do even more.

- Anchors customers around something familiar and important, whilst all else in the market, or in their personal world, continues to change.

- Evolves as markets and customers evolve, with the portability to move easily into new markets, and glue to connect diverse activities.

- Attracts the target customers, building preference, driving purchase behaviour and sustaining a price premium.

- Retains the best customers, building their loyalty, introducing new services and encouraging advocacy.

- Drives shareholder value, not only through profits, but also by improving investor confidence, credit ratings and reducing cost of capital.

Brand must reflect and engage people. If brands are about people rather than products, then the big idea around which they are formed is more to do with what it does for people rather than the company.

There are a million models of a 'brand' – however, there are three simple components they all have in common – they are functional, comparative and emotional. By collectively defining what it does for people, differently from anything else, and how it makes them feel, then we articulate 'the essence' of the brand. To be compelling and enduring is typically a far more profound idea than product-, company- or even sector-related benefits. It reflects aspirations rather than just needs, it provokes rather than just informs.

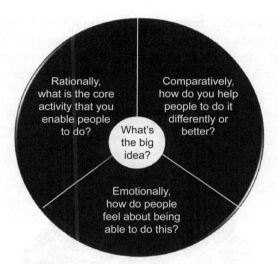

BRANDS ARE IDEAS THAT PEOPLE LIVE BY

Howard Shultz set up Starbucks out of frustration at the coffee quality in his native Seattle; however, the brand he created is much more than coffee. Shultz explains that he 'identified "the third place", which I really believe sets us apart ... not work or home, it's the place our customers come for refuge.' This drives the product range, the interior design, the service philosophy, the communications: the tall skinny latte is good, but the known routine and comfortable environment mean more.

Similarly, other brands give their organizations a core, engaging purpose, which connects all audiences emotionally in 'why we do business'. Brands stir emotions and energize people internally and externally to reach for the higher-order benefits that they are working towards. For Nike, it is 'to do your best'; for Coke, 'to refresh'; for Microsoft, it's 'to realize your potential'.

Brands enable people to do what they couldn't otherwise do. They should do more than simply endorse functional products, either by helping them to do something physically, or by building confidence and belief in their minds. Sony, for example, is all about helping people 'go create', encouraging their innovation and inspiring their action, helping them to do what they couldn't previously achieve.

BRANDS THAT DO MORE FOR PEOPLE

Brands can typically help people to do more in four different ways, to:

* *'Do'* what they seek to achieve better, through improved functionality or support.

* *'Be'* how they want to be perceived, through a strong identity that gives recognition and is admired by others.

* *'Belong'* to a community that they seek to be part of, through improved connections, real or perceived.

- '**Become**' somebody more than they are, adding personal esteem or the capabilities and confidence to do what they couldn't otherwise achieve.

Once a brand creates such a strong attachment with people, one that they find emotionally or practically essential to their lives, then the brand becomes an 'anchor' which becomes trusted and desired. Kevin Roberts, CEO of Saatchi and Saatchi, calls such brands *Lovemarks* and has created a fascinating collection at www.lovemarks.com of the brands that people love most, and why.

Insight 22: CHUPA CHUPS
Spanish lollipops that you can't stop sucking

'One of my first memories is of Chupa Chups. There would always be a half-globe of Chupa Chups sitting on the counter of every bakers shop. My family did not have much money so I rarely got treats but I would love looking at all the different flavors and color wrappings that were available. When I actually got one to eat by myself, it would take me hours to finish, the best, most enduring taste ever.'

The childhood memories of Chupa Chups are familiar to many of us – as recalled by this teenager when asked to describe her favourite brand on the *Lovemarks* website. The simple pleasure of the tastiest lollipops you have ever experienced – not great for your teeth, as your parents often reminded you – but worth an occasional, special indulgence.

Chupa Chups have been sweetening the lives of millions since 1958, although the origins of the world's best-loved lollipop are found a century earlier. In the 1850s, Josep Bernat established a small sweet shop in rambling streets of Barcelona and soon started making his own lollipops from a small factory at the back of his store. The business was sadly destroyed during the Spanish Civil War, but the art of lollipop was passed down through his family. In 1950, his grandson, Enric, decided it was time to revive the family business.

He opened his own small confectionery factory called Productos Bernat. Business was soon booming. A few years later, a family friend asked him to take control of Granja Asturias, a flagging manufacturer of over 200 products derived from apples. On accepting the challenge, the enterprising Enric agreed that if he was able to pull the company out of its difficulties, he would be entitled to 50% of its income and shares. By 1958, Enric was the owner of the profitable business.

Enric Bernat's insight was that the vast majority of the 200 products were not designed for their customers. His research showed that 67% of confectionary was bought by children, yet the vast majority was made for adults – the language (not even kids of the 1950s talked like that!), the taste, the shape, the packaging – it just wasn't geared towards sweets bought with pocket money, for eating in the streets.

His idea was simple: small, spherical and a stick.

His hand-rolled lollipops sold faster than he could make them. You suck and swirl. The flavour was intense, enduring and amazing. The stick, initially made of wood but soon of plastic, was practical and distinctive. Nobody else sold sweets like this. He named his lollipops 'Chups' but because of a catchy ad campaign enticing people to lick one – 'Chupa', Spanish for lick, was soon added – and the company became Chupa Chups SA in 1964.

Today, in Spain, all lollipops are called 'chupachús', reflecting the popularity of the brand.

The real success of Chupa Chups, however, came through its innovative distribution and retail displays. They get to places which their competitors would never think of – bakeries, bookshops, music stores, even banks – as well the more conventional retailers. They sit prominently on the counter next to the cashier, not in a jar, or alongside all their competitors.

Their eye catching displays, typically each lollipop slotted into a hemi-spherical stand, cannot be missed. They get there because of their passionate people – a huge, friendly and fun sales team that drive around in Chupa Chups cars, persuading individual retailers to take them. They even promise to replace free of charge any lollipops that disappear into wandering hands.

The business has grown over the years, but not at the expense of making the perfect lollipop. Their range has slowly diversified – with Smint, the innovative mint, the most significant addition. Still manufactured near Barcelona in Spain, the spirit of Bernat lives on – delighting the world's children and the occasional adult too.

One final touch of genius is the Chupa Chups daisy logo, designed by Salvador Dali.

8.2 PROPOSITIONS THAT ENGAGE YOU
Being more relevant and valuable to each customer

So how do you win customers in 2.6 seconds – the average time it takes a consumer or business decision-maker to make their purchase decisions?

- Brands that are memorable and engaging.

- Propositions that articulate the value to the customer.

- Context that is about their world, their issues and their ambitions.

- Benefits that are relevant and distinctive.

- Pricing that is fair for the benefits attainable.

- Narratives that start with issues and describe solutions.

- Language that is simple and practical.

- Memes that are compelling and memorable.

- Dialogues that sense and respond at the right moment.

- Relationships that ensure you are in the picture when it matters.

American Express has a corporate brand which is captured by the idea of helping their customers to 'do more'. They then have a portfolio of value propositions that more specifically define the distinctive benefits it offers to each target audience. These value propositions become the guiding force of the business and the way in which the inside aligns with the outside.

One brand can be delivered through many value propositions, each delivering it in more relevant ways. And many products can be delivered by one value proposition, each contributing to the bigger theme.

Propositions focus on what matters to customers. They are the high-level, benefit-driven themes or promises – delivered by the products and services, functions and processes – that enable the benefits to be realized. They create a 'pull' dynamic by which customer engage in what is relevant to them, rather than the typical 'push' of products.

So what sticks in customers' minds?

Rarely is it the tech specs and geek speak that lazy marketers rely upon – the processing power of the latest computer, the active ingredients inside your toothpaste, the meaningless serial numbers which define the latest mobile phone. Even a long list of benefits just creates a haze of irrelevance.

People remember what matters to them: logical arguments that explain how the offer solves their specific problems, articulates the most important benefits to them, in the language that they use, and in a way that makes sense, matters, and is memorable.

Customers perceive the value of a solution based on the relevance and applicability of the solution to them – the benefits that it creates, articulated in monetary gains or cost-saving, time efficiency or what they wouldn't be able to do otherwise.

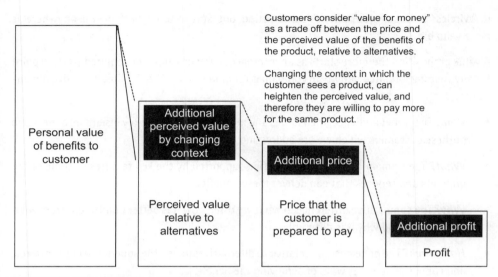

CUSTOMERS PAY MORE FOR A CONTEXT WITH MORE PERCEIVED VALUE

Consider an Apple PowerBook, the sleek and powerful laptop targeting graphic designers, agency creatives and other cool types. The absolute benefits to the customer include personal mobility, productivity and image. Comparative benefits then reflect how these are better than other brands. 'Value for money' is then judged on the comparative benefits relative to the price.

Slightly better perception of comparative benefits – expressed through a value proposition – therefore enables you to increase price, maintain the same value for money and directly improve profitability.

Whilst it might sound obvious, the key is to focus on the benefits – not the features. Benefits create value for customers; features don't. Products describe features, propositions describe benefits. So '24-hour home maintenance' is a feature; 'Peace of mind at home' is a benefit of it. 'Wireless emails on your phone' is interesting, but 'stay in touch with clients anywhere' is more valuable.

A value proposition therefore starts as an internal document – now the required starting point for any customer-related activity in companies ranging from P&G to Philips. It has five dimensions:

- *Who?* The target audience, their issues and motivations, and the key insight into the world of these customers which we are addressing.

- *What?* The primary benefits that we offer, supported by the key features of some of the products and services that can deliver these benefits.

- *Why?* The competitive difference in what we offer, how it is better or different from what others offer, and why it is different.

- *How much?* The price position relative to alternatives, given the superior benefits offered, and compared to other ways of achieving the benefits.

- *What not?* The trade-offs which the customer makes in choosing you compared to someone else, i.e. the differentiators of your competitors (although you wouldn't communicate this!).

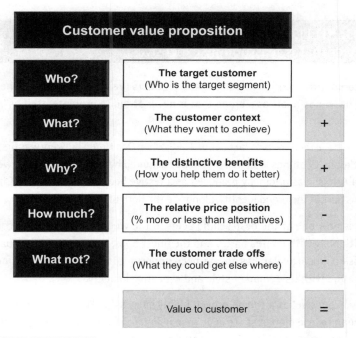

CUSTOMER VALUE PROPOSITION

Collectively, these dimensions articulate the superior value that we offer customers (usually not expressed numerically, although it could be).

The proposition is then often given a theme that brings the ideas together, internally at first, although the theme will then likely evolve into the basis of communication activity, so will need some additional thought to ensure that they are catchy and memorable.

Insight 23: STELLA ARTOIS
Belgian beer that is reassuringly expensive

In a highly competitive world where so many products are marketed on the cheapest price, Stella Artois has stood apart as a brand that is never afraid to promote itself as 'reassuringly expensive'.

Few brands can trace their roots as far back as 1366, when Den Horen brewery was first established in Leuven, Belgium. Centuries later in 1717, it was acquired by its then master brewer, Sebastian Artois. 'Stella Artois' was originally produced as a festive beer, named after the Christmas star which remains part of the brand identity, alongside the horn of the original brewery.

Stella Artois is now one of the best-selling beers in the world, sold in over 80 countries. It is brewed traditionally with malted barley and the finest hops, and famed for its quality and flavour. Advertising, in particular, has always been important to the brand – breaking the mould of beer marketing with its upmarket style and evocative imagery.

'Reassuringly expensive' as a theme proved highly successful. However, in the early nineties the brand began to lose market share in an increasingly crowded premium market. With more quality choices, a premium price alone seemed a risky differentiator to rely upon.

However, Stella Artois refused to abandon its position, instead opting to support it with an even stronger investment in product quality. Still using the line, but with more justification, Stella Artois has fought back from decline and is now re-established as the UK's biggest premium lager brand.

Design is a primary communication tool for this approach. Packaging initiatives such as embossing the can and re-designing the crate box in the style of champagne reinforce the brand's quality and prestige. A Stella Artois pint glass was introduced in 2001 and, within 12 months of launch, 66% of UK households possessed at least one glass.

Driven by a strong rise in draught sales, distribution growth has remained strong, with Stella Artois now being the most widely circulated lager in the on-trade. Marketing communications has focused on TV advertising, sponsorship, and price promotion in the off-trade markets, whilst using point of sale presence and new drinks delivery technologies to boost sales in the on-trade markets.

Between 1996 and 2003, Stella Artois has seen it volumes grow by over 200% in the UK compared with category growth of around 60%. This rise has made it the third-biggest lager brand and the biggest premium lager brand, selling 3495 million barrels in 2003. Stella Artois now holds an 8.9% share of the UK beer market, more than triple its 1996 share of 2.2%.

Committed to innovation, Stella Artois didn't rest on its laurels. In 2004 it launched Demi Artois, a half-sized bottle, and the following year the chalice glass, to drink the beer as it is traditionally drunk in Belgium. Bar staff were given extra training in traditional pouring techniques to create the authentic experience on tap.

2005 also saw Stella Artois linked to even more events, seeking to add more relevance between the brand and its modern day, non-Belgian audience. Its sponsorship of the Stella Artois Tennis Championships creates a clean-cut, exclusive image, whilst the Stella Artois Screen film festival connects it with cutting edge creativity and old favourites.

Advertising has always been important to sustaining the premium imagery. With its cinematic style, tone and subjects, it has create some memorable mime films about its origins and authenticity, and the sacrifices these have required. 2006, for example, saw Jonathan Glazer's depiction of ice-skating priests' frantic chase for an elusive bottle of beer and Frank Budgen's homage to the golden age of French surrealist film-making.

The focus on sacrifices, like the beer drinker of today makes in willingly paying more for some-thing special, connects with the audience. As the ad reminds its Anglo-Saxon audience, 'Ceci n'est pas un pint' – it's not just a pint.

8.3   EXPERIENCES THAT DO MORE FOR YOU
Connecting with customers in more compelling ways

Imagine that you are about to go into a sales presentation – the perfect opportunity to get your new proposition across, to engage your audience in a compelling and relevant way.

But it all tends to come out the wrong way.

We open our mouths and start talking about our world. Who we are, what we do, the products we offer, how we think they are better. We immediately go back into business world and forget customer world – their issues and ambitions, the benefits to them and how they are distinctive, in their language.

People are much more engaged when you talk about them. 'I know that your strategic priorities for this year are ...', then get them excited about how they can achieve their targets, sooner and better, and then work backwards to describe how you can help make this happen.

A 'customer script' is used to convey the proposition to the customer in a relevant and compelling way. However, it doesn't jump into 'this is us, and this is what we do'. It starts, not surprisingly, with the customer, and takes them through a logical path that will hopefully engage and inspire them to take the actions you seek. The customer script is simply structured, starting with:

- **Context** – about you, the opportunities and challenges you face.

- **Complexity** – the problem, why your current solution is not insufficient.

- **Challenge** – the question, how can you address the context better?
- **Core message** – the solution, the big idea I'd like to propose to you.

The core message would typically incorporate the proposition that you want to deliver, the solution which you believe is right for them and the big idea that you want to stick in your audience's mind.

The narrative might then go on to explain 'why' the conclusion is appropriate, or 'how' it can be achieved in a sub-structure of messages, often with specific evidence to support the case, or a more detailed description as to how it will be achieved.

The structure can be applied to anything from a script for a TV commercial, to the copy for a brochure, to the slides to support a sales pitch. And whilst it might run to many pages, it should also be possible to capture the essential narrative on one page.

At the same time, we want to find a narrative that is emotionally engaging and memorable.

Nike's Phil Knight was explained his passion for the endorsement of sporting icons by explaining:

> 'You can't explain much in 60 seconds, but when you show Michael Jordan, you don't have to. It's that simple.'

Richard Dawkins first coined the phrase 'meme' in his book *The Selfish Gene* to describe 'a unit of cultural evolution analogous to the gene', arguing that replication and mutation happens within our culture – in the language we use, the symbols we use, the behaviours we adopt – in a similar way to way to genetic evolution. He considers memes as the units of information that reside in the brain, and we see memetic structures in everything from catchy pop songs to new fashion designs.

Memes help turn brands and propositions into stories, symbols and slogans. They catch people's attention, they stick in their minds, quickly spread virally, by observation or experience, by word of mouth, email or text. In order to reach out to target audiences, to leverage the power of virtual or physical networks, and to be there in people's minds at the point of purchase, value propositions and communications needs to embrace memetics.

Memes stick in your mind and can be quickly accessed. They are constructs of memory that are more memorable, recognizable and contagious. Slogans such as Nike's 'Just do it' or colours such as the FT's pink paper; music such as Intel's five note jingle, or the 'Nokia tune', played by every Nokia phone; designs like Apple's translucent white computers, or illustrated by the use of numbers in Peugeot's trademarked central '0'; smell like Singapore Airlines, who bottle it; or typography such as the script of Coca-Cola. They all reflect the application of memes.

A meme should be catchy, memorable, easy to say and recall. It should imply a key benefit, something to describe it by. It should be different, original and easy to distinguish with emotional impact, imparting positive feelings. It might have shape, perhaps in terms of rhythm or rhyme. Most of all, memes should be simple, short and easy to understand, and therefore able to spread easily.

Propositions are then delivered through products and services that together form a customer experience. Harley-Davidson's CEO eloquently describes the experience by which he seeks to bring his brand and propositions to life:

> 'It's one thing to have people buy your products, it's another for them to tattoo your name on their bodies ... What we sell is the ability for a 43 year old accountant to dress in black leather, ride through small towns and have people be afraid of him.'

The brand idea is delivered through every possible medium that the organisation can utilize – from names and logos to leaders and buildings, products and services to advertising and brochures, colours and packaging to uniforms and interiors, culture and behaviours to training and rewards.

Every aspect of the corporate or product 'experience' can deliver the brand in tangible and intangible ways. As Jan Carlson, former CEO of airline SAS said, 'every person, every promise and every action is a moment of truth'. By design or default, every brand delivers an experience, although in the case of consumer goods, too often this is delegated to the retailer without too much thought or influence.

Experiences can take many forms, some where you are part of the experience yourself, and others where you can just observe:

- *Entertaining* experiences, from sporting events to rock concerts, far more dramatic than when edited and viewed remotely.

- *Educational* experiences, from historic monuments brought to life through re-enactments to training courses based on role-play and interaction.

- *Guiding* experiences, from art galleries that embrace all the senses, to health spas that stimulate and pamper them.

- *Coaching* experiences, from adventure sports to video games, that takes participants into extreme or imaginary worlds.

Any brand can embrace any of these types of experiences and engage customer like never before to bring the brand to life, uniquely, at that moment, for that individual.

Insight 24: TATE MODERN
London's art gallery designed to fit your mood

Solid and significant, modern or mundane, the Tate Modern sits on the South Bank of London's River Thames. Britain's best international collection of modern insight sits inside an old power station, built in 1947 and closed in 1981.

Approaching the modern art gallery from St Paul's Cathedral, crossing the river's newest bridge designed by Norman Foster, the power station is an imposing sight. It reopened in 2000, part of London's millennium celebrations, as an inspirational space for the young and old, art lovers and sightseeing tourists, and the simply curious.

In its short life, Tate Modern has become the most popular art gallery in the world. One visitor described what it meant to her:

'The South Bank is a wonderful arena for London's creativity. For many years I have walked along the Thames, from Dali Universe, to The Royal Festival Hall, The Hayward Gallery, the book market under the bridge near the Film Centre, past the OXO Tower and its plentiful creative outlets, up to the Tate and the Design Museum. The Tate Modern is a wonderful brand and catalyst for our future creativity.'

The works include Dali and Picasso, Matisse, Rothko and Warhol. Plus some even more contemporary artists – such as Gilbert & George, Viola, and Bourgeois. Unconventionally, the permanent collections, located on the upper floors, are not displayed in chronological order, but are rather arranged in themes. This was partly because of significant gaps in the collection, but also because it made more sense to the casual visitor.

The Turbine Hall is the most significant part of the building, having housed the electricity generators of the old power station. The enormous space is used for special exhibitions and events. This is where the true role of Tate Modern becomes apparent. Yes, there are visiting exhibitions by famous and emerging artists, but equally there is music and dance, a giant 100m helter-skelter slide, and weekend carnivals of fun and entertainment for all the family.

Tate Modern is not sitting back, a temple for the sophisticated and enthusiasts. It is going out and finding people – people who dislike the pretence of some galleries, and even larger audiences who would never have been seen dead in an art gallery. This is a place for the people –

the gallery itself calls it 'a big living room, where all the art is yours' – whatever their age and colour, background and interests, motivations and ambitions.

'Your Collection' is about giving art back to the people.

These collections are not designed around time or type. They are designed around real people, personal journeys that reflect you mood or enthusiasm. It is about redesigning an art gallery around people rather than art.

A distinctive advertising campaign reaches out to all types of people – on the tube, sitting in cafés, reading gossip magazines – with messages based on around 30 different moods including:

- The 'I'm Hungover' Collection

- The 'Rainy Day' Collection

- The 'I Like Yellow' Collection

- The 'First Date' Collection

- The 'I've Just Split Up' Collection

- The 'Happily Depressed' Collection

- The 'I'm an Animal Freak' Collection

- The 'Kids Only' Collection.

Based on motivational segmentation analysis of visitors and, more particularly, non-visitors, it selects small journeys through the huge gallery depending on who you are, and what you really want. It recognizes that some people just don't have the time, patience or energy for hundreds of works of art. Whilst others just want to impress somebody and others want to escape.

There's even a shortcut direct to the coffee and gift shops if art isn't really your thing.

Tate Modern is succeeding in bringing diverse new audiences to the world of art, on their terms. This matters because it is part of its remit, but also because it is its future, artistically and commercially. It recognizes that we are all different as people.

For the best hangover cure, live hip-hop, or chocolate muffins Tate Modern is the new place to be.

The power of networks and customer communities

'Like a force of nature, the digital age cannot be denied – it has four very powerful qualities that will result in its ultimate triumph: decentralising, globalising, harmonising and empowering'

Nicholas Negroponte

A more **intelligent** approach to **networks** that embraces a better *inside out* orientation	A more **imaginative** approach to **networks** that embraces a better *outside in* orientation
• Transactional business models are typically linear, one to one.	• Networked business models are more collective, many to one.
• Small, niche brands can be more effective than large, mainstream ones.	• Digital media complements traditional media, to create richer experiences.
• Digital media enable social networks that are user-centric and controlled.	• New business models can profit from facilitating user-generated content.
• User-generated content is shared between users and builds quickly.	• Community relationships are built between people in networks.
• Communication is more focused, relevant, collaborative and viral.	• Distribution is achieved through affinity and complementary partners.
• Advertising is more effective through carefully targeted media.	• Brands must be relevant and authentic built on stories and transparency.
• Customer loyalty is built on trust and affinity with the brand.	• The value of a customer network, or community, lies in its connections.

Networked markets are unlimited in reach, richness and relationship.

They spread like wildfire. Their content and connections grow exponentially. They are unlimited by speed or boundary, they are often free to use, and they create and sustain themselves.

No wonder that networks are described as the foundation of a new business age and the platform from which to drive fast, sustained growth.

We used to think of markets as ambient domains, patiently waiting to be served. We defined them by geography, category or socio-economic group. We established our space in the market, then hoped to attract as many people as possible to come to us. Our competitors similarly defined their areas and we were able to measure our relative success in terms of comparable market shares.

The best markets today are networks. Networks are organized and intelligent. They move easily across physical boundaries, and because they typically have collective reasons for being together, they also have collective needs and motivations, preferences and loyalties.

Networks come in all shapes and sizes – physical and virtual, structured and self-developing.

Networks can take the form of roads and flight paths, retail chains and radio stations, online communities and membership associations, fans of a certain football team or employees of a particular company, parents of the local school and people with a similar illness, or customers of the same brand.

Digital technologies create new pathways to link like-minded people once separated by geography, social or economic status, ethnicity or religion. These people do so with a deep passion for what they do. Their interest or activity binds them together, and drives their priorities. Their attitudes and behaviours, likes and dislikes are formed from each other, and by their collective role models. They talk and sometimes even act together.

9.1 THE POWER OF NETWORKS
Making more of the connections between people

It is said that everyone on the planet is separated by six other people. This is the power of networks.

Robert Metcalfe who founded 3Com proposed a 'law' during the frantic, excited times of the dotcom boom. Initially overlooked by the rush for domain names, 'eyeballs' and computing power, 'Metcalfe's Law' states that:

'The value of a network is proportional to the square of the nodes.'

The value of a network lies not in its size – how many people belong to it – but in the connections between these people. And the number of connections clearly grows much faster than the number of nodes – if one extra person joins a group of 7 people, then that creates not one but seven more connections, one with each person, and the value increases in the ratio of 49 to 64.

In the search for dotcom fortunes, websites were obsessed with the 'eyeballs' (the number of people to see a webpage or site), and gave little thought to connecting the people who came to their online music stores or gardening sites. However, the real opportunity lay in connecting the 'eyeballs' with each other, or rather, the interests and passions that these people share. That would add far more value than an online shop.

If the gardening website could tap into the world of rose lovers or flat lawn fanatics, then it could be special for them. If it could enable them to share their passions, they would be logging on every day. If the music site could identify a niche genre of music where passions were intense and loyalty to artists ran deeply, then they could attract the whole group. And if this group already had some form of network they could tap into, it would make it a whole lot easier and quicker.

233

Chris Anderson describes the reality of network power in his book *The Long Tail* where he asks what happens when there is almost unlimited choice, when everything becomes available to everyone, and when the combined value of the millions of items that only sell in small quantities equals or even exceeds the value of a handful of bestsellers. He argues:

> 'The future of business does not lie in hits – the high volume end of a traditional demand curve – but in what used to be regarded as misses – the endlessly long tail of that same curve ... Wherever you look, modest sellers, niche products and quirky titles are becoming an immensely powerful cumulative force.'

Look at the music charts – no longer governed by the best-selling albums within the confines of a music store, but driven more by the individual and eclectic choices of online downloads. Elvis Presley and The Beatles have both returned to the charts, not because they have a new release, but because there are enough people somewhere in the world who still want their music.

The story is the same in every sector – from books and clothing to cars and insurance. The mainstream, based on volume production that meets the average needs of customers, no longer drives success. Success lies in the margins, the niches, the eccentrics, and old favourites – as long as it's available, and people can find them. Networks, particularly digital networks, make this possible.

Insight 25: NET A PORTER
The new best friend for fashionable females

> 'Net a Porter gives you front row seats at the shows without the hassle ... If you can't contemplate a season without a pair of Jimmy Choo flip flops or a Chloe envelope bag, you'll feel very at home here.'

The Good Web Guide likes Net a Porter, as do an increasing number of trend-setting celebrities, high-flying female managers and clothes-conscious mums too.

Los Angeles born, raised in Paris, the former fashion stylist Natalie Massenet has created one of the best examples of a networked company, Net a Porter. An online luxury fashion retailer is insufficient to describe the business. It is as much a magazine, a community, an advisor, a best friend.

The online company boasts the best designers and latest fashions, combined with sharp editorial and deep insight into the latest fashion trends, what to buy and what not. It is like a personal consultant and shopper at the click of your fingers, or mouse, and delivered to your door in luxurious packaging, within 24 hours.

Fashion is Massenet's world, with a mother who was a Chanel model and a father who was a movie promoter. She originally worked for *Women's Wear Daily* in New York, and then *Tatler* in London, building up a great network of contacts in the business. However, deciding the bitchy, cut-throat world of fashion journalism was not for her, she decided to move on.

Net a Porter was born out of the gap she saw between women reading the glossy magazines and then searching in vain to actually find the desired items.

Launched in 2000, Massenet is proud of what she and some friends have created. Part magazine, part shopping site, she has managed to grow the business without treading on the egocentric toes of the fashion industry and its preference for high couture, glitzy boutiques and personal service.

It would not have been surprising if the likes of Chloe and Gucci would have resented her disruption to their classic retailing model, but instead they have embraced her new model, promoting the business and working closely on promoting their latest collections. In fact it is probably the first online experience for many of these brands, and they are intrigued by its impact.

Click on the site, and it feels much more like a women's fashion magazine – it has authority and gossip, recommendations and edited ranges, videos and interactive graphics, alongside the simplicity of a catalogue. The pages showcase the latest lines with stunning photography, all available to buy, which is often not easy in the niche distributed world of high fashion. Purchases are sent worldwide by express delivery from one of the global distribution centres, arriving in luxurious black packaging.

Net a Porter uniquely fuses content and commerce, advice and community. Commentary and opinion comes in the form of trend forecasters and fashion journalists straight from the likes of *Vogue* and *W*. The editorial team takes the uncertainty out of telling what's hot and what's not – a fashion or a fad, a smart choice or a fashion faux pas. There is also direct comment from real people – customer feedback, observations and suggestions.

The results are encouraging too, with 100,000 active customers, and around one million unique visitors to the site, who browse the latest fashions on average two or three times a month. Whilst the target audience is clearly affluent and female, men obviously have an important role to play too. Net a Porter's 'Santa' service sends an email to cheque-signing gentlemen, letting them know that their significant others have just identified a desired item, and how they can quickly bring a smile to their faces.

With sales of $75 million, the business has been profitable for the last two years. Employees have doubled in number each year, with around 300 people now split between London and New York.

Growing the business has required money. Perhaps helped by her hedge-fund managing husband, she has refinanced the company a number of times until it became profitable. Richemont, the owner of Cartier and Dunhill – as well as Shanghai Tang – owns 28%, as does the Venezuelan firm Baywinds. Alongside a number of private investors, Massenet is now left with 17%.

The real value of Net a Porter, however, lies in its growing and intimate relationship with a niche segment of wealthy females. Messenet, undoubtedly, has plenty more ideas to come on how to satisfy their fashion desires and luxurious aspirations.

9.2 CUSTOMER NETWORKS
Building communities that bring people together

MySpace, YouTube, Flickr, Second Life: often described as second generation websites (or Web 2.0), these sites enable collaboration between users, where content is largely generated by and shared by users. Similarly in the business world, companies like P&G have built networks of partners or business ecosystems, where new ideas and innovations are created in partnership.

They represent online communities that some regard as social networks but which also form the basis of collaborative production. Millions of people worldwide can participate in this economy like never before – selling antiques through eBay, uploading home-made documentaries to Current TV, remixing their favourite music for iTunes, designing new software, editing school homework, inventing new cosmetics, finding cures for diseases or sequencing the human genome.

The value of these networks is in the content that is developed through their connections.

The scale is awesome. Just in 2007, a staggering seven billion user-generated videos were streamed each month; 120,000 new blogs were created every day, adding to more than 70 million worldwide; in the US, 30% of all web users accessed YouTube, iTunes and Wikipedia each month. Meanwhile, Google paid $900 million to provide advertising on MySpace, but also got sued $1 billion by Viacom for alleged copyright infringement on its $1.65 billion acquisition, YouTube.

As broadband penetration soars and connection speeds accelerate, people are drawn to the rich and interactive, personalized and on-demand content of 'social' (or network) media.

The impact is not only digital and youthful. In 1995, there were 225 terrestrial TV shows across the UK which were watched by audiences of more than 15 million. Now there are none. Viewers have migrated to other channels, as their choice has mushroomed from 5 to 500. Similarly, advertising revenue has fallen dramatically as advertisers lost faith with traditional broadcast media and sought out more focused, more interactive ways to engage potential customers.

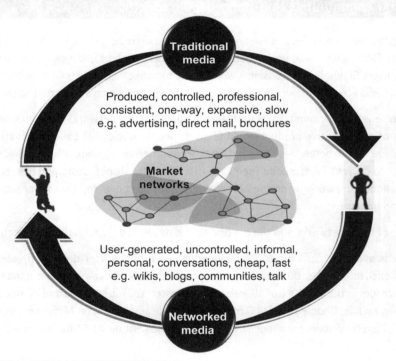

TRADITIONAL MEDIA VS. NETWORKED MEDIA

The difference between traditional and networked media is profound.

- *Traditional media*: access is controlled by location and time; content is produced, edited and distributed for a fee; the experience is professional and standardized, transactional and predictable. The audience is a passive consumer.

- **_Networked media_**: access is open to anyone, anywhere, anytime; content is self-gener-ated and shared freely; the experience is collaborative and multi-format, based on users' interests and relationships. The audience is an active creator.

As a business, a brand, you inevitably want to tap into part of these networks, particularly the ones which have the closest profile to your target customers. You'd like to create your own, based around your brand, but customers just wouldn't want this. Brands don't do enough for these people, certainly compared to what they can do for each other.

- You can't own customer communities, but you can influence and support them.

- You can't push messages at them, but you can listen and learn from them.

- You can't control them, but you can encourage them to want you.

Like traditional physical communities – imagine the way a small town develops – digitally based communities have characteristics that help them interact, organize and structure their worlds as they develop. Whilst a town might develop around common interests and events, groups and locations, rules and communities, an online community develops around participa-tion and common standards, decentralization and modularity of structures, where the user is in control of everything including his or her identity.

Insight 26: CURRENT TV
User-generated pods for the digital generation

'Current TV is about what's going on: stories from the real world, told by you'

Al Gore, former American vice-president turned Oscar-winning environmental campaigner, unveiled Current TV in 2005 as 'television for the internet generation'. He described the new service, which relies on viewer-created content for more than a third of its schedule, as the start of a media revolution that would prove as significant as the invention of the printing press.

Current TV is aimed at the digital-thinking, content-thirsty 18- to 34-year-olds who increasingly turn online, to mobile phones, and 500 or more TV channels, to complement their real life experiences. Instead of a traditional schedule, programming is made up of 'pods' of three to eight minutes duration, designed to be 'snacked on'.

Subjects typically range from a first person report from the war-torn villages of Darfur to insights on the role of graffiti as a respectable, urban art culture – sprinkled with more conventional segments covering, for example, a travel guide in partnership with Lonely Planet.

There is also a three-minute news bulletin every hour based on what users of the Google search engine are looking for, although on the day of UK launch, the most searched topics included a naked TV presenter and a man who has sex with cars.

However it is the user-generated content that should set Current TV apart. At least a third of the schedule will be made up of footage submitted by viewers through the www.current.tv website.

Viewers are encouraged to visit the website to vote on which ideas should be broadcast. If selected, they are provided with editing support to improve their films, and paid for their efforts (from $250 per segment). Even the advertising, with the support of paying sponsors, is viewer-created.

VC^2, or viewer created content, is made by anybody with a camera and a story to tell, and is eventually likely to fill almost the entire Current TV schedule. The content doesn't feel slick like MTV or an unruly mash-up like YouTube. But it does feel independent, interesting and individual.

Editors sitting at the San Francisco headquarters, or studios in London and LA, claim that the only filters imposed are legal and quality, trusting viewers themselves to embrace and follow a code of ethics. Critics claim it conveys a sanitized version of user-generated content as envisaged by baby-boomer politicians and broadcasting executives, while others complain that it too closely adheres to the 'youth TV' conventions established by the likes of MTV.

Current TV evolved from the cable channel *Newsworld International* which Gore and some colleagues bought in 2004 for $70 million. Gore became the chairman, whilst the investors also included CEO Joel Hyatt, and Silicon Valley luminary Bill Joy, the co-founder of Sun Microsystems.

In its first year, the accessible audience grew quickly from its original 17 million households to more than 50 million households, as more networks embraced the new channel. It is already thought to be profitable. The first international launch in 2007 in the UK is part of an expansion plan designed to create, in the words of Gore, 'a global conversation'.

At the launch Gore talked about Current TV reflecting a fast-shifting media landscape in which the power of monolithic broadcasters was being challenged by the ability of individuals armed with cheap cameras and laptops to make their own films. 'It's compelling, it's entertaining and it's relevant. It's made by the people who are out there living their lives,' he said. 'Decades ago television supplanted the written word. It was so interesting and magical that it took us a while to realise it was one way. Our democracies depend on a vibrant, multi-way conversation where new voices can be heard.'

Wired magazine called Current TV 'a media smorgasbord of quick, slick and sometimes very interesting short-form video segments targeted at the iPod generation ... combining the immediacy of video blogging with the voyeurism of reality TV'.

9.3   NETWORK MARKETING
Unlocking network power for business impact

Networks fundamentally transform the way you communicate and distribute products and services, how you attract new customers to you and deliver a brand experience, and the way in which you support and build customer relationships.

Whilst we shouldn't get carried away with the latest fad – you need to create your company's MySpace site, or its virtual version of your business in *Second Life*, or your CEO better hurry up and start writing a blog – we should see networks as a complementary channel, and an important growth platform for the future.

Networks offer new opportunities – to reach new audiences across physical boundaries, to target specific segments accurately, to collaborate with them more personally, to offer more comprehensive solutions with partners, to eliminate many of the frictions of conventional channels and to deliver a richer brand experience for each customer.

- *Ideas* spread virally amongst target audiences, particularly trend-setters and other 'hyper-connectors'. Compelling concepts built around 'memes' (catchy, memorable techniques such as graphics, sound and words) build interest and instant demand. Stories and legends build brands, helping people to identify with personality, beliefs and values.

- *Communication* becomes instant and interactive, customized and collaborative. Rather than push expensive ads or mail millions of brochures in pursuit of a 1% response rate, you can target people more personally, and even wait for them to start talking – rather than trying to sell what and when they don't want.

- *Distribution* channels are no longer stove-pipe structures that push products and services at customers. They create a multichannel, multimedia environment where channels inter-act together and complement each other. Syndication of content, for example through RSS technology, is free and easy.

- *Affinity* partners offer tremendous opportunities to access whole communities of target audiences, attaching the values and loyalties of people to the partner brand to your own brand. Franchising and licensing spread a brand appeal quickly, without the need for infrastructure and capital investment.

- **Solutions** are broader and customized. You work with partners to really solve problems rather than sell products – the one-stop, broad-knowledge, multibranded solution. Customization of content, products and service becomes the norm; personal service and support, whilst modular production and logistics enable rapid assembly and delivery.

- **Experiences** are richer and ongoing. Brands do more for you, enabling interaction with experts and other users, developing new skills, and providing online resources to do the task better. Networks enable experiences to be personal, shared, collaborative, and global – playing the latest, sharing an interest, finding the answer to a problem.

- **Relationships** are collaborative and between users. The old CRM idea of seeking to persuade customers to have a relationship with your company is quickly replaced by the much more attractive option of getting to know somebody else like you. People become loyal to networks not brands. Brands are the new relationship facilitators.

- **Reputation** is driven by customers. In the past, brands were trusted, enduring icons. They still can, but come under far more scrutiny. Transparency enables customers to dig beyond your brochure ware, and any inconsistencies, one bad experience, can spread quickly. Reputations can take years to build, but can be destroyed in seconds.

Networks enable organizations to behave in fundamentally new ways – to develop new business models, to be a small, niche yet global and famous brand – it's about much more than just establishing a website. Of course, you can abuse networks too – the torrent of spam in your inbox is no better than the deluge of junk mail. But thoughtful, collaborative and value-adding marketing will result in customers from Auckland to Alma Mata logging on to track down brand.

Insight 27: NEWS CORPORATION
Ready to reinvent the networked media world

Rupert Murdoch described his spectacular $5 billion takeover of the *Wall Street Journal* as the crowning moment of half a century's deal-making and empire-building.

Not everyone was happy. As one of the newspaper's journalists anonymously blogged, 'I am now an underling in the world's most evil corporate empire', and others were said to have held impromptu wakes. Readers were not happy either, emailing to say they would cancel their subscriptions, whilst another imitated Murdoch's tabloid-style headlines with 'D'oh! Simpsons boss Homers in on Journal'.

Yet the Australian-born American citizen, who built up his business empire from an assortment of media assets (including the *Adelaide News*), which he was left when his father died in 1956, establishing the News Corporation in 1980, is a remarkable visionary. He has brought dispersed content and networks, audiences and titles together from all corners of the earth. He has turned round failing newspapers and TV stations. He has been a pioneer of digital technologies and deregulating markets. He has shaped his world in his vision.

From printed titles like *The Times* and the *New York Post*, cable and satellite broadcasters Fox Networks and Sky Television, film studio Twentieth Century Fox and publisher HarperCollins, to online community MySpace and business information source Dow Jones – Murdoch is at the heart of the digital and networked media revolution.

Perhaps what his detractors fear most is his success. They fear he is rich enough, powerful enough and audacious enough to get anything – anything – that he wants. Now that his empire is absorbing the second best-selling newspaper in the US (and one of its most politically influential), he is more powerful than almost anybody without access to a nuclear button.

The *Wall Street Journal* was the missing piece of his American jigsaw, where his influence on the news was limited to the country's most watched news channel, Fox News. Whilst some feel that its content is politically biased and generally low quality, it has utterly changed the landscape of US television news, blurring the boundaries between facts and comments. His tabloid, the *New York Post*, which he rescued from bankruptcy, is more like a guilty pleasure for many New Yorkers. A similar story can be told in many other countries. In the UK, for example, he reigns across the range, from tabloid *The Sun* to broadsheet *The Sunday Times*, whilst Sky continues to shape the face of sport and entertainment.

Perhaps the most intriguing puzzle is how he, or maybe his sons and daughters, will bring together their physical and digital networks even more powerfully.

How will the world's leading social networking site MySpace come together with satellite and print content, from *The Simpsons* to sporting events? How will the online business information of Dow Jones, plus a global network of business newspapers and satellite channels, enable him to influence the way stock markets behave and companies work? How will he influence the world of advertising, as well as politics, now that he owns such diverse media and can access such huge audiences? How will it further embrace user-generated content, in the way we now see at YouTube or Current TV, to transform broadcast and publishing models?

To understand how News Corp is likely to shape the future networked world, we should look back at an astonishing 25 years of business growth.

Murdoch's first foray into the US market came in 1974 with the purchase of the *San Antonio Express-News*, soon followed by the *National Star*, a supermarket tabloid, and the *New York Post*. In 1981 he bought Twentieth Century Fox, and soon after, the Metromedia group of stations, which resulted in the 1986 launch of Fox Broadcasting Company.

That year also saw Murdoch's subsidiary News International at war with the British newspaper industry – its move from the traditional home of the press, Fleet Street, to Wapping in London's Docklands, was the flashpoint that saw him challenge the highly restrictive work practices of the printing unions. Nightly battles ensued until the unions agreed to Murdoch's changes.

By 1991, News Corp had amassed huge debts, which forced it to sell many of the American magazine interests. This was mainly due to its stake in Sky, the loss-making satellite broadcaster in the UK, eventually sorted out by merging with the rival BSB to form BSkyB on a firmer financial footing.

Fox Networks came under scrutiny in 1995 after claims that Murdoch's ownership was illegal, and that although Murdoch had taken American citizenship, it was owned by an Australian company. The courts favoured Murdoch. In the same year, he launched a news website with MCI, and the Foxtel pay television network in Australia in a partnership with Telstra.

News Corp became a major player in the music industry in 1999 – acquiring and merging Mushroom Records and Festival Records, then giving them to his son James to manage, one of several apprenticeships. In late 2003, News Corp acquired a stake in Hughes DirecTV, the largest American satellite TV system for $6 billion.

MySpace came under the Murdoch spell in 2005, snapped up by his subsidiary Fox Interactive Media for $650 million. It is now the world's sixth most visited website, third in the US, and has over 100 million accounts. Its vast, youthful network, desperate to view and share each other's interests and opinions, music and video, has become a popular phenomenon – the best place for music artists to launch a new single and to engage with the youth of today.

Murdoch, now well into his 70s, surveys his physical and virtual world from an enormous apartment on Manhattan's Upper East Side which once belonged to the Rockefeller family. With his wife, Wendi Deng, half his age, who he met at Star TV in Hong Kong, Murdoch has been extending his dynasty, with two young daughters. However he shows no signs of handing over to a new generation just yet – Lachlan, his eldest son, was seen as his likely successor, but the money is now on the younger James, who currently runs the Sky Television business.

One thing is for sure. With the global assets now in place, the connected story of News Corporation is probably only just beginning.

Radical ideas, practical action

PART 4

Radical ideas, practical action

'Whatever you can do, or think you can do, begin it. Because boldness has power, genius and magic in it'

Johann Wolfgang von Goethe

Deliver high performance more intelligently with **practical action** that has maximum impact in the market and drives profitable growth.

Deliver high performance more imaginatively with **radical ideas** that are energizing, transforming and value creating.

- ► It is one thing to have a great idea, quite another to make it happen practically and profitably. As insights flow through organizations, ideas emerge and innovations evolve, we pass the magic that initially came from the market, like a relay race. The difficulty is that sometimes the baton is dropped or another one replaces it. Ideas get compromised and powerful concepts become diluted.

- ► 'Genius' lies in the thinking and the doing. Not only can bright ideas lose their magic in implementation, but conversely an ordinary idea can sometimes be delivered in extraordinary ways.

- ► Delivering radical action takes people with a deep belief in new possibilities, energized by the ability to solve problems and make lives better, and with a relentless passion for doing it. It requires teams who work together, individuals who can think strategically as well as act tactically, and leaders who can nurture and protect, accelerate and deliver the best ideas into practical action.

- ► Business needs the 'heads up' people who think beyond conventions and act without compromise. People who are naturally entrepreneurial, who are 'people' people, who are motivated and inspired to do what nobody else has done before.

Creating the greatest place to work

'I think that business practices would improve immeasurably if they were guided by "feminine" principles – qualities like love and care and intuition'

Anita Roddick

A more **intelligent** approach to **people** that embraces more *practical action*	A more **imaginative** approach to **people** that embraces more *radical ideas*
• People are focused and engaged on what creates value for all stakeholders.	• People are inspired by leaders working to make the compelling vision their reality.
• Managed with clear and open structures, communications and resources.	• Empowered by managers, creating trust, flexibility, accountability and speed.
• Creating internal collaboration through common purpose, values and goals.	• Stimulating new ideas through diversity, collaboration and new partnerships.
• Delivering the brand promise at every point of customer interaction.	• Living the brand in way that builds a distinctive personality and culture.
• Building intellectual capital in the sense of capability, knowledge and innovation.	• Building intellectual capital in the form of talent, new ideas and relationships.
• Linking benefits and rewards to the short- and long-term priorities of the business.	• Creating an environment that encourages risk, entrepreneurship and agility.
• Ensuring that a great place to work delivers growth and value creation.	• Enabling a fulfilling and rewarding lifestyle for everybody in the business.

People matter more than ever.

In a business world where the economic value of an organization is largely intangible – based on knowledge and innovation, relationships and brands – then the market capitalization is ultimately driven by your ability to attract, nurture and retain the best talent.

It's not just about having the people, it's about how you work with them. Whilst the old man-ufacturing world required manual skills where people could either do a job or not, today's knowledge-based, service-based business depends on getting the best out of people.

Getting the most out of people, applying their talents, and recognizing and growing their potential is a more subtle art. It is about emotions and influence rather than process and instruction. It requires us to think of each employee as a unique individual, an emotional and complicated human being.

As leaders, our challenge is to engage, enable and energize people with unique ideas and tal-ents, who build reputations and relationships, and share their passion and energy with others. A motivated, energized business is tremendously powerful. As Walt Disney once said:

> 'In my organization there is respect for every individual. Whatever we accomplish is due
> to the combined effort. I feel there is no door which, with the kind of talent we have,
> could not be opened, and we hope we can continue to unlock these barriers.'

Employee engagement can sometimes be taken for granted by leaders who live and breathe the organization and are intimate with the challenges and objectives. This is often not the case further down the organization. As tasks get more specific and regular, there can feel less of a 'cause' for the business, less of a need to change, to improve, to perform better.

In the US, a Gallup survey revealed that only 29% of employees feel actively engaged and committed at work. Yet, according to research by the Corporate Leadership Council, if people are committed to the organization they work for, they try 57% harder, perform 20% better and are 87% less likely to leave.

The financial impact of employee engagement and business performance can be quantified using value driver analysis to articulate the cause-effect impact of people's attitudes on behaviours, on customer service and satisfaction, retention and advocacy, profits and growth. Whilst the effect will differ for each company, depending on its markets and structures, there is a common flow that can simply be described as the 'people – service – profit' chain.

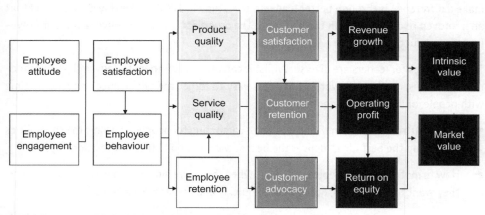

EMPLOYEE, CUSTOMER AND FINANCIAL VALUE DRIVERS

Sears Roebuck, the international retailer, was one of the first to evaluate this impact, and articulated its 'people service profit' chain in its own way: 'a compelling place to work', creates 'a compelling place to shop', creates 'a compelling place to invest'. According to research by Rucci, Kirn and Quinn in *Harvard Business Review*, Sears found that a 5% increase in employee attitude drove a 1.3% improvement in customer perception, which drove a 0.5% increase in revenue growth.

A marginal increase in the satisfaction and engagement of your people – an extra smile each day, starting work with a buzz, or a few percentage points' improvement on the employee satisfaction index – could be worth, in large companies, $100 million to the bottom line.

Whilst there are many different structural ways to improve the lives of your employees – better workplaces, better development, better rewards – the biggest and simplest way to make a difference is through better leadership. A study in 2006 by the Hay Group found that an improved relationship with the leaders of the organization would deliver a 30% improvement in productivity.

The challenges for leaders are diverse. Whilst it can often seem that strategy and performance require every second of the working day, it is easy to forget the importance of spending time with people, and in particular addressing:

- How to attract and retain the best talent – competing for people who have the capabilities to develop the best ideas, deliver the best service and build the best relationships.

- How to motivate your people every day – when they have big ambitions and little patience, they want to learn faster, get promoted quickly and constantly earn more.

- How to engage people in the collective goals – when work is becoming more individualistic and people are more independent, entrepreneurial and personally ambitious.

- How to bring together dispersed teams – globally located, mobile workers, home workers – to stay in touch with and in control of them, so that they add to and benefit from the team.

- How to retain more flexibility – balancing employees and self-employees, so that you can tap into specialist skills as needed, scaling teams up and down according to demand.

- How to get the best out of people – to find the right role for them and most effective style of leadership, encouraging them to deliver great service and bring the brand to life.

- How to brand yourself where teams are more transient, and competition for the best projects and jobs are high, building your personal network and reputation.

You need to think about yourself too. How can you be most effective as a leader? How can you add most value? And if that means you can't do everything, then where are your priorities for the business and yourself? What ignites the passion and energy inside you?

10.1 BUILDING A PASSION FOR PEOPLE
Unlocking the talent and dreams of your people

The business already has a wealth of developed structures, skilled resources and scientific techniques to connect with people. Yet because they are largely deployed only to engage customers with the business, the brand and its products, managers forget that such rigour and approach can equally be applied internally.

There has been much written about creating an 'employee brand'. The reality is that there is only one corporate brand and it is far better to develop that single brand in a way that has relevance to all stakeholders, including employees and shareholders, rather than solely for customers.

A core brand idea that defines the organization and captures its purpose and personality can then be delivered in different, relevant ways to each audience internally and externally, just as it is already adapted to different customer segments. If the big idea is to 'humanize technology' or 'bring dreams to life', then by engaging employees in this goal, they are far more likely to be motivated and focused on engaging the customers that they service in it too.

The brand effectively acts like a 'magnet' engaging each audience in a core idea – in a way that is visible, emotional and energizing. The brand facilitates a relationship with each, and between each, stakeholder. In the employee's case, this means that people deliver great work in return for a range of benefits, serve customers with a common cause, and understand the role of shareholders too.

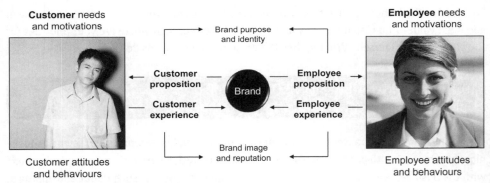

ENGAGEMENT BRANDS BRING PEOPLE TOGETHER

The magnetism is based on an idea that engages each audience emotionally. In the same way that we explored how to engage customers through the 'energizer pyramid' (Chapter 7, p. 192), we need to look your employees' energizers, enablers and essentials – what are their essential needs and wants from coming to work? What is enabling to them, helping them to achieve their goals? And what energizes them?

Obviously not all employees are the same – just as not all customers are the same. Not all employees are of equal value (although not an easy thing to say, sometimes), just as there are good and less good customers. Therefore segmentation of employees based on physical-ity (function, level, geography), motivation (needs, wants, ambitions) and value (specialist skills, potential, performance) helps us to target and tailor our approach appropriately.

Each target segment of people can then be addressed distinctively – by developing 'employee value propositions' that take exactly the same format as customer value propositions. They identify what matters most to the particular group and then describe the most important and relevant benefits of working for the company to that audience.

The proposition conditions the whole approach to each segment. It becomes reality through 'products and services' – or the role and activities, contracts and salary, targets and rewards, environment and management relationship that collectively deliver the 'employee experience' – what it's like to work for the company. The processes and structures are the same as delivering a personal, compelling and memorable experience for customers.

Internal communication becomes an ongoing dialogue with your people – founded on their issues and focused on the benefits to them. Like external communication, it should embrace the most appropriate media, enabling people to initiate dialogue, fast and openly. From business television and magazines to websites and blogs, physical events and online communities, it should facilitate openness between managers and employees, and between employees.

A diverse workforce needs can be engaged in very different, and much more relevant ways. Personalization of contracts, benefits and work experience is then entirely possible through effective management-employee relationships.

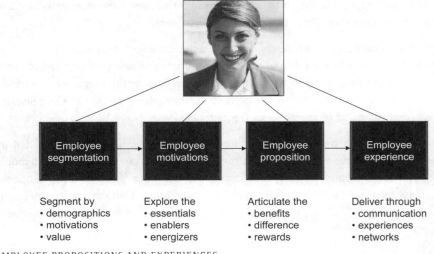

Employee segmentation	Employee motivations	Employee proposition	Employee experience

Segment by	Explore the	Articulate the	Deliver through
• demographics	• essentials	• benefits	• communication
• motivations	• enablers	• difference	• experiences
• value	• energizers	• rewards	• networks

EMPLOYEE PROPOSITIONS AND EXPERIENCES

Insight 28: GOOGLE
The hyper-active brains behind one hundred zeros

'Googol' is the mathematical term for a 1 followed by 100 zeros. It perhaps symbolizes the magnitude of Google's ambition, and increasing impact on the whole dynamic of markets and marketing.

In 1995, Larry Page and Sergey Brin created, in their Stanford University bedroom, what would already be dealing with 100 million Internet searches every day within five years, and make them multi-billionaires in less than a decade.

Google has a simple but daunting mission: 'to organize the world's information and to make it universally accessible and useful'. As Page puts it, 'the perfect question and answer machine – one that understands exactly what you mean and gives you back exactly what you want'. With well over 10 million users, searching through 10 billion webpages, Google is well established as the world's leading search engine.

Google is also the best place to work.

Maybe that doesn't surprise you, particularly when you learn that the tech company only has a 2% turnover within its 5000-strong workforce each year, and receives almost 500,000 applications for that handful of vacancies. More significantly, when the people from 'Best Company to Work For' arrived to evaluate Google's Mountain View headquarters, they decided it really was the best workplace.

Ninety-five per cent of people, 'Googlers' as they call themselves, said 'Taking everything into account I'd say this is a great place to work'.

Sitting in one of Google's eleven gourmet restaurants within the campus, you might reflect on what makes this such as extraordinary place. Maybe it's the long list of unique benefits that enable people to learn, grow, travel and have a truly fantastic day. Maybe the free breakfasts, lunches and dinners, or the unlimited sick leave, the gym, or the 27 days paid leave each year. Or the more conventional aspects, such as the free WiFi-enabled bus to work, the on-site medical and dental care, the car and bike repair shop, and the lunchtime language classes.

As the culture audit states:

> 'There is no hard data that can ever prove that a free lunch and a multicultural, campus-like environment contribute to the organization's success and profit. What can be proven is that Google is growing at an immense pace – retention of employees is high, attrition is low and revenues are strong. People are eager to work at Google and applications to our job openings are exceedingly high (approximately 1300 résumés a day).'

Yet this is also an organization that works and grows at break-neck speed. It is constantly developing new products, entering new markets, extending its portfolio. It is a stressful, hard working but exhilarating place. As one Googler commented:

> 'Google is a great company and I am very proud to be a part of it. The perks are extraordinary and this is the most unique working environment I have ever been in. The products, ideas, creative minds that we have continue to amaze and inspire me.'

When Sergey Brin and Larry Page founded the company, all those short years ago in 1998, they believed in a better way of doing business – certainly better than their Stamford University bedroom, which doubled as their global headquarters at the time. They established their motto 'Don't be evil' and always believed that a creative business needs to treat people with respect and support if they are to unlock their talents.

Since the early days, the two founders recognized that the success of their business fundamentally lay in being able to attract and retain the world's best technologists, and indeed the world's best business people too.

Their CEO Eric Schmidt is given this as a primary responsibility, in the belief that if they get this right, then operational and financial success will follow. He seeks out 'brainy, creative, entrepreneurial people', well-rounded people, not narrow-minded tech geeks, then puts much effort into supporting their personal development and performance. He also works hard to ensure that they have a lot of fun – to relieve stress, improve collaboration and drive creative solutions.

So what else would I experience working in the Google world?

- TGIF is the weekly company-wide get-together, often with the founders themselves. A time to welcome new recruits, update on key activities, and most importantly, a no-limits question and answer session which is webcast around the world.

- Google Ideas is a website where Googlers add, connect and discuss their ideas. Anything is possible, and better to get it out there, rather than in somebody's head. Colleagues rate ideas from 0 (dangerous) to 5 (do it now).

- Quarterly 'kick-offs', mainly for the sales teams, when goals are set for the next three months, people are focused on target prospects and products, inspired by guests, and encouraged to attend specialist training clinics, ready to drive growth even further and faster.

- Professional development is also provided in the form of $8000 budgets for each employee to find what they believe is right for them, from anywhere in the world, be it technical training or a one-year MBA.

- The education leave program goes even further, enabling people to take up to five years (a long time in Google world!) off to follow a program of study, and to be reimbursed up to $150,000.

- Pre-launch access to new products, so that employees can start using the best new applications, such as Gmail, Froogle, Toolbar or Local – as well as testing and feeding back improvements.

- 20% projects are what all Googlers are encouraged to spend 20% of their time working on – things outside their responsibilities, wacky ideas they believe in, or getting involved in the developments going on in completely unrelated areas.

- New parents are looked after too – all those sleepless nights, and no time to look after yourself when a new baby arrives. Google makes things a little better by paying for $500 worth of take-out meals during the first four weeks.

- Compensation is structured in a way that supports primary business objectives – attracting and retaining the best talent, encouraging collaborative working, taking more responsibility, and being like a 'start-up' entrepreneur, but with all the other benefits of being in a large company.

- The Founders Award is incredibly prestigious within Google world. It goes to the team that has created enormous value for the business, and is rewarded with shares in the business – last year, $45 million-worth was divided between 11 project teams.

- Community activities matter greatly to Google. Encouraging females and minorities to embrace technologies at school or home is a key diversity initiative, whilst $90 million was donated through google.org to projects that utilized Google skills charitably.

- Office décor is not forgotten either – this is definitely a place for lava lamps and pink sofas, bicycles on the ceiling and exercise balls under the desks, giant Lego sets and the best coffee machines, T-shirts and flip-flops.

- 'Googleyness' is the special quality Google seeks in its people – those who can work well in small team, in fast-changing environments, are well-rounded but with unique interests and talents, enthusiasm for Google, and in making the world a better place.

'To organize the world's information' doesn't sound like the most exciting job in the world, but Google is a truly amazing, inspirational place to work.

10.2 LIVING THE NEW WORKSTYLE
Bringing a better lifestyle to the workplace

'I choose to work on Tuesdays to Fridays, because it suits my social life. On waking I check my inbox and schedule, take the kids to school, then arrive around at the local business hub at around 0930. I wear T-shirts and trainers some days, but others might be a shirt and suit. I spend time with the team, talking over priorities, new ideas and last night's sports results. I head to the gym at 1200, followed by lunch round the kitchen table with my personal performance coach.

'The afternoon is spent with customers, working on my personal projects or building new international partnerships. At 1700 I have a video-chat with project colleagues in

Bangalore and Tallinn, then ensure my shopping has been delivered to my car downstairs. On the way home I catch up with my CEO letting her know about my latest investment decisions, and arrive in time for dinner. Later I spend a few hours logged into my social network, exploring my new business venture, leaving just enough time for an episode of *Lost* then bed.'

We live in very different world from the nine-to-five corporate man, the one who succeeded by fitting in, keeping his head down, playing the game. Sitting in hour-long meeting after hour-long meeting, mostly talking about agendas and minutes, rather than doing anything of substance. He (he was a he) was like all the others, and that gave them comfort. A slave to the 12-month planning cycle and the performance metrics. They didn't like diversity or change, challenge or tension. They were in the company for life, motivated more than anything else by their pension.

Is it really healthy for people to follow the rules? Do all those endless meetings help or hinder us? What if it was 20, not 60, minutes long? Is a pension really an aspiration that drives young people to do great work? Don't we want as many different and interesting people as possible?

Today people want to be happy. The pursuit of corporate happiness sounds a little too soft and cuddly for a high performance workplace. 'HAPIE' also stands for:

- **H**umble – leadership that is genuine, personal, inclusive, and inspirational.

- **A**daptive – employees are enthusiastic and creative, and embrace change.

- **P**rofit – all stakeholders all share in value creation for mutual benefit.

- **I**nvigorated – people are energized by a shared and compelling purpose.

- **E**ngaged – there is a genuine sense of team, citizenship and community.

Google gave new meaning to bringing the home into the workplace, the work-lifestyle. Arrive at Mountain View and you can enjoy three free meals every day in any of their gourmet restaurants. You can work on any project you like. You can take as much time off as you want. You get to busk with Sergey and Larry every so often. You get the latest cool product leases before anyone else. There are even new T-shirts twice a week.

The story across at Genentech's campus, or at P&G in Cincinatti, and at Microsoft Campus in Redwood is very similar – or they hope better, as they are all in competition for the same great people, less defined by physical skills, more defined by who they are.

It's not just about money. That's too rational. It's about engaging people emotionally too. It's about being part of something – both in the sense of a sharing in a cause that will transform society, and in being a member of a high-energy, high-performing community.

At the Infosys Technologies campus in Mysore, India, the story is the same. Thousands email in their applications to share the new Indian middle-class dream. The tech leader is incredibly people-centred, big on learning, big on support, big on benefits. You might think that this is the land of the limitless, low-paid workforce. Not so. Infosys' campus is dominated by a huge white dome – not the reception or the executive suite – but four food courts surrounding a 96-bedroom employee hotel. A state of the art gym, pool hall and bowling alley run alongside.

In Shanghai, the competition for talent is even more fierce – the local managing director of Cisco, for example, maintains a huge map behind his desk with red dots reflecting each worker – not their task or performance, but where they live, so that he can schedule more shuttle busses – and thereby make Cisco the nearest, easiest place to work.

The stories of corporate 'theme parks' are endless – gaming rooms, nap stations, media lounges, good old bean bags and bikes on the walls – but it's not just about sociability and well-being.

So what really energizes an organization? Stanton Marris specialize in helping companies to build organizational energy that drives engagement and performance. They use a simple five-step approach:

- Being open: sharing the big strategic challenges with everyone.

- Opening up: seeking suggestions from all stakeholders.

- Letting go: giving local teams the freedom to contribute.

- Being supportive: showing continuous and consistent interest.

- Maintaining focus: monitoring progress and holding on to the big picture.

Sounds obvious? Of course it is, although not necessarily to a manager of the twentieth century. Jack Welch would be squirming in his spreadsheets. Other factors that bring twenty-first century organizations to life, that create an enduring buzz inside and out, that create a new 'workstyle' include:

- Personal and flexible – everything from role and benefits to working hours and location.

- Partners and networks – stimulating and extending ideas by tapping into the outside world.

- Trust and empowerment – few rules, no time sheets, asking for forgiveness, not permission.

- Flat and accessible – decisions are not by hierarchy, anybody can talk to anybody, any time.

- Team and collaborative – sharing challenge and rewards, sparing and sparking with others.

- Resources and tools – the best tools for the job, be it computers, phones or stationery.

- Learning and support – work and personal interests, with peer-partnering and mentoring.

- Health and well-being – healthy buildings, food and fitness, lots of rest and medics on tap.

The workstyle will evolve quickly – with the best talent taking ownership of their employment, and developing portfolios of work, jumping across sectors and functions, from healthcare to technology, from marketing to finance. The best talent is infinitely transferable. Virtual talent networks will form to pursue their common interests and collectively negotiate the most interesting, most valuable projects.

Organizations need to rethink many of the factors which created their old glue, and start working in faster, knowledge-based, connected ways themselves.

Insight 29: FERRARI
Creativity that drives fast and fanatical performance

In 1919 an Italian muleskinner decided to follow his real passion for cars and became a test driver for the small Milan-based car manufacturer Costruzioni Meccaniche Nazionali. A decade later, he was ready to start his own business and founded the company that would go on to produce the world's best racing cars, and most desirable sports cars.

Today, Enzo Ferrari's name is synonymous with speed, glamour and performance.

From Monte Carlo to Monza, the world's F1 Grand Prix circuit is defined by the red cars with the prancing horse logo that lead the snake of manufacturers around the winding circuits. They win more often than any other, the car of choice of world champions.

However, a new award sits alongside all the Formula 1 trophies and other accolades that the company has won over the last 60 years, an award that Enzo would probably be as more proud of than any Grand Prix win. This award is not based on superior technologies and engineering. It is based on how it manages and inspires its 3000 people.

In 2001, the company's president Luca di Montezemolo launched 'Formula Uomo'– not a new generation of racing cars, or highly tuned engines, but an internal initiative to improve the lives and work of Ferrari people. A budget of €200 million was allocated to the project, news of which had a significant impact on employee morale in itself.

The project took its inspiration from the company's racing ambitions and successes. Ferrari recognized that if it wanted to keep its position at the front of the F1 championship – where 1/1000th of a second can determine winners from losers – and which then directly affects the desirability and perceived worth of its retail vehicles – it had to be at the forefront of work practices and performance too.

'Formula Uomo' covers three basic areas: workplaces and structures, professional training and international growth, and personal and family benefits. It is designed to put people at the heart of Ferrari's business and its future, seeking to enhance the broader 'human capabilities' of employees at all levels, and in particulate to stimulate creativity across the business.

Some of the benefits relate directly to the outside world, offering participation in company events such as the 'Finali Mondiali' and the unveilings of new cars, VIP seats at the various Grand Prix, sports groups, and discounts with many different third parties. Personal services include medical check-ups for employees and their children, specialist preventative medicine, and well-being programmes.

Eighty-eight per cent of all employees now participate in new ongoing training activities, all of which are voluntary, some in traditional formats, and others more informal. Employees can start their day improving their language skills with english@breakfast (there is also @lunch and @tea if they miss the early morning start). Other languages are offered too, and are free for anybody to join.

Meanwhile, the Creative Club is one of the most popular initiatives – bringing together an eclectic mix of painters and sculptors, musicians and writers, DJs and actors to introduce new skills, new perspectives – encouraging people to think more radically and innovatively.

Senior managers and engineers, sales people and warehouse people, they all come along to learn about the world of sculpture, or talk about the big issues in life with the nightclub DJ.

It breaks down the barriers, and gets them curious and thinking differently, and collaborating in new ways. There is no facilitation, no forced connection between the world of hip-hop and finely tuned engines. Translating the new energy and behaviors back into a work context is natural, particularly when the subject matter of Ferrari is the stuff of normal people's dreams.

However it is the new buildings that really symbolize the new spirit of Ferrari.

Employees can now live in the magic kingdom day and night if they want, with the development of Maranello Village, a high-specification housing complex exclusively for staff. Situated only 4km from the factory, the two are connected, perhaps oddly for Ferrari, by a bicycle path.

Each Ferrari home (there are 22 studios, 42 two-bedroom and 58 three-bedroom flats) comes fully furnished, not completely in red. The village also has a fitness centre, a wonderful restaurant and an impressive bar. And of course there is plenty of indoor and outdoor parking for those specially priced and highly prized cars.

In 2007 the transformed and high performing world of Ferrari was voted Europe's Best Place to Work, and yet again they won the F1 championship too.

10.3 IGNITING YOUR OWN POTENTIAL
Making the most of yourself in the new business world

What sparks you? What is the ignition that enables you to energize your business?

A deflated leader is the quickest way to drain all the energy out of an organization. But an inspiring, energizing leader – one who is naturally an energy 'giver' rather than 'taker' – is the quickest way to turn potential energy (the latent but inert power of the organization) into kinetic energy (the power of action that builds momentum and becomes self-sustaining).

When Renzo Rosso comes down from his mountain vineyard and works with his people in their offices and design studios, when A.G. Lafley sits down to discuss a brand's strategy, when Ray Davies walks into his latest coffee shop-looking bank, then their passion and enthusiasm is catching. It might not seem like a crucial use of their time, but it certainly makes a difference to their people.

As an individual, you too need to have a personality – who are you? What do people know you for? What do you believe in most? Why should they trust you, want to work with you?

Whether you are the CEO or a leader at any level in the organization, you need to throw off your grey executive image, and create a more distinctive, more personal aura. Whilst you are part of the organization, you are also uniquely you. Your personality, your beliefs, your ideas should complement but also stand out from those of the organization. Try these three steps to get started:

Define yourself. Consider what you most want to be known for. Whilst your CV might be long and impressive as a list of experiences and achievements, it is unlikely to be memorable.

- What's the thing you want people to remember – 'He's the guy who created the 'Just Do It' slogan for Nike', or 'She took Google into eastern Europe', or 'He ran the Boston Marathon'.

- Similarly, what do you want to achieve – your personal ambition, your big idea? What do you stand for in the organization – what's your particular interest, passion or big idea?

- Prepare your mental 'elevator pitch' – what you say when you briefly meet someone that will leave a lasting impression – no more than three things that they will remember you by.

Get connected. There is nothing like building your own personal networks to stay in touch with humanity, meet new and diverse people, broaden your perspective and spark new ideas.

- Build your network inside and outside at every level, with suppliers and peers – 'Have you got 15 minutes for a quick coffee?' – or through online through sites like Facebook and LinkedIn.

- Get involved in non-functional activities – champion a new initiative, look for cross-functional projects, get into sporting or social activities.

- Stay connected with people you have met. In your address book, note down something interesting about them, and send an occasional 'Hi – how are you?' email.

Be different. Get known for what you do, not in an ego-driven publicity-seeking way, but by doing something different, being visible and vocal, memorable and distinctive.

- Build awareness, for example by speaking at events internally, run a training course, speak at an external conference. Inspire and maybe provoke. Write articles, maybe even a book.

- Be memorable by developing your own style – be it a dress sense (like Steve Jobs and his black turtle necks), or a saying (like Lafley's 'the customer is boss'), or even a nickname.

- Get out there, in the outside world. Take off the blinkers of your own organization, join professional or industry networks, read and write blogs, see the bigger picture.

Whilst these may seem like trivial actions compared to the priorities in your inbox, they will help you become a more effective leader, build stronger relationships with people, and thereby deliver better team and business performance.

People create the energy of organizations, and ideas are sparked by diversity of people. We do things for people who we care for, and who motivate and inspire us. But we need to be authentic, let people know who we really are, rise about the organization structure like a lighthouse in the sea.

Insight 30: FEDEX
People who deliver, absolutely positively

FedEx is a people business through and through. In 1971, when former US Marine Fred Smith founded the company in Little Rock, Arkansas, he knew better than most the importance of people on the front line.

From his military experience he knew that great strategies, great offices, great officers, can be worth little in the heat of the battlefield. He knew that it was about being prepared and equipping the real people – the operational staff, the customer service agents, the drivers and counter staff, the sales guys – with the beliefs, capabilities and tools to deliver great service every day.

Whilst studying business at Yale, he had put together a plan for a logistics business that would change the industry. At first he developed it for a spare parts business, where getting items quickly was essential and depended on incredibly rapid supply structures across many locations. He plotted out a 'hub and spoke' operation, whereby packages could be brought together in one location, and then redistributed to where they were to go, all within 24 hours.

It was a great plan, but it would require lots of resources – most significantly aircraft, warehousing, and great people who could see the vision, and make things that were simply deemed impossible happen. In 1973, FedEx began operating 14 aircraft to 25 cities, and grew its network year by year. It was not all easy-going – there is the legend of staff who sold their watches to buy fuel, or used their own credit cards in a difficult moment. Smith himself is said once to have gambled his last few dollars in Las Vegas casino, winning $20,000 and enough to pay his people that week.

FedEx is now the world's leader in overnight delivery, with 140,000 employees and the world's largest cargo fleet of 600 aircraft. It claims to handle a third of all US international trade, to 325 airports in 212 countries.

It delivers three million packages every day with a 99.82% on-time delivery record.

'Absolutely, positively' is the slogan of its overnight delivery service, derived from the original promise 'When it absolutely, positively has to get there overnight'. Employees will do anything to achieve this. If a package missed a flight for some unavoidable reason most companies would just send it the next day. At FedEx, a team member would jump their car and make a 500km round trip to make sure it got there next day.

So how does FedEx 'put people first' in order to serve their customers with such passion? There are many similarities to other companies, but a few special cultural ingredients too:

- The 'people-service-profit' chain is at the heart of Fred Smith's philosophy, focusing the business on people who are committed, motivated and well trained.

- Every employee gets at least 40 hours training every year, with call centre agents required to train for six weeks before taking a live call.

- Staff are empowered to spend up to $2000 on the spot, to solve problems, to offer refunds, so that customer problems are not allowed to fester.

- Everybody in the company takes an annual exam, delivered electronically. If they don't pass they are required to take more training or leave.

- Annual performance reviews link compensation to performance. Goals are set and evaluated around customer orientation, enthusiasm, team fit, loyalty, flexibility and expertise.

- The annual staff survey is based around 32 questions, and each manager is evaluated on their performance based on their teams' responses, which are then acted on.

- There is a clear 'fair treatment' policy for handling staff complaints, with a three-step appeals process that seeks to resolve all issues fairly.

- Communication is open and two-way, continuous and human. FXTV, the in-house television service, broadcasts daily around the globe, regularly featuring Fred himself.

- Management development is based around internal promotion which is gained through a rigorous and ongoing assessment process linked to a vacancy website.

- Leadership has a particular focus across the business – seeking people who are charismatic, intelligent, considerate, courageous and dependable, flexible, respectful and with integrity.

- Most visible is the recognition processes that FedEx has institutionalized, based around awards that employees wear on their uniforms with enormous pride, including:

  - Five Stars – the 150 top performing staff in the annual reviews.

  - Golden Falcons – people who are recognized by customer feedback.

  - Humanitarian Award – for bravery and kindness to people in distress.

  - Bravo Zulus – managers rewarding staff on the spot, including $150 cash.

Fred Smith himself is more determined than most to make the business a success, and believes that everybody is motivated by more than money. On returning from his military service, he found that he had inherited a $4 million fortune, meaning that he could have lived comfortably without ever creating FedEx. But for him, like his people, it is about much more than that.

Making change happen, and making it stick

'You've got to figure out a way to manage the complexity of large projects yet still allow your core teams to focus on the essentials'

Steve Jobs

A more **intelligent** approach to **change** that embraces more *practical action*	A more **imaginative** approach to **change** that embraces more *radical ideas*
• Defining the change required to achieve the inspiring vision.	• Developing an inspiring vision and how it is different from today.
• Engaging people in the case for change, making it essential.	• Engaging people in the need for change, their hearts and minds.
• Identifying the priorities for change, what to start, stop and continue doing.	• Being open and honest with people, building an ongoing dialogue.
• Implementing the change as a clearly managed process.	• Leaders understanding how they will need to change themselves too.
• Managing the complex activities, timescales and milestones.	• Building energy and momentum so that it overcomes resistance.
• Sustaining the change as the new 'business as usual'.	• Identifying symbols of change that represent the new ways.
• Realising the performance benefits and value creation.	• Delivering 'quick wins' and celebrating success.

Is your business more like a jigsaw, or is it a bucket of Lego?

There is only one way to solve a jigsaw puzzle, and once it's done it is a little bit useless. Lego succeeds because of its infinite versatility – constantly building new shapes, more sophisticated and interesting as time goes on.

At Google, everyone plays with Lego.

Organizations in dynamic markets need constant reassembling. Often it's about reassembling the blocks in new ways, sometimes about throwing away some old ones, sometimes about getting new ones. Strategies help us to design the new structures, but we also need a good process to rebuild.

'Change' is about transforming the way the business works – both in terms of its 'harder' structures and processes, and its 'softer' attitudes and behaviours. It can be complex and hard work, and could easily go wrong – 'why break an organization, when it's not broken?', particularly when you need to sustain and grow revenues at the same time as making the change happen.

'Change management' is the process for doing it effectively. Whilst change used to have more of an internal focus, to improve the quality and efficiency of whatever the business does, today change is much more externally driven, typically with factors beyond the organization's control driving the need for change, and a clarity of purpose and priority driving the direction of change.

In Japanese, change is now much more about 'kaikaku' (radical reform for a specific purpose), rather than 'kaizen' (continuous improvement because it's good for you).

Andy Grove, chairman of Intel, calls significant market change – such as the arrival of the Internet, wireless mobility and social networks – 'strategic inflection points' which occur when '10x' forces alter a market with '100x' impact. He recalls how Intel itself almost missed the

Internet, and in the same way that Microsoft initially poured scorn on Netscape, Intel ignored the rise of Japanese microprocessor manufacturers.

He now realizes that reacting to external change is not enough, and argues that organizations will regularly have to make one of three choices:

- Not to change.

- To change only when forced to.

- To take charge of your destiny and seek to change before, or differently to, others.

Business leaders therefore need to become change agents – sensing the need to change, then galvanizing, leading and managing the process of change in their organizations as this is essential to future growth, and before it becomes essential to their survival.

Change is a journey that leaders will need to persuade, cajole, inspire, support and manage their organizations through. It should be driven by market and business strategy, staying true to the compelling purpose and direction of the business, but also recognize that little else is sacred.

Change will require decisive leadership and rapid action. Everything in the organization should be open to challenge, and if necessary, change. It might require innovation, to start doing new things, but even more importantly, will be to decide what to stop doing. It will take time, and sometimes be painful, hence the need to do it quickly. It must be driven and managed, with clarity of purpose and actions, and continuous dialogue with all stakeholders.

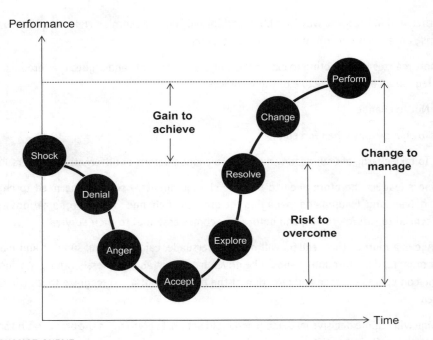

Performance

THE CHANGE CURVE

The result of change, getting from 'old world' to 'new world', is rarely, however, an end point. The benefits need to be realized, which means the change needs to stick. It would be easy to regress back into old ways, or even to remain stuck in between the two worlds. Change becomes regular, and maybe even continuous, as in the world of Intel where the market is driven by relentless innovation.

11.1 THE AGENDA FOR CHANGE
Making change essential and inspiring for everyone

'The most emotionally wrenching and terrifying aspect of any major organizational change is getting people to realize that change is essential, building the extreme intensity that people have to feel if they are to step into the void, step onto the journey.' Prof. Noel Tichy is author of *Control Your Destiny or Someone Else Will*, the story of GE's transformational journey over recent decades. His most significant insight is that, every time, GE has struggled to wake people up to the need to change.

Everybody likes the status quo – it is familiar and comfortable, and we find a way to succeed within it. But then change comes along, and pulls the rug from under our feet, threatening our jobs, projects, bonuses and careers. We don't like change.

Making the case is much easier when there is a crisis. But then it's too late.

As Charles Handy will always remind you, a frog that jumps into a bucket of boiling water will jump out, but a frog that sits in cold water that is gradually heated to boiling point, will not sense the danger until too late. There are plenty of organizations, plenty of executives, who are happy to sit tight and hope things don't get too hot, at least before they move on to their next job.

Change therefore needs leaders and managers. Leaders must inspire people to take the brave step into the unknown, to define an inspiring vision, and to guide them on the journey. Managers need to coordinate and control what can often be an incredibly complicated process and transition a multi-billion dollar enterprise from one state into another.

One simple but effective way to think of making the case for change is in the following formula, demonstrating what is required to overcome people's natural resistance:

Change will happen if **A x B x C > D**

Where:

A = an inspiring vision of the what the future organization will be like.

B = the reasons why the current organization cannot continue.

C = the first practical steps to get towards the future organization.

D = people's resistance to change, and preference to stay as they are.

The case for change should be made simply and definitively. The vision should be engaging personally, so that people can quickly recognize the benefits to themselves. The reasons why the organization as it is today is not sustainable might be financial or logical – a declining share, rising cost-base, new competitors – these factors need to be extrapolated so stakeholders can see how they would severely restrict the business's future without change. A business case might be helpful, but people step into their known patterns until they truly understand the consequences, to them, of resisting change.

John Kotter in *Leading Change* has some even more direct tactics for overcoming the resistance of your people to change, including cleaning up the balance sheet to take a significant loss in the next quarter; moving the head office to disrupt old habits and symbolize a new start; telling business units they have 24 months to become number one or two in their market or face closure; and toughening up the performance targets of senior managers to provoke 'honest' discussions.

Insight 31: PROCTOR & GAMBLE
Transforming a global market leader

A.G. Lafley is in the midst of engineering a remarkable turnaround. The first thing Lafley (his first name is Alan) told his managers when he unexpectedly stepped up to the CEO job in 2000 was just what they wanted to hear: focus on what you do well – selling the company's major brands such as Crest, Tide and Pampers – instead of trying to develop the next big innovation.

Now, old staples of the P&G stable have done so well that they are again the envy of the industry. So is the company's share price, which climbed 58% to $92 a share in the six years since Lafley started, while the overall stock market has declined 32%. Profits are almost $6 billion on sales of $44 billion, having outgrown most rivals for the past five years.

Maybe softly spoken Lafley was the antidote P&G needed after 18 months of Dirk Jager, the previous CEO, who had flown into Cincinnati from the Netherlands on a mission to shake up the company. He stuck up 'Old World, New World' posters, asking people which world they were in. The share price plummeted. He rammed through an agenda of change, and whilst he was absolutely right that the business need a new, and much more external culture, he ripped apart everything that P&G's insular culture was built on, and alienated almost everyone. Instead of pushing P&G to excel, his torrent of slogans and initiatives almost brought the company to its knees.

Lafley, in his 23rd year at P&G, wasn't supposed to be a radical change agent; he was supposed to bring some stability back to the business. Having spent his early years managing Tide and a decade running the Japanese business, he had recently returned to head up North American operations. He recognized the need for change, the need for more speed and agility, a deeper understanding of consumers, and a more radical approach to innovation. But he also understood that P&Gers – some of the best trained, brightest managers in the world – would only embrace such change in a P&G way.

On taking up the job, Lafley pushed through Jager's agenda even faster and more radically than his predecessor had dared hope. However, he did it in a way that engaged people, that built on what they had spent their careers doing, that offered hope and personal gain rather than despair and pain.

In his short time in charge, P&G has not only experienced transformation internally but has absorbed some of its largest competitors too – buying Clairol for $5 billion in 2001, followed by Wella for $7 billion, and Gillette for a huge $54 billion in 2005. He has replaced at least half of his most senior managers and his top 30 officers, and cut 10,000 jobs. However this is just the beginning. If one unguarded memo is believed, 25,000 more jobs could soon go, based on the idea of turning P&G into a virtual brand-owning company, with marketing as its core business and most other activities – from innovation to manufacturing – done in partnership with others.

Lafley's rallying call is incredibly simple, almost embarrassingly so, as he reminds people in meeting after meeting that 'the consumer is the boss'. With this phrase he is turning P&G inside out – or, more precisely, outside in.

Symbolically, he tore down the walls of the executive offices, including his own. He moved people about, for example seating marketing and finance people together to drive faster, more collaborative, more commercial, much more customer-driven ways of working. He himself spent hours talking to real consumers in their homes around the world – about how they live, how they cook, how they clean. When his managers came to him with an idea, he was ready to respond with a consumer's mindset.

He is a listener and sponge, and when he communicates, he does it in very simple *Sesame Street* terms, but people love him, because they believe he is trying to do the right thing. He only ever writes one-page memos, and most meetings are scheduled for 20 or 30 minutes, rather than the conventional hour. He brought in Meg Whitman, CEO of eBay, as a non-executive director, and hung out with GE's new CEO, Jeff Immelt, himself joining GE's board.

Innovation, in particular, has come under the microscope. Despite battalions of scientists and engineers, P&G hadn't delivered a real innovation in decades, even with millions of dotcom-style dollars being pumped into internal ventures. When they tried to innovate, it was always based on a technically-advanced product offer rather than something consumers actually wanted.

He insisted that at least 50% of new products should come from outside, compared to 10% at the time. This would require a seismic culture change, and putting your future in the hands of others would be risky too. The new 'connect and develop' approach is about collaboration, with partners who have specialist skills that P&G doesn't, and with consumers.

Lafley's own eyes were opened to the need for change when he worked in Asia. P&G was a minnow compared to the might of Unilever and Nestlé in that market. Brand names long on American heritage and short on real difference just did not sell. Indeed, what sold in the American market was never likely to excite the Indian consumer, as even the likes of Coca-Cola have found the hard way. P&G lacked insight, relevance, differentiation and creativity. Performance was respectable, but not sustainable.

Changing a huge, global business is not easy. He recognized that he couldn't do everything. He quickly focused his change agenda on 'the core' business – the select few markets, categories, brands and capabilities that defined the business. Core meant being a global leader, leading economics, high growth and strong cash flow. Other areas would have to wait, telling them to 'just keep doing a great job'.

He was clear and direct with people – 'These are our core business – fabric care, baby care, feminine care and hair care' and 'Everything else is non-core'. He wanted to unclutter the thinking.

Whilst his approach was hands-on in the early years, he has increasingly stepped back to become more of a coach and facilitator. He wants his managers to learn to make their own choices – to embrace his passion and focus in their own ways, as he can't possibly manage everything. However he demands a strategy from every team – including a 'to-do' and 'not-to-do' list – and every decision must be based on sound consumer insight, not just some manipulated financial projection.

He regularly reminds people of the their enduring purpose: 'To improve the everyday lives of people around the world with P&G brands and products that deliver better performance, quality and value'. He points out that this has not changed, nor have the values and principles of the business.

One thing Lafley has carefully avoided is setting out a vision statement. He doesn't believe it is necessary, that the purpose of the business is clear and that is sufficient, and otherwise it is about the consumer not the business. He calls it managing from the 'future back' – his eyes and ears on today's world, and his back to the future, believing that the consumer is his best navigator.

11.2 MAKING CHANGE HAPPEN
Preparing and implementing significant change

The change must be driven by business leaders, be managed to mitigate risks, release energy that mobilizes people, make a difference to customers, and deliver results quickly to give confidence, and long term to drive a step-change in performance. There are four phases to the change process:

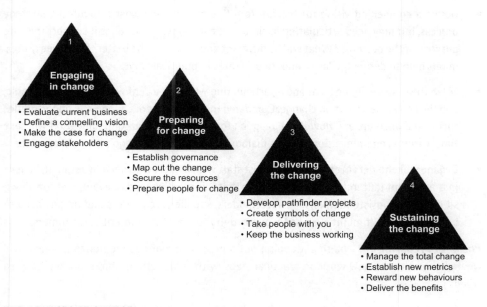

THE 4 PHASES OF CHANGE

Phase 1: Engaging in change. All stakeholders need to understand and hopefully support the change – why it is needed, what it will involve and how it will happen.

• Evaluate the current business – how effective is it currently, and compared to best practices competitively and more broadly? Where are the strengths and weaknesses? What needs to be sustained, changed and eliminated? Benchmarking, strategic alignment and gap analysis will be important in achieving this.

- Define a compelling vision for the future – this may already exist through the strategy process, but may need articulating in simpler, clearer ways – how does it support the core purpose of the business? What will be different and why will it be better? Employee groups might help to define the 'as is' and 'to be' states in practical ways.

- Make the case for change – as above, articulating why the current world is not sustainable, and the consequences of no change. Compared to the benefits of change, the opportunities this would open up, and how it will be good for people too. This communication will take time, careful communication, regular dialogue at all levels and ongoing reinforcement.

- Engage stakeholders in change – this must start with leaders who need to design it, believe in it and want it. It must be bottom-up, so that it is practical and relevant, and top-down so that it is consistent. Sponsors, shareholders, suppliers, regulators and unions need to be engaged too. It might even be an opportunity to signal your intent to customers.

Phase 2: Preparing for change. Mapping out a programme of change horizons – how will we move from to the new world in practical steps, with what actions and resources required when?

- Establish a governance structure – who will sponsor the change (ideally the CEO)? By mapping out stakeholders, you can shape a steering group to oversee the project, lend support and keep them engaged. Define a project leader and manager, and recruit a project team with representatives from across the business. Define roles and responsibilities.

- Map out the change – balancing the financial imperatives, with what makes more sense logically and for people. Develop horizons of change, so that the change becomes less daunting, more manageable and simply articulated. The 'change plan' should include milestones, timelines and 'quick win' business results that will build confidence.

- Bring together the resources for change – acquire the budgets, people and other resources to support the change. You may need specialist external help – either technically or to provide a fresh, independent view. Consider the legal implications, including employee rights. This will require business cases and their approval.

- Keep preparing people for change, with ongoing communication. Don't just say there will be a organization restructuring, with new job roles and reporting lines. Engage them in the wider reasons and opportunities, maybe let them define what new processes or behaviours should be like, and then discuss the choices and changes required to implement their ideas.

Phase 3: Delivering the change. Making the change happen comes down to people and effective management, sustaining the momentum of change to overcome resistance and barriers.

- Develop pathfinder projects that introduce the change in chosen areas first, then build on these as examples, transferring skills from one area to another, and showing people practically what it will be like. Learn from the 'pilot' cases how to do it faster and better next time, evolving the change as you go, making it real and simple.

- Create symbols of change. Identify small or significant parts of the programme that reflect the bigger idea. As CEO, decide to give up your large office and move to an open workspace, deliver a new service to customers, consider refreshing the corporate brand at the same time, launch new learning and development programmes so that people know they matter.

- Take people with you. Letting go of the old world and overcoming fears of the new world is not easy. Focus on hearts and minds – making change in culture and process at the same time, so that people have the tools to do what they now believe is right. Keep talking to them, encouraging dialogue, addressing their concerns, share your own, be their coach.

- Ensuring that the business keeps working. The worst aspect of change can be that the organization grinds to a halt, unsure of its future, employees stop working or at least slow down. This could be the death of the business. Functional managers need to stay focused on today, weaving in new process and behaviours as soon as appropriate.

Phase 4: Sustaining the change. The change must be seen through to completion, sustaining commitment for it, and ensuring that it becomes the new 'business as usual' as quickly as possible.

- Managing the change, with a dedicated change team that is taken out of the 'business as usual' mindset. The programme, built up of many supporting projects, needs active coordination and delivery – actions and resources, budgets and risks. Steering groups need to review progress frequently, making adjustments as required. Sustain the change momentum.

- Develop sustaining mechanisms to reinforce the new ways of working. Introduce a new approach to strategy and decision-making, stating clearly the new priorities and measures of success. Encourage new habits and rituals. Tell the story of how the organization moved from old world to new world, and find reasons to celebrate success.

- Reward the new behaviours by restructuring people's key performance indicators, career progression, capability frameworks, benefit packages, incentives and rewards to reflect and encourage the new behaviours. What gets measured gets done, but what drives an individual's bonus will quickly become their new priority.

- Ensure that the change delivers business impact, a step change in business performance, more effective and efficient ways of working, bringing to life a new brand or competitive position, resulting in a better customer experience. Communicate the success, reinforce the messages of the better world, and keep adjusting and improving.

The changed organization is a compelling place to work. It creates a fresh start to build a new reputation in the outside world, to drive innovation and new levels of service, to change the opinions of analysts and investors, and to shine as a business leader.

Insight 32: MARKS & SPENCER
Bringing a business back from the dead

M&S had fundamentally lost its way. Sales were falling, the share price had dived, the stores were grey and shabby, the advertising tried to tell women that it was okay to be 'big' and that now they could buy 'big' pants especially designed for them, and consumers walked quickly in the other direction.

In 1998, M&S was the success story of British retailing – the first store chain to reach $1 billion profit – and they could seemingly do nothing wrong. However a new breed of retailer was catching up quickly – fast and fashionable, cheap and cheerful, the likes of Top Shop and Next, H&M and Zara were more in tune with the market, with fashion, and offered consumers a better deal.

Blinded by their ego, the old, stuffy M&S – the one with its 'St Michael' brand name; the one with rails upon rails of ladies' trousers in 45 different styles but all in brown or navy; the one where the directors decided which new foods to sell, not consumers; and the one that refused to accept credit cards – looked the other way. Profits fell to $145 million.

In 2004 Philip Green launched an $8 million hostile bid for the company. Stuart Rose, an M&S veteran who had, in more recent years, built his reputation as CEO of the Arcadia Group, had always wanted to run the company. Within a few days his wish was granted and the existing chairman and CEO had been ousted. The next six weeks were a frantic battle, waged mostly in the press, to fend off the bid. Eventually Rose succeeded, stating that he would grow the value of the business way beyond what Green wanted to pay, and now he had to set about doing it.

He found that he needed to change work practices quickly.

Decisions were being made by people with little experience – junior buyers were spending $30–40 million without much control from above. The business was carrying far too much stock, leading to a huge surplus which eventually had to be sold off at a loss. Suppliers were in losing, uneconomical relationships going back many years. Underperforming stores were allowed to continue underperforming. And most frustrating to Rose, a raft of consultants was trying to drive through 31 'strategic projects' and few seemed to be having any impact.

His initial plan was to focus on the core values that had made M&S an icon, but rearticulated for the twenty-first century. He would sell off the financial services arm and buy the Per Una contemporary womenswear brand, which they exclusively sold, from its founder, George Davies. The business was already moving to new high-tech headquarters near Paddington, which Rose pushed through but as more of a catalyst of the change he wanted in his management.

He refined his focus to three areas – product, store environment and service. They had to be fixed, and fast.

He dispensed with all but ten of the 'strategic projects' underway, and handed over responsibility from the consultants to his own managers. He closed the newly opened, ultra-trendy 'Lifestore' concept in Gateshead, and recognized that supply management was probably his biggest challenge. He brought in two former colleagues, Charles Wilson, who would oversee supply chain, IT and property; and Steve Sharp, who would look after marketing, store design and a refresh of the corporate brand. Rose himself took hands-on control of products, pricing and delivery.

'Your M&S' was launched at breakneck speed, a modern, stylish interpretation of the tired brand. Black, lime green and white replaced dark green all over.

The pace of change was phenomenal. Rose met the 30 top suppliers, one by one, agreeing that it was 'change or die' for both of them, and finding new win-win relationships with each one. He opened five global sourcing offices around the world to coordinate sourcing from the most efficient places globally. He had a complete store clear-out, throwing out the mishmash of cardboard signs that cluttered the store, and replaced them with clean, stylish navigation. Twenty per cent of staff were let go, too.

2005 saw a £500 million investment in store refurbishment and a further £800 million soon followed. Some changes were significant and structural. Others were cosmetic and inspired. Black tiles rather than white tiles for the food halls were unconventional, but looked amazing under halogen lighting. One hundred new escalators and twenty miles of new fridges were ordered. Walkways and displays became less structured and more zoned. Stylish black uniforms were introduced. Window models wore black sunglasses, adding a touch of attitude.

Products improved dramatically too – more stylish, more relevant and easier to access. Pricing was positioned at three levels – 'good', 'better' and 'best' – each representing good value.

Service has always been a hallmark of the good old M&S. But pay had fallen from the top quartile to bottom quartile, and they needed to get it back up with the best. Staff clocked on and off as they wished, rather than in regular, simple to roster, patterns. Pay and bonuses were based on years of service rather than performance. Career structures were fragmented and complex and needed simplifying. More accountability was needed on the shop floor. All of this was addressed, alongside a refresh in the basics of customer service – customer first, making eye contact, working as a team.

It was time to tell consumers about the improving M&S. The food business had always been one of the strongest business units, and so initial advertising – almost unheard of in the old M&S – was commissioned to showcase the food. The camera zoomed in on every morsel, and the sensual voiceover could not have been more engaging. It quickly became labelled as 'food porn'. Consumers loved it, as did staff, and investment analysts too. One ad for M&S chocolate puddings drove a 3000% increase in sales.

Rose recognized that he needed to take a step back from some of the decision-making. He needed to get his manages to improve their judgement, their gut feel as well as analysis, and has become much more of a coach and catalyst rather than controlling boss.

One of the initiatives of which he is most proud is his environmental initiative – 'Plan A. Because there is no Plan B.' The £200 million, 100-point plan focuses the business on reducing carbon emissions, avoiding landfill waste, ensuring goods come from sustainable sources, being ethical and supporting the health and well-being of its customers.

As the high-profile, media-smooth Rose frequently reminds people, his most important role as CEO is to be the guardian of the business and leave it in a better condition than he found it.

11.3   TRANSFORMATIONAL LEADERS
Changing yourself to change your business

The entrepreneurial leader is a change agent. He or she recognizes that the only way to sustain growth – to move through the Seven Lives of Business – is to drive regular changes in how people work, and what the business does. The changes are very much embodied in the behaviours and vision of the leader. However, many entrepreneurs fail to realize that as organizations get larger, they need to change too. This can be the greatest barrier to their ambitions.

An effective change programme therefore also requires leadership change – either different leaders, or at least a shift in mindset and behaviour of the existing leaders. This is almost a prerequisite for change. Change agents need to change too.

The most effective way to engage leaders in a personal change is to place it within the business context. As this last track showed, leaders can be so wrapped up in the business and other people that they become blind to their own weaknesses, which can often be the biggest inhibitors of change and growth. If leaders can consider business change and what it will mean for them, then they are far more likely to objectively evaluate themselves, and consider how they might change.

The development of a change programme should therefore embrace the leadership change programme in which leaders 'toggle' between the business and personal challenges and opportunities. Through the facilitated process, the leaders become more open and collaborative, recognizing that they all need to change in order to achieve a collective vision.

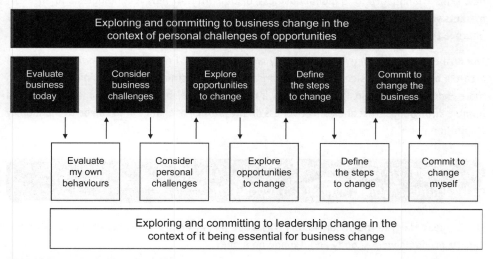

TRANSFORMING LEADERS TO TRANSFORM BUSINESS

Leadership has traditionally been transactional – about decisions and actions – whereas transformational leadership is more about context and change. By encouraging leaders to see the bigger picture – to stop and think about where the business is going, how it needs to change, and their own roles in it – they see that they too have a bigger role to play.

This, of course is not easy. Many traditional leaders are uncomfortable with change, however good it sounds to them when they talk about doing it to others. They don't like exposing their personal sides, admitting to a weakness, exposing their frailties. This is, of course, the only way they will change. It is why ego-driven, chest-beating, macho-talking leaders don't succeed in growth businesses.

A transformational leader recognizes that they need to work in a new way – collaboratively rather than hierarchically, empowering rather than controlling. They might realize they need new skills – languages for a global business, or to learn how new technologies and different markets work. It might even be that they need to get a life – go home earlier, do more sport, improve their diet.

The authentic leader, one who genuinely wants to move their business forwards, wants to create a better world inside and outside, and wants to constantly personally improve, is much more endearing to people. Recognizing their need to change shows them in a more human and humble light, builds trust and collectiveness on the journey of change, and can be tremendously inspirational too.

Insight 33: HAIER
The Chinese worker who led a revolution

The Qingdao Haier Refrigerator Factory was a dump. Its workers were unpaid, its factory smelt bad, its products were shoddy and it made no money.

Zhang Ruimin had worked his way up through the disorderly and demotivated ranks to become a senior manager of the company. In 1984, he convinced Chinese Communist Party officials to let him take control of the struggling business.

Today it is simply Haier, a home appliance giant, and one of China's best known global companies.

Zhang, its transforming CEO, has proved to be one of the world's great leaders and survivors of change. Thanks to his obsession with quality and innovation, Haier has since become the leading producer of white goods in China and the fourth biggest in the world.

In 1984, the future of the company was at stake. It was RMB 1.47 million in debt, it was on its fourth leader within a year, and its 800 staff hadn't been paid for several months. His first action was to borrow money, which he used to pay the workers. It might not seem an enlightened way to get a business out of trouble, but it was much appreciated.

At Chinese New Year he borrowed again to give each worker a gift of five kettles of fish. It gave him a chance. He now had his former colleagues, his people, on side. They believed that it might be possible to turn the business round. He even invested in a new staff bus to replace the truck that used to take workers to the factory each morning. It made them think they had a chance. They were prepared to support their leader; they could see things getting better.

He demanded hard work in return for this goodwill, promising to pay them on time as long as they stuck to his new disciplines. No more half-hearted work. No more stealing company goods. No more urinating on the production line. And those who did continue to abuse his trust were put on probation, denting their pride and shocking their peers.

Zhang knew that he had to lead with confidence if he wanted to build confidence in his people. He recognized the risks he was taking, but as a former worker himself, he knew that gaining the hearts of his people mattered most to making change happen.

Quality improved with motivation, and without significant financial investment he was able to reorganize production processes, reduce costs, and improve productivity. His debts started to ease and he even started to make small amounts of money, which he shared with the workers, and otherwise invested in essential plant and infrastructure.

In 1991 he borrowed again to move production to a new location, with new, standardized production techniques, and enormous capacity to meet what he believed would be exponential future demand. Many thought he was crazy – the business was now profitable, so why seek to make more, when they were happy with what they had?

Zhang had succeeded because he could take the perspective of his people. He knew from the worst times, and through change, how they felt. Now he was also demonstrating a highly commercial perspective, one that still seemed alien to his colleagues who had lived through the Cultural Revolution.

In 1993, the Chinese economy really took off. Haier was well-placed to seize the new opportunities, meet the new aspirations of a changing society and target markets worldwide. He has embraced the latest production methods, the best technologies, cutting edge design and direct channel sales and support too. Today, many talk of Haier as the Chinese version of GE, an Asian powerhouse, the Samsung of white goods.

Zhang attributes his leadership style to the ability to energize each of his people. With this goal, he focuses his leadership on giving people room to learn and grow, encouraging flat and cross-functional project working, empowering people to make their own decisions and develop their own ideas. At the same time he ensures that rewards are team-based, rather than individual, related to project performance rather than hierarchy or experience.

In the outside world, Zhang recognizes that market leadership is not only achieved through people, but through serious innovation. His 'three season product innovation' cycle focuses on product improvement for the existing market, technology-driven developments over a three-year horizon and basic research that drives longer-term breakthroughs.

Perhaps, as you might expect from our man of the people, Zhang identifies management talent as Haier's most important differentiator. Not necessarily highly qualified graduates, but people who can drive change from a human perspective and who could also take a dilapidated, debt-ridden factory and turn it into another RMB 100 billion business.

Delivering high performance today and tomorrow

'Intellectual capital is the sum of everything everybody in a company knows that gives it a competitive edge'

Thomas Stewart

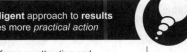

A more **intelligent** approach to **results** that embraces more *practical action*	A more **imaginative** approach to **results** that embraces more *radical ideas*
• Short-term focus on attracting and retaining the best customers.	• Long-term focus on shaping the best markets to your advantage.
• Sustaining growth through customer and portfolio management.	• Creating value by unlocking the potential of intangible assets.
• Managing the performance inputs for efficiency and optimization.	• Managing the performance outputs to maximize business value.
• Managing delivery to ensure promises are delivered consistently.	• Managing perceptions of the business reputation and potential.
• Using metrics and controls to focus the business on high performance.	• Using success and rewards to inspire the business to high performance.
• Harnessing the value drivers to focus resources for most impact.	• Staying true to the core values to focus on what makes you different.
• Delivering results for shareholders short- and long-term.	• Sharing value with stakeholders as a dynamic value exchange.

The twenty-first century business is largely intangible.

Measuring and managing the performance of an intangible business is different. Quarterly results are easily manipulated and even financial accounts do not reflect the real value of the business. This makes strategy and decision-making, management and evaluation more difficult.

To understand the 'invisible business' we need to return to 'value'.

The business seeks to create economic value – to generate a return on investment, beyond the cost of that investment. It grows and sustains this value by working with a range of stakeholders – shareholders, customers, employees and others – and, when successful, shares value with them.

The value of a business, or 'enterprise' to be accurate, reflects its potential to generate cash in the future. This potential is influenced by how it is likely to grow, how quickly, and the likelihood of this happening. A fast-growing, reliable business will be very valuable.

The 'enterprise value' of a business is the business's own calculation of the net present value of the sum of its future cash flows, adjusted for the risks involved in delivering them. The 'market value' is the stock market's own version of this, based on its perception of the company. A company that manages its investor relations well will find agreement between the values. An 'undervalued' business needs to convince investors, an 'overvalued' business should caution investors so as not to disappoint them with the actual future performance.

12.1 BUILDING THE INVISIBLE BUSINESS
The value of today's business is in the intangibles

In the past, companies were largely tangible – they were manufacturing businesses which owned factories and equipment, making and selling definitive products. The future potential was simple to estimate, based on how many products could be sold, and the value of the plant.

Today's business is based on its brains rather than its brawn.

The most valuable assets in a business are no longer the hard things but the softer attributes, the more subtle or intellectual aspects of business that are hard to copy – ideas, knowledge, brands, relationships, design, patents. Non-core activities such as manufacturing, systems and logistics can be done in partnership with others and are therefore less valuable.

In his book, *Intellectual Capital*, Thomas Stewart defines three main categories of intellectual capital, the building blocks that collectively represent the intangible assets:

- *Human capital* – the talent that lies in your employees – the knowledge, skills, experience and ideas inside people's heads.

- *Customer capital* – the relationships you have with customers – and the positive reputation and advocacy they have for you.

- *Structural capital* – the retained knowledge in the organization, in its databases and manuals – technical data, process maps, product patents and publications.

To understand the value of these assets, we need to quantify what likely 'uplift' will be gained in future performance due to the ownership and application of each. For example, what are the additional revenue, margin and reduced costs due to having long-term relationships with key customers rather than having to continually attract new customers?

In accounting terms, the international standard 'IFRS 3' defines an asset as a controlled 'resource' expected to provide future economic benefits.

It goes on to define an 'intangible' asset as such a resource which is non-monetary, non-physical and identifiable (meaning that they can be separated; for example, sold off, transferred or licensed). Of course, this definition excludes a wide range of other attributes – such as people and their talents – which are often included in a more general definition.

The International Financial Reporting Standards define five categories of intangible asset:

- Marketing-related (including trademarks, domain names, uniformed dress, etc.).

- Customer-related (including customer lists, orders, contracts, relationships, etc.).

- Contract-based (including contracts for services, leases, rights and licensing, etc.).

- Technology-based (including patented technology, software, databases, etc.).

- Artistic-related (including books, magazines, music, lyrics, photos, video, etc.).

'Intangible assets' now account for around $22.2 trillion, 61% of the overall value of the world's quoted companies, according to the *Global Intangibles Tracker* published annually by Brand Finance.

And the intangible proportion of a business' value is increasing. In the last five years, these companies – which represent a total of $36.2 trillion in terms of enterprise value – have grown by $9.4 trillion, with 64% of that growth due to intangibles. In some sectors, such as media (91%) and pharmaceuticals (89%), it is virtually all intangible. Similarly, in certain geographies – such as Switzerland and India – business is almost completely composed of this 'soft stuff'.

As an example, consider the acquisition of Gillette by Proctor & Gamble in October 2005. P&G completed the largest ever acquisition in the consumer goods sector by paying $53.4 billion for Gillette, which generated profits of $2.5 billion. The preliminary post-purchase allocation is shown below:

Gillette	$ billion
Purchase price	53.4
Tangible fixed assets	4.5
Intangible assets	29.7
Brands	25.6
Patents and technology	2.7
Customer relationships	1.4
Working capital	0.6
Long-term liabilities	(16.2)
Residual goodwill	34.9

Source: Brand Finance

An invisible business, one where the majority of the assets is intangible, requires a different form of management from traditional, physical organizations. Investment should be focused on these intangible assets rather than traditional buildings or stock, even if they are harder to see and measure. This increases the need to measure them.

Each organization must find its own ways to unlock and apply these assets, relevant to their goals, and distinctive from others. Owning the assets is no guarantee of their effective use.

Intangible assets need to be addressed together. Their value can rarely be locked in isolation. Branding is an example of the collective application of assets. They are cross-functional tools, requiring collaboration and collective responsibility – from product innovations or customer relationships.

Human capital has established the most sophisticated measurement and reporting techniques, championed by the HR department. Other assets need more dedicated management. Customer capital can be the most significant asset, but is also the most fragile. Reputations and relationships can take years to build, but can quickly become unravelled.

More generally, value-based management will apply these ideas to every aspect of running the business – for example, ensuring that strategy is focused on the long-term value creating activities, and that people are measured and rewarded on their long-term performance. An executive bonus scheme, for example, that ties business leaders into the 3- or 5-year value growth of the business, overcomes the urge to take short-cuts and forget the future, whilst also retaining your best people.

Insight 34: GREEN & BLACK'S
The luxurious chocolate with accelerated growth

Green & Black's makes the most mouth-watering, organic chocolate you have ever tasted – and epitomizes the new triple-bottom line focus of the enlightened business, one that delivers sustained profitable growth for its shareholders, but also measures its impact on society and the environment too. Yet, however 'green' you are, consumers still want a great product – so if you can make these factors work together, the results can be staggering.

'I was born on a farm in Nebraska. I learnt the fundamentals of business as a paperboy, for the *Omaha World Herald*. In 1966, before moving to England, my Uncle Floyd offered me a deal on 1000 acres of rich riverside land in Iowa and a 700 head beef feedlot if I would join him in the farming business after I graduated from Wharton. Instead, like many of my contemporaries, I discovered the macrobiotic diet and developed an awareness of the unsustainability of the way that food and farming was going. I didn't want to be part of the problem and I aspired to help bring about the solution.'

It was 1967, Britain was at the peak of flower power, and Craig Sams arrived in London to set up a macrobiotic restaurant in London. Two years later, a retail store, and another year later he launched the Whole Earth brand of brown rice and macrobiotic foods. A wholefood bakery followed with organic peanut butter and jams – he typically sought out finding healthy and sustainable alternatives to the foods he loved most. Most of all, he loved chocolate.

In 1991 he was sent a sample of organic dark chocolate from Africa. His wife, the environment columnist Josephine Fairley, found the half-eaten bar on his desk and sampled some for herself. The intense flavour was unique and unlike anything she had tasted before. She was convinced other chocolate lovers would appreciate it too and they set about making the world's first organic chocolate.

The final product was a high-quality, bittersweet dark chocolate bar, packed with 70% cocoa solids made with organic cocoa beans grown in Togo, West Africa. It was organic and fair-trade, the legacy of a French foreign aid project to stop environmental degradation in Togo's highlands.

They needed a name. They wanted something that sounded English and with heritage, like their childhood favourites such as Barker & Dobson. They eventually seized on green to symbolize organic, and black to represent the rich, dark chocolate.

Sales rose gradually, although it was still very much a niche brand serving a narrow customer base. It was initially embraced by chefs who valued the intense flavour in their cooking and by health food addicts who went out of their way to find 'good' products. Its distribution was therefore mainly through small, independent stores and it was very much a chocoholic's secret.

Eventually, the business recognized that it needed to do something different to grow, but without compromising its values. The insight they gained from consumer research was that whilst 'organic' products – which their marketing and packaging focused on – was appreciated, it was the flavour that mattered much more. They switched emphasis from green to black. The brand was repositioned as the most luxurious, most intensely dark chocolate around.

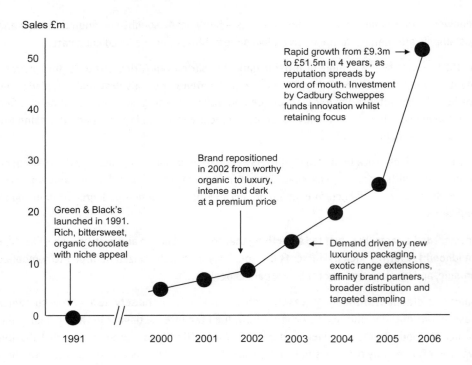

Sales £m

Rapid growth from £9.3m to £51.5m in 4 years, as reputation spreads by word of mouth. Investment by Cadbury Schweppes funds innovation whilst retaining focus

Brand repositioned in 2002 from worthy organic to luxury, intense and dark at a premium price

Green & Black's launched in 1991. Rich, bittersweet, organic chocolate with niche appeal

Demand driven by new luxurious packaging, exotic range extensions, affinity brand partners, broader distribution and targeted sampling

1991 2000 2001 2002 2003 2004 2005 2006

Growth was phenomenal. The insight was profound. From 2002 to 2005, sales grew from £4.5 million to £29 million – at 544% it became the UK's fastest growing consumer food brand. The brand could more than hold its weight against the much larger, more widely advertised competitors. Through word of mouth, eye-catching repackaging, clever advertising and targeted sponsorships, the brand took off, and by mid-2006 held 7.4% share of the UK chocolate market, whilst the average selling price rose from £1.19 to £1.54.

In 2005, Green & Black's became part of confectionary giant Cadbury Schweppes, rewarding its founders and investors with a £25 million return on their passion and perseverance.

The chocolate company is still run as an independent business – with its own small, funky offices near London's Waterloo Station, caring entrepreneurship, and with Sams as chairman. The parent company keeps its distance, providing support in terms of new packaging techniques, for example, and the financial resources to enter new markets around the world, but otherwise the business stays true to its original principles in respect of organics, fair trade and corporate social responsibility. Has Green & Black's sold out to the big commercial world? As Sams says:

> 'Some people have said that ultimately we will have engineered a sort of reverse takeover, on a cultural level, of the world's largest confectionery company. Remember that Cadbury's were founded on the Quaker belief that a steaming cup of cocoa would help wean the working classes off beer and gin. There are still no pubs in Bourneville, the town they built as their corporate headquarters, manufacturing base and for housing their workers!'

12.2 MANAGING FOR HIGH PERFORMANCE
Intangibles require a different style of management

The old adage that 'what gets measured gets done' is still true, and even more so 'what gets rewarded gets done'.

Targets, metrics and rewards should not, therefore, be considered the end point, but the starting point.

The wrong performance indicators, an unreasonable performance target, or a badly balanced 'Balanced Scorecard' (measuring people, customer, financial and improvement factors) will drive business in the wrong direction. Strategic decisions will be based on false criteria, investments will not deliver optimal returns, people will become demotivated by their inability to hit targets and investors will lose confidence.

Get the right measures, then you can make the right decisions, people and resources are focused in the best places for high returns, and everyone can share in the rewards.

Market share, for example, is increasingly meaningless, depending entirely on how you define your boundaries – you could have a 100% share of one market and a 0.1% share of another. As customers' needs change, and market profitability varies, markets are not equal. Rarely are two companies in the same market – P&G and Unilever might be big competitors in some sectors or segments, but irrelevant to each other in others.

There is, of course, a better way, as Diageo demonstrated, in using what some call the 'ultimate measure' of business performance – the total long-term return to investors (in both the form of capital growth and dividends) – measured across sectors, against a group of peers.

This gives the big picture and a unifying goal, but is less practical in enabling day-to-day decision-making. Developing a business scorecard, the right portfolio of metrics should be based firstly on the 'value drivers' of the business. These will differ by company, but in simple terms there are:

- **Inputs** – such as operating costs, headcount, and time to market – factors that can be managed directly because they relate to decisions and actions.

- **Throughputs** – such as productivity, sales growth, customer retention – factors that are direct consequences of operations and can quickly be influenced.

- **Outputs** – such as profitability, return on investment and share price – factors that are more complex to influence, but are clearly driven by the previous metrics.

Another dimension is to consider the implications of short- and long-term actions and effects in the organization – a sales promotion will give an immediate return, building a new brand will take longer for its impact to be seen, investing in new product development will take even longer.

Short- and long-term both matter – which is why a simple comparison of this year's costs and revenues is a rather simplistic way of looking at business – particularly when most of the value lies in intangible assets, which typically deliver long-term returns.

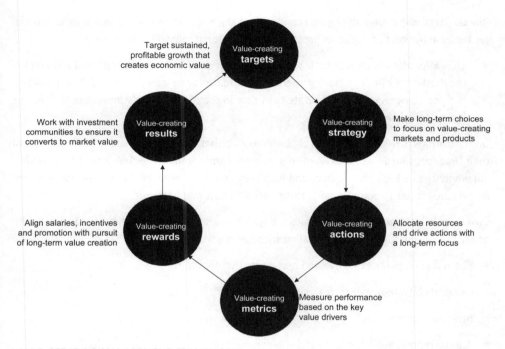

VALUE-CREATING MANAGEMENT FRAMEWORK

'Value' provides the answer – calculating the sum of likely future cash flows, embracing both the short- and long-term. Value-based decision-making therefore becomes crucial to deciding:

- ***Strategically*** – which are the right businesses and brands, markets, products and customers to focus on for the longer-term? Out of the business portfolio, which businesses 'create value' and which 'destroy value'?

One business might have strong sales and market share, and even operating profits look good, yet because the cost of capital is greater, every additional sale will destroy value.

- *   ***Operationally*** – what is the most effective allocation of budgets of people and resources in the short-term? Whilst long-term performance matters, the markets might still be immature, and the business needs to generate cash flow in the meantime to survive, and to fund the longer-term investments.

One of the most perverse attributes of boardrooms is that they typically spend less than 10% of their time focusing on where 90% of their success comes from. Little time is spent on discussing where the revenue comes from and how they could be improved, before the conversation quickly progresses to operational performance and cost management.

Customer-related performance metrics are typically more informative about the future health of the business, whilst most financial metrics look backwards.

- Board meetings for executive and non-executive directors.

- Quarterly business reviews for managers and staff.

- Investor relations briefings to analysts and media.

- Annual reports available to all stakeholders.

Imagine the CEO standing up at the next board meeting, or the first page of the annual report, with customers and brands being the focus of commentary, their current performance, and the investments that are currently been made to secure and enhance future results.

This might seem an obvious and engaging place to start in reviewing a business, yet the vast majority will start with costs, processes and supply chains.

One retailer was amazed at the impact it made when it went into the investor briefing and started describing the financial impact of getting new fashion from catwalk to clothes rail in two weeks less than anybody else on the high street, and the incremental sales and margins that this drives.

Of course, at the end of the day, business is not a machine and performance does not come out of a calculator. Business needs to bring together internal and external insights, financial and non-financial information, business and personal beliefs in order to make the right decisions.

Insight 35: PORSCHE
Small in stature, big on impact

'The mouse and the elephant' is how *Fortune* magazine described the tiny sports car maker Porsche, in comparison to its much larger cousin, Volkswagen. The elephant, which has the mouse as its largest shareholder, is 15 times larger in revenue. However, the mighty mouse has superb profit margins (dwarfing the elephant's seven times over) – the best in the world.

Ferdinand Porsche grew up in Bohemia, in Vratislavice, which is now part of the Czech Republic. After learning his business as technical director at Daimler-Benz, he left the company having failed to convince the company to make small cars. At 55, he started his own design firm for all sorts of vehicles, and became a charismatic although hot-tempered entrepreneur. In 1934, he was asked to develop a cheap and reliable family car by the German regime. He called it the 'people's car', the Volkswagen. In 1948, Porsche launched its first independent car, the 356. Made in Stuttgart, Germany, it was distinguished by its aluminium frame, rear-mounted engine and roaring high speeds.

In 1954, Porsche, now run by its founder's son, also called Ferdinand, launched its first racing car, the 550, and began to create a global reputation. The 911 followed shortly after in 1964. Designed by the founder's grandson, Bultzi, it became a design legend and still lies at the heart of the range today. In 1972, when the Piech family bought a share of the company, Bultzi left to form an independent design studio, 'Porsche Design'.

Porsche's expensive cars made it vulnerable to global economic health, and it struggled in the late Eighties and early Nineties. The company worked its way through many different leaders, with much in-fighting between the Porsche and Piech families. However in 1993, 38-year-old Wendelin Wiedeking became CEO, and has stayed there ever since.

Wendelin Wiedeking is passionate about cars, having learned to drive at the age of 11 and claiming to have made over 1500 model cars during his childhood. At the time, Porsche didn't make that many more, around 15,000 a year. He quickly made his mark. Using his production expertise he brought more focus to the business, and sales and the brand's reputation quickly improved.

He believed in clarity and direction, in openness and commitment. He sent his managers to Japan to study Toyota's lean production methods. He slashed overhead costs, laid off management and introduced new models. In 1996, he launched the Boxster, and a year later, an all new, liquid-cooled 911. Meanwhile, all around him, competitors like Jaguar and Lamborghini, Alfa Romeo and Aston Martin were being gobbled up by the big car makers like Ford, Fiat and GM. Porsche was determined to stay independent.

'Size alone is not a prerequisite for survival or success,' Wiedeking famously reminded everyone.

Today, Porsche is the high performance benchmark of every automotive business. Whilst the brand with the Stuttgart black horse (the same as Ferrari's) in its logo is by no means the largest company in the industry – it's the 34th largest car manufacturer in the world – it delivers some of the best returns to shareholders. With 12,000 employees producing around 100,000 cars every year, Porsche delivered $1.7 billion profit on sales of $9.1 billion in 2006. The profit margin of 19.2% is the highest in the industry, compared for example to Toyota's 6.9% and BMW at 5.9%.

	Porsche	Volkswagen
Employees	11,400	325,000
Cars produced	102,000	57,000,000
Revenue	$9.1 billion	$132 billion
Net profit margin	19.2%	2.6%

Source: Fortune, 2006

The comparison to Volkswagen, however, is much more significant. Not just financially, but because it reflects the fortunes of two companies – one big and one small, both admired as successful brands – which have become entwined by family connections.

Ferdinand Piech, another grandson of the Porsche founder, became CEO of Volkswagen in 1993, and after a decade stepped up to be chairman. Whilst he is dedicated to the success of the company that produces the enormously successful Golf and rejuvenated flower-powered Beetle, his family – the Porsches and Piechs – own 100% of Porsche, which makes him Wiedeking's boss.

Most significantly, in 2005 Porsche took a €15 billion stake in Volkswagen for 30% of the business, and became the largest shareholder. Wiedeking took a seat on Volkswagen's board and is determined to introduce a new energy, and in particular new production ideas, into the underperforming – as he sees it – business. You can imagine the tension between the two men, both with vast fortunes and reputations at stake.

Wiedeking, however, is relaxed about the relationship and future. In fact he is most interested in the performance of his potato farm and his small hand-made shoes business. He is Germany's highest paid executive; he has a formidable reputation in the car-making world; and he is bursting with ideas for the future, to drive up the performance of both companies.

12.3 SEARCHING FOR THE EDGE
A little bit of magic that makes all the difference

Extraordinary results rarely come out of a formula. As with Einstein and Picasso, Jobs and Buffett, there is typically something unusual that drives them. Perhaps some of the 'quirks' of the best performing companies will inspire you to dare to deliver:

- *Talent Shows* – the traditional interview process is less concerned about your qualifications and more interested in whether you can sing, dance or perform (First Direct).

- *Group Hugs* – start the day with a song, a joke, a hug or a challenge; everyone together, same time, every morning; and it also means that people are rarely late (UPS).

- *Graffiti Walls* – let the walls become the voices and minds of your people, to express their views and ideas, their words and pictures, uncontrolled and instant (3M).

- *Silver Networks* – keep in touch with retired staff, tapping into their capabilities and contacts, time and experience: give them a laptop rather than a gold watch when they go (Intel).

- *The Street* – bring the town to your people, from supermarkets to dry cleaners, dentists and fitness centres, saving time and making their lives a little easier (GSK).

- *Catalyst Kit* – all the materials, gadgets and tools you need to stimulate new ideas and articulate innovative solutions anytime, anywhere (IDEO).

- *Corporate Fool* – play the devil's advocate with your best ideas, be ready to challenge every decision and action, and recognize it as a positive activity (Google).

- *More Complaints* – encourage complaints, immediately or by email/phone, the quicker you can solve the problem, the more likely you are to retain the customer and learn for next time (British Airways).

- *Extreme Measures* – obsessively measure yourself against the very best of the competition in each thing that you do, not just direct competitors (Ford).

- *Phone the Boss* – demonstrate that you really do care about what customers think by publishing your home phone number on your business website, although few will ever use it (Midshires).

- *Beat the Plan* – if frontline teams can do their jobs cheaper or faster than planned, then share the gain with them: put a bonus in their pay packet, or let them go home early (Whole Foods).

- *Action Meetings* – don't let review meetings become nice rubber-stamping exercises; make them no-holds-barred debates and innovation sessions (P&G).

- *Team Bonuses* – encourage collaboration rather trying to measure each hour and every action of individual people, and instigate bonuses based only on collective results (Egon Zehnder).

- *Peer Pressure* – who knows who would make the best team leader? Well, the team, of course, so let peers rather than superiors decide who should be boss (Pret a Manger).

- *Value Sharing* – earning a stake in the business through high performance, encouraging equity rather than profit share, building ownership by your best people (Microsoft).

But the edge is really about you.

Whilst we have focused largely on the business attributes of a marketing genius, performance ultimately comes from people, and an inspired individual in business derives that energy from all aspects of their life and well-being.

Paula Radcliffe, the world record holder for the marathon, uses the analogy of five balls to reflect on her unbelievable success in obliterating the competition in her first three marathons, knocking almost four minutes off the previous record time. She pushed the boundaries to the limit, training 150 miles per week, lifting weights well beyond her own, jumping into an ice cold bath after each run to help stimulate her blood flow. Yet all this seemed wasted when she failed to finish the 2004 Olympic Marathon in Athens.

In trying to rationalize her excellence, but misfortune, she mused that life is about juggling five balls in the air. They are health, family, friends, integrity and career. However these balls are not all the same; the important thing to remember is that the career ball is made of rubber but the others are more fragile.

You can take more risks with the rubber ball. You may try to throw it through higher and higher hoops because if you do drop it, it will eventually bounce back. Normally, this ball does not suffer long-term damage. The other four balls need to be looked after more carefully. If you drop one of these it will be damaged and it may even shatter.

In sport, athletes constantly take risks with that career ball, throwing it higher and higher, pushing themselves into the unknown to get an edge on their competitors, to strive for excellence, to realise their potential.

In business, it is no different. Indeed, Brian Dyson, the CEO of Coca-Cola Enterprises, uses the same five balls analogy to inspire his marketers to greater things. He urges his people to recognize and achieve that balance in themselves as a route to achieving personal and marketing excellence. He encourages them:

'Don't undermine your worth by comparing yourself with others. It is because we are different that each of us is special. Don't set your goals by what other people deem important. Only you know what is best for you.

'Don't take for granted the things closest to your heart. Cling to them as you would your life, for without them, life is meaningless.

'Don't let your life slip through your fingers by living in the past or for the future. By living your life one day at a time, you live all the days of your life.

'Don't give up when you still have something to give. Nothing is really over until the moment you stop trying.

'Don't be afraid to admit that you are less than perfect. It is this fragile thread that binds us to each other.

'Don't be afraid to encounter risks. It is by taking chances that we learn how to be brave.

'Don't shut love out of your life by saying it's impossible to find. The quickest way to receive love is to give it; the fastest way to lose love is to hold it too tightly; and the best way to keep love is to give it wings.

'Don't run through life so fast that you forget not only where you've been, but also where you are going. Don't forget, a person's greatest emotional need is to feel appreciated.

'Don't be afraid to learn. Knowledge is weightless, a treasure you can always carry easily.

'Don't use time or words carelessly. Neither can be retrieved.

'Life is a journey to be savoured each step of the way.'

Radcliffe, for one, has used the story of the five balls in good times and bad – to maintain a sense of balance and humility whilst all the world went crazy about her stunning world record-breaking performances, and to put failure into perspective and to pick herself up again, in her case by rebuilding her reputation only months later by winning the New York City Marathon, and the next year becoming World Champion.

Insight 36: BERKSHIRE HATHAWAY
A final word from the sage of Omaha

He played the ukulele, sang with dancing fruits and appeared in a spoof interview with an NBA basketball star. It was even better than last year, when he had appeared in a home-made version of *The Wizard of Oz*. Every year is different, but loyal investors, global economists and the simply curious all make their annual pilgrimage to the shabby theatre in the centre of Omaha, Nabraska. He calls it 'the Woodstock for capitalists'.

Warren Buffett followed his entertaining performance by fielding questions from his shareholders. This was, after all, a formal event – the annual meeting of Berkshire Hathaway. For six hours the 76-year-old billionaire and his even older business partner, Charlie Munger, addressed a diverse range of internal and external issues before a crowd of roughly 28,000 – everything from the rise of private equity deals, the opportunities of China and Russia, to plans for his death.

The so-called Oracle of Omaha is chairman of the board of Berkshire Hathaway – which has averaged a phenomenal 25% annual return to its shareholders – for the last 25 years. Every share bought for $175 in 1978 is now worth about $110,000.

In the early days, Buffett focused on long-term investments in publicly quoted companies, but more recently he has turned to buying whole companies. He now owns a diverse range of businesses ranging from confectionery to jewellery, newspapers to encyclopaedias, home furnishings to vacuum cleaners, beer to executive jets, and uniforms to footwear.

Berkshire Hathaway began its charmed life as a clothing manufacturer, founded in 1839 by Oliver Chase as the Valley Falls Company in Valley Falls, Rhode Island. In 1929 the company merged with Berkshire Fine Spinning Associates of Massachusetts, creating a $120 million textile business, although it struggled to break even. In 1962, Buffett began buying shares in the company, and after some clashes with the owning family, he soon had enough to seize control. Whilst retaining the core business (until 1985), he diversified into insurance in 1967 by acquiring the National Indemnity Company and the Government Employees Insurance Company, which forms the core of his insurance operations today. It also generates the capital required for all his other investments.

Buffett issued an 'Owner's Manual' to all Berkshire Hathaway's shareholders in which he set down 13 owner-related principles that he hoped would help owners understand the business and its managerial approach. The full manual can be downloaded from this book's website. Here, summarized, are some of the more profound extracts:

> 'Although our form is corporate, our attitude is partnership ... We think of our shareholders as partners, whilst Charlie and I think of ourselves as managing partners ... we do not think of the company as the owner of our assets, but as the conduit through which shareholders own them ... We hope you don't just think you own a piece of paper whose price wriggles around daily, a candidate for sale at any time ... but as something you expect to own indefinitely, like a farm that belongs to your family.'

> 'Most of our directors have the majority of their net worth invested in the company. We eat our cooking. Charlie's family has 90% of its net worth in Berkshire shares. I have 99%. Whilst many of our relatives – my sisters and cousins – have done similarly ... We feel totally comfortable with this eggs-in-one-basket situation because Berkshire owns a wide variety of truly extraordinary businesses ... We can't promise you results, but we can guarantee that your financial fortunes will move in lockstep with our own.'

> 'Our long-term economic goal is to maximize Berkshire's average annual rate of gain in intrinsic business value on a per share basis ... Our preference would be to reach this goal by owning businesses that generate cash and earn above average returns on capital ... Our second choice is to own parts of similar, wonderful businesses, attained through the purchase of shares by our insurance subsidiary businesses ... Overall Berkshire and its shareholders benefit from a sinking stock market – don't panic or mourn – it's good news for us.'

Examples of Berkshire's shareholdings in other businesses (as at 31 December 2006) include:

	Ownership	Market value	Earnings growth
American Express	12.6%	$9.2 billion	18%
Coca-Cola	8.6%	$9.7 billion	9%
Wells Fargo	6.5%	$7.8 billion	8%
Proctor and Gamble	3.2%	$6.4 billion	11%

Source: Berkshire Hathaway

Buffett describes the CEOs of the companies that he invests in as the people he admires most – people like Ken Chenault, Jeff Immelt and A.G. Lafley – but he doesn't think he could do the job that they do. 'I wouldn't enjoy many of the duties that come with their positions – meetings, speeches, foreign travel, and government relations'.

He says, 'For me, Ronald Reagan had it right when he said "It's probably true that hard work never killed anyone – but why take the chance?"' So he takes what he calls the 'easy' route – sitting back and working with the great managers who run the shows. He sees his task as to cheer them on, whilst shaping his own business and making the right investment decisions.

His investment strategies, like his personal values, are decidedly off-beat. He rejects the complex trickery of day-traders and hedge funds, instead founding his business choices on common sense, information and intuition – famously saying he didn't understand technology, and still prefers to avoid investing in it. His knack of spotting undervalued companies with low overheads and high growth potential is renowned. He buys them on the cheap and watches them grow.

As his ukulele playing and folksy humour demonstrate, he is no ordinary billionaire investor or chairman. He still lives in the grey Stucco house that he bought in his twenties for $31,000. He dines on burgers and Coke, plays bridge with Bill Gates, and frequently quotes Mae West. He doesn't use the Internet, and only recently acquired a mobile phone. His only extravagance is his fondness for luxury air travel and his Gulfstream IV-SP jet.

For all this eccentricity and earthiness, he is one of the world's most respected business leaders, and his annual letters to shareholders are read by millions for their insights and inspiration. His personal wealth is estimated at $52.4 billion, according to *Forbes* magazine, making him one of the world's top three richest people, depending on the rise and fall of the world's stock markets. He did however, recently pledge much of his fortune to charity, donating $30 billion to the Bill & Melinda Gates Foundation.

He ended his 2007 letter to shareholders on a personal note:

> 'Charlie and I are extraordinarily lucky. We were born in America, had terrific parents who saw that we got good educations, have enjoyed wonderful families and great health, and came equipped with a business "gene" that allows us to prosper in a manner hugely disproportionate to other people who contribute as much or more to our society's well-being. Moreover, we have long had jobs that we love, in which we are helped every day in countless ways by talented and cheerful associates. No wonder we tap-dance to work. But nothing is more fun for us than getting together with our shareholder-partners at Berkshire's annual meeting – our annual Woodstock of Capital-ists. We'll see you there.
>
> Warren E. Buffett, Chairman of the Board.'

The Genius Lab

The Genius Lab

'I never did a day's work in my life, it was all fun'

Thomas Edison

the
genius
lab

Genius Tools

Genius Books

Genius Live

Genius Works

The pursuit of high performance involves a multitude of challenges, whether you are the leader of a small or large business. If we take one definition of genius as the ability to hold two conflicting ideas in your head at the same time, then you probably feel like you need to be a genius many times over.

From entrepreneurship and growth, strategy and innovation, customers and propositions, to change and performance, we have explored the essential challenges for business.

I truly believe that a small business can take as many ideas away as a large business, and whilst they might seem like big company ideas, smaller organizations can often make them happen quicker and better, to seize an advantage over lumbering giants who struggle to turn their organizations around.

THE MAKING OF GENIUS
How can you become a 'business genius'?

We started off by exploring genius as the four balances – at a personal level, bringing together left and right brain thinking, radical ideas and practical action; at an organization level, connecting future back with now forward, outside in and inside out approaches. In each track we have considered how these balances can deliver more intelligent and imaginative approaches to business.

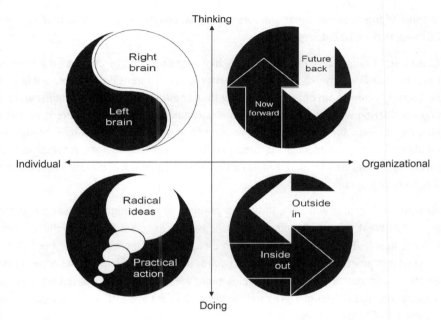

THE 4 DIMENSIONS OF 'GENIUS'

However it is worth going slightly further back to remind ourselves of how 'genius' has delivered extraordinary results in other walks of life, and the more fundamental approaches that these world-changing people bravely embraced. Geniuses are generally:

1   **Original.** A genius starts with an open mind, uncluttered by conventions, taking new perspectives, deconstructing a problem then reassembling it in better ways. Many great ideas have been rejected because they don't fit with conventional thinking, denounced as impractical or 'ahead of their time'. The Swiss watchmakers who rejected the idea that timepieces could be built through electronics rather springs and gears are one example,

or think of the floppy disk manufacturers who just couldn't see the disruptive coming of CDs and, in turn, USB drives.

2   **Conscious.** A genius has an exceptionally high state of consciousness, a greater awareness of what is going on, and look for patterns like a forensic detective. Some of the best insights come from observation rather than enquiry, like an anthropologist watching and considering what is happening. This is particularly useful when there is no current language or logic for explaining the phenomena or behaviour. Alexander Fleming found mould on his exposed medical cultures, just like many other doctors, yet instead of just throwing it away, he considered what caused it, an observational curiosity that led to the discovery of penicillin.

3   **Analytical.** A genius will work through a problem or idea progressively and rigorously, as well as creatively, challenging the mathematical or scientific logic. Whilst a genius reaches new levels or dimensions through creative leaps, there is still the need to make sense of it in practical terms. This often requires a pure mental logic as the current mathematical formulae or scientific principles might well themselves be based on some false assumption. 'Breakthroughs' are rarely achieved by derivation of convention, but it does require proof of the new concept.

4   **Creative.** A genius is always open to possibility, seeking to solve problems by hypothesis, taking a mental leap and then seeing whether it proves to be true or not. Einstein often used hypotheses to jump out of his mathematical derivations, to conjure a possibility that he could then seek to prove or disprove. Logical derivation will take you down certain avenues of thinking dependent on where you start. Constantly having the curiosity and confidence to ask 'what if?' rather than seeking safety in what is close or known.

5   **Dual.** A genius can think in parallel, to tolerate apparent ambiguities, to bring together opposites and connect the unconnected. New solutions are often contradictory, either with conventions, or within itself, and indeed F. Scott Fitzgerald's definition of what makes

a first rate mind is 'the ability to hold two opposing ideas at the same time'. Niels Bohr, the Danish physicist, imagined how light could be thought of as both particles and waves. This seemed entirely contradictory, yet his discovery of 'photons', intangible particles that behave like waves, led to his 'theory of complementarity'. Similarly da Vinci combined the sound of a bell with the ripples when a stone hits water, to arrive at the idea that sound travels in waves.

6   **Holistic.** A genius can take a broader perspective to see the holistic problem in context of its environment and piecing together its many parts. Einstein brought together different strands of our natural world, uniting apparently diverse attributes such as energy, mass and speed of light. Picasso's abstract work sought to represent much more than a simple image. His works built personality, context, feelings and vision into his observations. He sought to provoke more holistic and deeper thought, rather than simply replicate what he saw. Indeed the ability to see the bigger picture, or to fill in the spaces, can often mean that a genius 'sees what everybody else can see, but thinks what nobody has thought.'

7   **Prolific.** A genius searches for many solutions – rather than just finding one – building on or challenging each of them, constantly searching for a more perfect solution. A genius has a constantly active and fertile mind; the sheer quantity of their output can be intimidating, which is why it sometimes takes some years to identify the best from the also-ran. Mozart wrote 600 pieces of music; Bach one every week even when sick. Einstein published 148 papers, although he's best known for one of his earliest. The enormous work rate of Picasso in his final years was initially denounced as the senility of an old man trying to maximize his legacy; however, many years later we actually recognize this most productive period as also the one that was the most creative.

8   **Pragmatic.** A genius recognizes that ideas and solutions are of little use in the abstract, that the theory or concept must be made real, that it must practical and useful. A genius is constantly thinking, exploring, inventing and discovering. However, genius is only genius

if it can be put to practical action and can add value in some way. Edison held 1093 US patents, more than anyone else to this day, and demanded of himself one minor invention every 10 days, and a major one every 6 months. Similarly most successful entrepreneurs will have many failures behind them before they succeed, most innovators will develop far more new ideas than see commercial success.

9   *Visual.* A genius is able to express their ideas more clearly – typically visually, through diagrams and analogy – to make sense of complexity in comprehensible ways. The creative explosion of the Renaissance was marked by a multitude of drawings and diagrams, as Galileo and da Vinci graphically illustrated their revolutionary ideas. These captured people's imagination far more than words or numbers. Pictures enable connections to be made more quickly, concepts to be demonstrated far more easily, and the holistic system to be explained.

10 *Belief.* A genius must have the inner strength, belief and confidence to stay true to what they believe, whilst conventions and colleagues will challenge them. From Galileo and da Vinci, to Einstein and Picasso, genius requires an inner strength of conviction to stand by the radical ideas and actions that are at odds with received wisdom, that challenge the status quo, that could easily be compromised by a lesser-willed person. In any walk of life, it is rare for people to immediately like significant change in their surroundings, practices or beliefs. We prefer the safety and convenience of what we know to what we don't. But we gradually see the possibility, the logic, and the benefit in different thinking, and we accept it, and eventually engage in it. A genius often reaches out beyond today, and slowly people will follow and embrace what is new, different and better.

The 'genius' needed to excel in business lies in the fusion of intelligence and imagination. New business leaders work with their people to focus and stretch these characteristics in everything they do. They connect ideas and actions to deliver extraordinary results, accelerating growth and creating superior value. They create an inspired organization.

Evaluating and building the high performing business

The *Business Brainscan* is a diagnostic approach to understanding how you and your team can embrace the balance and stretch of more intelligent and more imaginative approaches to each fundamental aspect of business.

It is delivered through a combination of team workshops and personal assessments that measure current performance and future potential, identifying strengths and weaknesses, individually and collectively.

Together we define where the issues and opportunities for high performance lie within your team and within each person. By aligning this gap analysis with the strategy and priorities of your business, we collaboratively build a programme of development actions that will be relevant and valuable to you. You can then track progress and balance over time, refocusing as needed to deliver results.

The starting point is the four dimensions of genius, the four fusions or balances to get right at organizational and individual levels:

GENIUS TIME = FUTURE BACK + NOW FORWARD

This is the timeframe by which an organization explores and defines where it is going.

Does your organization address strategy and innovation by exploring the future possibilities, or by blindly and incrementally evolving from where it is today? What is the relative importance of the long and short term in making decisions and investments, measuring and reporting performance? Do you work more to maximize long-term value or short-term profitability?

High performing businesses require many perspectives, although the future back view matters most, and is the context in which to act now forward.

GENIUS SPACE = OUTSIDE IN + INSIDE OUT

This is the orientation by which an organization senses and responds to customers.

Does your organization start by thinking outside in, or inside out? Is the business driven more by the opportunities and challenges of the market, or the efficiency and improvement of capabilities? Does it do business when, where and how customers want, or does it prefer to do it in a way that is most convenient and efficient for itself?

High-performing businesses require both orientations, however outside in is the primary driving force in today's markets.

GENIUS THINKING = LEFT BRAIN + RIGHT BRAIN

This is the mindset by which an individual senses issues and understands them.

Do you start by thinking rationally or creatively? Do you rigorously analyse specific facts, or do you explore the possibilities and bigger picture? Is your thinking linear and progressive, quantifying issues and opportunities, or is it more holistic and random, seeing the possibilities and bigger picture?

High-performing people require both mindsets, although the right brain creates the quantum leaps and uniqueness that wouldn't otherwise exist.

GENIUS ACTION = RADICAL IDEAS + PRACTICAL ACTION

This is the action bias by which an individual responds to issues and adds value.

Do you have a bias to ideas or to action, to contribute more by the power of your thought or by the practical application of the ideas into effective business actions? Is the output of your thinking more visionary, innovative, strategic and long-term, or is it more grounded in today, tactical and short-term? Do you have the confidence and determination to make great things happen?

High-performing people require both action types, with the ability to create radical new ideas, which can then be implemented successfully.

A 'genius' business must embrace the extremes and achieve new balance in all four of these dimensions. There is little point in being superb in one extreme (the ultimate analytically, structured and measured business) at the expense of others (if there is no passion, energy or magic).

Balance, as in the famous yin-yang, is about positive reinforcement, rather than neutralization. It is about ensuring that $1+1 = 3$ rather than $1-1 = 0$.

Indeed 'space-time' is a fundamental precept on which Einstein based his understanding of the physical world. He showed that distance and time are connected, can be influence each other, and can traded off, or equally can come together in to support each other. The 'space-time' of organizations, and similarly the 'thinking-doing' of individuals, are the platforms from which to create new and unusual solutions, and why it is not unreasonable to seek results more than ordinary.

HIGH-PERFORMING ORGANIZATIONS

If we bring together the 'space-time' dimensions, those relating to the balanced and inspired organization, then we can consider the activities which need to be evaluated more practically.

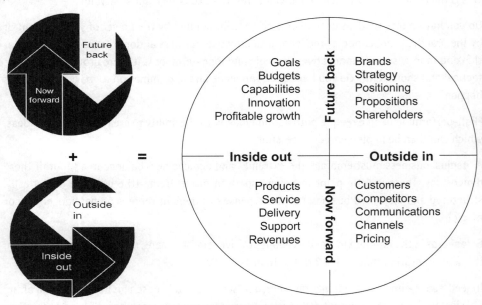

THE 'SPACE-TIME' DIMENSIONS OF HIGH PERFORMING ORGANIZATIONS

High-performance businesses are effective in all four quadrants, although some will be more unusual than others. Market shaping strategies (OI+FB) emerge from one quadrant, but the organization also needs to succeed today, both in terms of efficiency (IO+NF) and sales (OI+NF). And whilst the business needs stability and evolution (IO+FB), it is the market perspective that matters most, and where marketing can add significant value, becoming the driver of business direction and focus.

Brands (OI+FB) are built over time to reflect the needs and aspirations of chosen audiences, rather than the company or its products. These audiences are more sustaining than the products that service them. Operational delivery (OI+NF) is initiated by the specific needs of customers, within the competitive context of today.

Performance is measured in term of the long-term value created for stakeholders, most significantly shareholders (OI+FB), although this is only achieved by creating value in a mutually reinforcing cycle for customers, driving improved margins and sustainable growth. Of course cash flow matters too (IO+NF), but only as a means to this end, working in double time to deliver today, whilst creating tomorrow.

HIGH-PERFORMING PEOPLE

The 'thinking-doing' dimensions focus on the way in which the individual senses and responds to business challenges and opportunities.

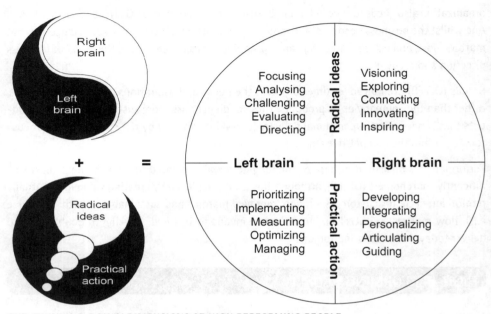

THE 'THINKING-DOING' DIMENSIONS OF HIGH PERFORMING PEOPLE

High performers work in all four quadrants, although their personal capabilities and preferences for work might be in some areas rather than areas, complemented by other team members.

Perhaps even more significant are the aspects which people have been conditioned to think are more important to focus on. Convention suggests that people who are radically creative struggle to make their ideas happen practically, or that highly analytical people could never have an innovative thought in their mind. This is nonsense, and whilst stereotypes are hard to break, the impact of people who can connect these perceived anomalies will speak for themselves.

Developing market strategies through rigorous analysis (RI+LB) will always be limited by where you set your context, whereas we know that adjacent markets rapidly merge with existing markets, and it requires the exploratory mind (RI+RB) to see this bigger picture. Complexity of course can be analysed into many components, but if not connected (RI+RB) they will not make much sense.

Success, of course, is only achieved if the radical ideas can be made reality. However, implementation cannot be a standard process (LB+PA) into competitive markets. It requires constant rethinking and creativity. Whilst people have typically relied upon spreadsheets or consultants to give them the results, they now need to take the lead (RB+PA). The focus, however, has to be on integration, bringing together ideas and people to create initiatives and solutions that have more impact.

Leadership exists in all quadrants, adding value in different ways in each.

EVALUATING YOUR 'GENIUS' POTENTIAL

The actual diagnostic process is based on evaluation of current and future performance on each of the intelligence/imaginative factors introduced at the beginning of each track in this book. These calibrate to map individual and collective performance.

The resulting attributes for your *Business Brainscan* are derived by matching your strategic priorities against the overall set of characteristics. Current and future profiles enable a gap analysis, which drives priorities for action. The map is relevant and practical for you and your business, driving an action plan that might involve refocusing activity, new team structures, recruitment and new work practices.

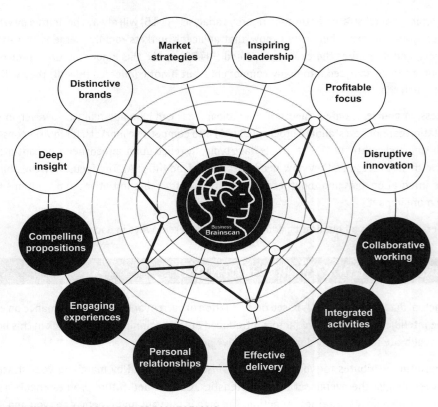

THE *BUSINESS BRAINSCAN* FOR ORGANIZATIONS

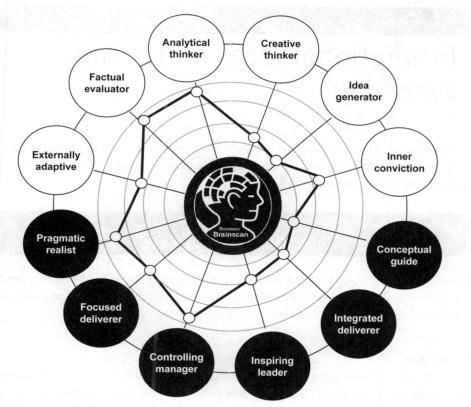

THE *BUSINESS BRAINSCAN* FOR INDIVIDUALS

More than anything, however, the brainscan inspires the business as a whole – to raise its game, to work with heads up rather than heads down, to shape markets rather than be shaped – and to be bold, brave and brilliant.

Inspirational ideas and action every day

A book is just a beginning. It will hopefully introduce new ideas, make you think differently, help you to make them happen and inspire you to do them in extraordinary ways. There are a range of other 'genius' resources to help you.

GENIUS LIVE
Updates on the best ideas from around the world

From Crocs to Umpqua Bank, business is a living, shifting story. Be inspired by the new genius: the new ideas as they emerge, the best practices as they evolve, the people and stories that inspire you think differently. Visit thegeniusworks.com for live updates:

Genius Blog
The best 'yin-yang' anecdotes from around the world. A real-time diary of new experiences from unusual business places. Remember, ideas are found in the margins not the mainstream. Learn about the Baltic entrepreneurs, latest technology trends, or celebrity brands of LA.

Genius Events
An ongoing programme of inspirational speeches, in-house workshops and master-classes

from around the world – exploring the new agenda for business, the customer challenge, how to design business from the future back, and how you can be a business genius too.

Genius Downloads

Over 250 free downloads including the latest research and trends, case studies and reports, all together in one place – one of the best collections of leading-edge papers on strategy and leadership, customers and marketing, growth and innovation, people and performance.

GENIUS WORKS
Practical support in making your ideas happen

It's not easy to stretch your mind, think in new ways or challenge your conventions from the inside. You need the right environment, processes and support to do it. A number of practical 'genius' approaches can help you to address business issues and opportunities in more powerful ways. See www.thegeniusworks.com for more information:

The Fusion Lab

A three-day creative event that that inspires your people to think creatively – to challenge and shape, innovate and focus business strategies and customer propositions. The lab is built on a high-energy, interactive environment where people work fast and collaboratively to reach beyond normality.

Business Accelerator

An intensive strategy and innovation process that enables you to develop business or market plans quickly in a structured, dedicated environment – instead of taking three months to complete plans, engage managers actively and do it all in two weeks.

The Fast Track

Explore the very latest ideas and best emerging practices in the areas of strategy and leadership, customers and innovation – a series of one- or two-day development workshops that combine inspirational thinking with practical application.

GENIUS BOOKS
More insights and ideas to help you think differently

You can explore more 'genius' ideas and insights from by Peter Fisk. Each combines a more intelligent and imaginative approach to specific aspects of business, exploring the emerging ideas and very best practices from around the world.

Marketing Genius – how to compete with your left and right brain

Marketing is the most important and exciting part of business today; brands and relationships are the most valuable assets, engaging customers and delivering differentiation. From Apple to Coke, Jones Soda to Virgin, we explore how to shape new markets in your vision and build brands and customer solutions that deliver extraordinary results.

Customer Genius – how to do business from the outside in

Become a customer-centric business – use your intelligence and imagination to attract, serve and retain customers where, when and how they want. From Amazon and Best Buy, to Toyota and Singapore Airlines, we explore how to engage customers more personally and effectively through their experiences and in their communities.

Creative Genius – how to innovate from the future back

Strategic innovation transforms business and markets, harnessing the power of creativity and design. We explore the four creative zones of business, and how you can combine the intelligence of P&G with the imagination of D&G, the creative culture of Google with the innovative practices of Zara, to make your best ideas happen.

All books are published by Capstone, available from Amazon and all good bookshops from early 2008. Read more at www.thegeniusworks.com.

Index